"Carefully researched an(
that the community in A(
audience is to identify, th
the art of theological interpretation. The community is the necessary bridge for communication between the Spirit and Scripture, as well as the nexus that generates theological understanding in dialogue with the Spirit and Scripture. Pruitt's monograph is a must read for those interested in theological hermeneutics in general and Pentecostal and Renewal hermeneutics in particular because he moves the conversation forward on how community functions in the interpretive process in significant ways."

—KENNETH J. ARCHER
Professor of Theology and Pentecostal Studies, School of Divinity, Barnett College of Ministry & Theology, Southeastern University, Lakeland, FL

"The dissertation makes an original contribution in that it extends our understanding of how memory theory can be utilized to understand and reconstruct how the early church employed collective memory of sacred events to construct identity/ies. Not only does the work of Pruitt make an original contribution to the field, but it successfully evaluates and critiques the current research on this topic."

—CORNÉ J. BEKKER
Dean & Professor, Regent University School of Divinity

"Building cordially upon prior work in this field, Pruitt's book represents another important addition to the chorus of voices calling for, even demanding, a more mature approach to biblical and theological hermeneutics within Pentecostal/Charismatic traditions. His combination of clarity, nuance, and irenic tone allow for an accessible-yet-evocative appraisal of the role of the community in the theological process, an appraisal that bears significant implications for the application of Scripture in the contemporary world."

—RENEA C. BRATHWAITE
Dean of Graduate and Professional Education, North Central University

"What role does the community play in theological creativity? In the context of current uncertainties, Pruitt uses Luke-Acts to show that the community can have—must have—a decisive role in theological creativity. With close attention to the text, Pruitt shows that, for Luke, the community functions as a hermeneutical bridge between its testimony of the Spirit's work and its application of Scripture to a theological problem. This is an important book and should be read by all concerned with theological creativity, particularly in the Pentecostal and charismatic traditions."

—GRAHAM H. TWELFTREE
Academic Dean, Professor of New Testament and Early Christianity, London School of Theology

"Demonstrating the importance of the first-century community for theological development in the Acts of the Apostles, Theology through Community issues a clarion call to Pentecostals and others to focus attention on our communities as central to our theological identity and creativity, thereby demanding a renewed interest in the heritage, stories, and testimony that shape the church."

—WOLFGANG VONDEY
Professor of Christian Theology and Pentecostal Studies, University of Birmingham, UK

"This persuasive study informs us that Acts is about much more than the acts of individual leaders, but rather describes an engaged community creatively involved in the act of interpretation to better understand the divine activity they had witnessed. Its portrayal of early Christian communities presents us with the challenge to develop similar communities trained in the Scriptures and attentive to the Spirit so that we can realize the promise of the prophetic community envisioned at Pentecost."

—BLAINE B. CHARETTE
Professor of New Testament, Northwest University

Theology
through
Community

Theology
through
Community

Luke's Portrayal of the Role of the First-Century
Community of Believers in Theological Creativity

RICHARD A. PRUITT

WIPF & STOCK · Eugene, Oregon

THEOLOGY THROUGH COMMUNITY
Luke's Portrayal of the Role of the First-Century Community of Believers in Theological Creativity

Wipf & Stock
An Imprint of Wipf and Stock Publishers
199 W. 8th Ave., Suite 3
Eugene, OR 97401

www.wipfandstock.com

PAPERBACK ISBN: 978-1-5326-6401-4
HARDCOVER ISBN: 978-1-5326-6402-1
EBOOK ISBN: 978-1-5326-6403-8

Manufactured in the U.S.A.   02/05/19

The Greek text, except where otherwise noted, follows Nestle-Aland, 28th edition.

Contents

List of Figures

PREFACE

IN THIS STUDY, WE will demonstrate Luke's portrayal of the role of the first-century community of believers in theological development, or more aptly stated, theological creativity. By approaching Acts as a form of first-century novel and by applying literary conventions of storytelling, we will show that theological creativity for Luke is the act of reformulating formerly held theological concepts as the believing community adjudicates between their understanding of Scripture and their experience of the Spirit's evidential work. As a result, we will see that Luke's method of characterization reveals the role of the first-century community of believers in an interpretive process involving Spirit–Community–Scripture.

In order to establish the manner in which Luke characterizes the role of the community in his narrative tale, we will utilize the literary categories of action and conflict as inherent qualities within narrative characters. In so doing, we will see how the community, as a character in Acts, interacts with both Scripture and Spirit in the process of theological creativity. The selected passages, (1) Acts 1:12–26; (2) 4:23–31; (3) 6:1–7; (4) 15:1–35; and (5) 11:27–30; 13:1–4; 21:4, 8–14, feature the community as an active and important character in Luke's story. In each episode, the community as a character is substantive, identifiable, engaged in the action and conflict, and not passive or merely assumed. As we focus on each passage, we will see how Luke, as a storyteller, uses the community to engage other characters and confirm divine actions.

With special concern for the Renewal Movement's interest in the community's function in the interpretive interaction between Spirit–Community–Scripture, this research will demonstrate that Luke's view of the community in theological creativity offers balance to any concern that the community overshadows either Scripture or Spirit in the interpretive process.

Acknowledgments

I COULD NOT HAVE completed this project without the support and love of my wife and family. Thank you, Judy, for never giving up on me. Your timely nudges enabled me to push forward. I am also grateful for the persistence of Dr. Graham Twelftree and the countless hours he spent reading, rereading, and supervising my work. His attention to detail is unwavering and I was fortunate to have him as my advisor. I am also grateful for the seminal works of Dr. Amos Yong and Dr. Kenneth Archer. Their works concerning the interpretive process served as a catalyst for this project. Finally, a word of appreciation is due to all the librarians who came to my aid time and again, especially the ILL staff at Regent University Library. Their efforts in the task of research were invaluable.

LIST OF ABBREVIATIONS

AB	Anchor Bible
BA	*Biblical Archaeologist*
BDAG	Bauer, Walter, Frederick W. Danker, William F. Arndt, and F. Wilbur Gingrich, *Greek-English Lexicon of the New Testament and Other Early Christian Literature*, 3rd ed. (Chicago: University of Chicago Press, 1999)
Bib	*Biblica*
BMI	The Bible and Its Modern Interpreters
BSac	*Bibliotheca Sacra*
BTB	*Biblical Theology Bulletin*
CBQ	*Catholic Biblical Quarterly*
CurBR	*Currents in Biblical Research* (formerly *Currents in Research: Biblical Studies*)
DNTB	*Dictionary of New Testament Background*
EBC	Expositor's Bible Commentary
ERT	*Evangelical Review of Theology*
ExpTim	*Expository Times*
HTKNT	Herders Theologischer Kommentar zum Neuen Testament
HTR	*Harvard Theological Review*
IBS	*Irish Biblical Studies*

IEJ	*Israel Exploration Journal*
IJST	*International Journal of Systematic Theology*
JBL	*Journal of Biblical Literature*
JEH	*Journal of Ecclesiastical History*
JETS	*Journal of the Evangelical Theological Society*
JH	*Jewish History*
JJS	*Journal of Jewish Studies*
JLT	*Journal of Literature and Theology*
JPT	*Journal of Pentecostal Theology*
JRH	*Journal of Religious History*
JSNT	*Journal for the Study of the New Testament*
JSNTSup	Journal for the Study of the New Testament Supplement Series
KEK	Kritisch-exegetischer Kommentar über das Neue Testament (Meyer-Kommentar)
LNTS	Library of New Testament Studies
NAE	National Association of Evangelicals
NC	Narrative Commentaries
NIDPCM	*The New International Dictionary of Pentecostal and Charismatic Movements*
NovT	*Novum Testamentum*
NTS	*New Testament Studies*
PRSt	*Perspectives in Religious Studies*
RB	*Revue biblique*
RevExp	*Review and Expositor*
RevQ	*Revue de Qumran*
SBLDS	Society of Biblical Literature Dissertation Series
SNTSMS	Society for New Testament Studies Monograph Series

SP	Sacra Pagina
ST	*Studia Theologica*
StABH	Studies in American Biblical Hermeneutics
SymS	Symposium Series
TDNT	*Theological Dictionary of the New Testament,* edited Gerhard Kittel and Gerhard Freidrich, translated by Geoffrey W. Bromiley, 10 vols. (Grand Rapids: Eerdmans, 1964–1976)
THKNT	Theologischer Handkommentar zum Neuen Testament
TLG	Thesaurus Linguae Graecae: Canon of Greek Authors and Works. Edited by Luci Berkowitz and Karl A. Squitier. 3rd ed. New York: Oxford University Press, 1990.
TR	*Theological Renewal*
TQ	*Theologische Quartalschrift*
WTJ	*Westminster Theological Journal*
WUNT	Wissenschaftliche Untersuchungen zum Neuen Testament
ZNW	*Zeitschrift für die neutestamentliche Wissenschaft und die Kunde der älteren Kirsch*

Principal Manuscripts Cited

LXX	Septuagint
SP	Samaritan Pentateuch
ℵ01	Codex Sinaiticus
B03	Codex Vaticanus
D05	Codex Bezae (Greek)
d5	Codex Bezae (Latin)

INTRODUCTION

SINCE THE 1980s,[1] RENEWAL scholars[2] have focused considerable attention on the role of the believing community in the interpretive process.[3] A broad

---

1 When the Society for Pentecostal Studies (1970) formed its peer-reviewed scholarly journal, *Pneuma: Journal for the Society of Pentecostal Studies*, in 1979, it opened a new avenue for Pentecostal and Charismatic writers to engage in theological conversation beyond the local conference setting. Other journals, such as *Theological Renewal* (1980) and later publications including *Journal of Pentecostal Theology* (1991) and *Journal of the European Pentecostal Theological Association* (1991), contributed to the proliferation of scholarly ideas focused on Pneumatological and other so-called renewal interests.

2. In the context of this research, the term *renewal* refers to Christian traditions that emphasize the work of the Holy Spirit within creation in general and in the life of the Christian community in particular. Generally speaking, these include Pentecostal and Charismatic traditions. According to Spawn and Wright, the so-called renewal tradition "refers to global charismatic movements and scholars in these groups who maintain that Pneumatological commitments and experiences have implications for the hermeneutical project." Spawn and Wright, *Spirit and Scripture*, xvii, also n. 1. Also see the definition in Kärkkäinen, *Spirit in the World*, xv–xviii. For a more extensive consideration of "renewal tradition," see Burgess, "Neocharismatic Movements," *NIDPCM*, 928.

3. For example: Smail, "Sign and the Signified," 2–8; Smail, "Decision and Discernment," 2–3; Robeck, "Prophetic Authority," 4–10; Mühlen, "Theological Aspects," 22–36. Emphasis on the role of the community in the interpretive process gained a new emphasis with Ricky Moore's influential challenge to directly engage the cooperative nature between "the text, the community, and also the ongoing voice of the Holy Spirit." See Moore, "Canon and Charisma," 75–92 esp. 75 n. 1. Earlier hints of Moore's position are recognizable in a 1987 campus publication. See Moore, "Pentecostal Approach to Scripture," 4–5, 11. I am grateful to Moore for discussing his early reflections with me by phone and for sending an unpublished conference paper concerning a Pentecostal use of Scripture. In it, he credits his views as further developments of two papers given in 1985 at the Society for Pentecostal Studies by Michael B. Dowd ("Contours of a Narrative Pentecostal Theology") and Francis Martin ("Spirit and Flesh"). Further developments include S. Porter, "Why Hasn't Reader-Response Criticism Caught on in New Testament Studies?" 278–92; Israel, Albrecht, and McNally, "Pentecostals and Hermeneutics: Texts, Rituals and Community," 137–61; Pinnock, "The Role of the Spirit in Interpretation,"

consensus has emerged that a triad involving Scripture, the Spirit, and the believing community harmoniously forms a cooperative relationship resulting in theological development followed by commensurate action, what this research identifies as theological creativity.[4]

Various attempts to explain the interplay between these aspects are generally conceived in hierarchical terms with either Scripture or Spirit at the top (or side by side) and the community of believers below (underneath), who are in some manner subject to the directives of Scripture or Spirit.[5] Such a mental configuration seems adequate enough for those with a high view of Scripture or whose perspective envisions the Holy Spirit leading a community of believers. But a top-down view of the interpretative process in this configuration is inadequate since, in practical terms, a community (or individual) must negotiate or interpret the meaning and function of both Spirit and Scripture.[6]

Efforts to promulgate a harmonious or more balanced interplay between Scripture, the Spirit, and the community of believers have struggled (1) to explain it without relinquishing the primacy of Scripture or Spirit or (2) to demonstrate it in concrete terms. For example, Terry Cross suggests

---

494–95; J. Thomas, "Women, Pentecostals and the Bible," 41–56; Arrington, "The Use of the Bible by Pentecostals," 101–107; R. Moore, "Deuteronomy and the Fire of God," 11–33; J. Johns, "Pentecostals and the Postmodern Worldview," 13–96; R. Baker, "Pentecostal Bible Reading," 34–48; Goldingay, *Models for Interpretation*, 233–50, 251–65; Stibbe, "This is That," 181–93; Lyons, "The Fourth Wave and the Approaching Millennium," 169–81; Ellington, "History, Story, and Testimony," 245–63; Hey, "Changing Roles of Pentecostal Hermeneutics," 210–18; Cross, "A Proposal to Break the Ice," 44–73. For more extensive treatments, see Yong, *Spirit-Word-Community*; Archer, *Pentecostal Hermeneutic*; Spawn and Wright, *Spirit and Scripture*.

4. Cartledge, "Text–Community–Spirit," 130–42; Cross, "A Proposal," 44–73; Yong, *Renewing Christian Theology*, 337–39, 341–42; Yong, *Spirit-Word-Community*, 311–15; Archer, *Pentecostal Hermeneutic*, 133–48; Stibbe, "This is That," 181–93; Goldingay, *Models for Interpretation*, 233–50, 251–65; Moore, "Canon and Charisma," 75 n. 1.

5. For example, Spawn and Wright, *Spirit and Scripture*, despite being an excellent treatment of the subject from a renewal perspective, the word "community" is left out of the title altogether. For an evangelical attempt to bring the community's role into sharper focus while still subordinating it to the role of Scripture see Vanhoozer, *Drama of Doctrine*; and Green and Turner, eds., *Between Two Horizons*, which includes contributions by Pentecostal and Charismatic authors.

6. On the nature of the community as the negotiator of meaning see Ricoeur, *From Text to Action*, 118–24; Corrington, *Community of Interpreters*, 47–68; Fish, *Is There a Text*, 1–17, 167–73, 305–12. For an evangelical refutation of Fish, see Vanhoozer, *Is There a Meaning*, 169–71, 438–41. Cf. Porter, "Why Hasn't Reader-Response Criticism Caught on in New Testament Studies?" 278–92.

"wholly subjective" concerns in the hermeneutical process may be mitigated "if bolstered by a text, a community and the Spirit." However, he does
not elaborate on how this may be accomplished.[7]

In a more recent treatment, Kevin Spawn and Archie Wright concede,
"Despite the attention paid to the topic . . . biblical interpretation as a task of
the community is still a work in progress, while the distinctive contribution
of the broader renewal movement remains to be defined."[8] Consequently,
a common argument against emphasizing the role of the community in
theological creativity is that it replaces the Spirit or Scripture as the rule
of normative Christian experience.[9] For example, if the community's role
in theological creativity is approached contextually (i.e., from the "eye of
the beholder") or sociologically (i.e., from a cultural and linguistic point of
view), the role of the community inevitably overshadows the role of both
Scripture and Spirit.[10] Either position creates difficulty for achieving a balanced view in which the community functions cooperatively and does not
overshadow the role of Spirit and Scripture in theological creativity.

Some have endeavored to analyze New Testament and patristic writings concerning the community in decision-making, drawn upon examples
of the first-century community of believers engaging in theological creativity.[11] Conversely, others have taken a more philosophical approach to
the interaction between Spirit, Scripture, and the Community.[12] However,

7. Cross, "Proposal," 52, also see 56 n. 25.

8. Spawn and Wright, *Spirit and Scripture*, 3–22, esp. 16, also see 131–33, 191–98.

9. Vanhoozer refers to "the normative Christian experience" as the "Rule of Faith."
Vanhoozer, *Is There a Meaning*, 97–100. Also see Fee, "Hermeneutics and Historical
Precedent," 118–32, esp. 21. For an alternative perspective concerning "normative Christian experience," see Frei, "'Literal Reading' of Biblical Narrative," 36–77; Lindbeck, *Nature of Doctrine*, 104–8. For an analysis of differences between the theories of Vanhoozer
and Lindbeck see Pruitt, "Rethinking Postliberal Theology," 161–75.

10. For agreement see Vanhoozer, *Is There a Meaning*, 55–57, 154; Vanhoozer, *Drama
of Doctrine*, 10–12, 98–99, 120–33, 174–75. With regard to hermeneutical concerns
and contextualization, see Hesselgrave and Rommen, *Contextualization*, 170–79. For a
sustained defense of contextual and cultural principles in hermeneutics see H. Yung,
Mangoes or Bananas, 1–9, 76–96, 234–40.

11. For sustained discussion concerning decision-making, see Johnson, *Scripture and
Discernment*; Brown, *Corporate Decision-Making*. See also Thomas, "Reading the Bible,"
108–22; Thomas, "Women, Pentecostals," 41–56.

12. For a philosophical example see Yong, *Spirit–Word–Community*, 315. Although
Yong offers a succinct theoretical outline of the philosophical complexities involved in
a "triadic, trialectical, and trialogical" theological hermeneutic, he does not provide a
concrete biblical (or otherwise) example. Also consider the work of Hinze and Dabney,

attempts to describe how a community of believers function in the triad of Scripture, Spirit, and the community of believers are less developed and understood.[13] And none have focused their inquiry on Luke's characterization of the role of the first-century community of believers engaging in theological creativity.

Given the importance of Luke-Acts in renewal studies, can, therefore, Luke's portrayal of the function of community in theological creativity offer an acceptable solution to the concern of community overshadowing Scripture or Spirit in the hermeneutical process of interpretation? We will argue that Luke's portrayal of the first-century community of believers in theological creativity can benefit hermeneutics in general and renewal hermeneutics specifically, particularly since the Pentecostal and Charismatic experience of Spirit-baptism remains essential to its self-understanding and interpretive position.[14]

Thesis and Anticipated Conclusions

This study will demonstrate that the first-century community of believers in Luke's narrative functions as an indispensable character in the formation of theological creativity in Acts.[15] In the context of this research, theological creativity is the act of reformulating formerly held theological interpretations resulting from testimony concerning the Spirit's evidential work (i.e.,

---

eds., *Advents of the Spirit.*

13. As noted above in Yong, *Spirit–Word–Community*, 315; Cross, "Proposal," 52, also 56 n. 25; Spawn and Wright, *Spirit and Scripture*, 16.

14. The nomenclature *Pentecostal* encompasses North American denominational communities emphasizing the role of the Holy Spirit in the life of the believer and Spirit baptism with initial physical evidence of speaking in tongues. For further clarification and analysis, see Oliverio, *Theological Hermeneutics*, 5–11. The term *Charismatic* includes main-line denominational communities emphasizing the role of the Holy Spirit within the life of the believer and Spirit baptism, not dependent on tongues as initial physical evidence. Both groups are part of the wider (so-called) global Renewal Movement. For clarification on Pentecostal and Charismatic self-understanding and interpretive concerns, see Archer, *Pentecostal Hermeneutic*, 147; Arrington, "Use of the Bible," 104–5; Thomas, "Women, Pentecostals," 41–42, 51–56; F. Martin, "Spirit and Flesh," 30; Ervin, "Hermeneutics," 33.

15. As we will see, the community in Luke's narrative is an identifiable group of believers living in disparate places between the time of Jesus' ascension (Acts 1:9–11) and Paul's detention in Rome (28:30–31). For Luke, the community in his story is not a single group of believers but various groups of believers who share a commitment to the apostles' message concerning Jesus Messiah and to each other.

divine activity), an emerging understanding of applicable Scripture, and followed by commensurate action.[16] Moreover, theological creativity is the outcome of the interpretive process since it is theology in action, functional in nature, and situationally pragmatic in scope. It involves the process of theological justification and action or reaction to current circumstances. In this sense, to be creative with theology is to take an existing theological assumption and broaden or adapt it to current circumstances in light of the Spirit's evidential work and a consensus understanding of Scripture.

By approaching Acts as a novel (or "novel-like" in nature)[17] and by analyzing the community as a character and its actions in the story,[18] we will see Luke's view of the believing community in theological creativity as it interacts with both Spirit and Scripture. The selected passages include (1) Acts 1:12–26, (2) 4:23–31, (3) 6:1–7, (4) 15:1–35, and (5) 11:27–30, 13:1–4, and 21:4, 8–14 and feature the first-century community of believers as an active and indispensable character in Luke's narrative tale. In each episode, the community as a narrative character is easily identifiable and integral to the plot.[19] The community of believers, by affirming or rejecting the words or deeds of other characters or by corporately addressing issues impacting the community's experience, is able to confirm and acknowledge its testimony of the Spirit's evidential work followed by commensurate action in Acts. Thus, in story-form, Luke portrays the community as an active agent in theological creativity.

Finally, concerning renewal interest in the interpretive process, it will be argued that Luke's view of the first-century community of believers in theological creativity does not overshadow Spirit or Scripture in the interpretive process. Rather, as we will see, the community in Luke's story is positioned between Spirit and Scripture and, so to say, "balances the

16. Since identifying the Spirit's work, or the Spirit's activity, is a subjective event we will refer to the Spirit's activity as testimony of the Spirit's evidential work. The Spirit's evidential work (evidence of the Spirit) in Acts is expressed through the testimony of the community of believers (e.g., Acts 1:26; 2:2–4, 14–16; 3:3–9, 12–16; 4:7–10, 24–25; 6:5–6; 7:55–56) or revealed by the narrator (e.g., Acts 1:2; 2:5–11, 41; 4:7–8, 31; 5:11–16, 19–21; 6:7, 15; 8:18–24, 26, 39–40).

17. Specifically, a *novella*, a prose narrative normally longer than a short story but shorter than a novel. See also Abrams, *Glossary of Literary Terms*, 198, 295–97. For further analysis see excursus in Witherington, *Acts*, 376–81. Cf. Keener, *Acts*, 1:62–83, esp. 62, 82–83; Pervo, *Profit with Delight*, 135.

18. For example: characterization by Luke, analysis of dialogue, action, conflict, plot, point of view, and narrative time and setting.

19. That is, the community's role in the plot is not passive or merely assumed.

equation" by functioning as a bridge through which its testimony of the Spirit's evidential work and its application of Scripture interact. In order to illustrate this balancing act, we will use a modified configuration of the triadic notion: Spirit–*Community*–Scripture.[20]

Characterization in Luke

Throughout this study, we will use the word *character* to identify a persona in a literary work that possesses moral qualities, traits, or aspects attributed to a real or fictive person[21] or to a group of people[22] within the story.[23] Weaving personality traits, actions, and other information together constitutes the warp and weft of character development.[24] Such character traits are inferred or discerned through what characters say and what they do, whether directly or indirectly revealed in the story.[25] To *characterize* is to give a narrative character substance (e.g., traits) in a story, which ultimately moves the plot (story) forward in grand and minute ways.[26] In order to describe Luke's development of the community of believers as a character, we must first establish our view of Luke's characters in general followed by a method for how he characterizes them in particular.

According to Baruch Hochman, the process by which readers and hearers apprehend and identify with characters is, "virtually identical in

20. For a similar but less developed configuration, "text–community–Spirit," see Cross, "Proposal," 52. Cross echoes Moore's earlier construct. See Moore, "Canon and Charisma," 75 n. 1. Building on Cross, Cartledge engages the issue more recently, but only methodologically. See Cartledge, "Text–Community–Spirit," 130–42, esp. 131–33.

21. Such as "Paul" or "Agabus."

22. Such as "community of believers" or "sect of the Pharisees."

23. For a similar character approach see Aristotle, *Poet.* 6.7–21; Aristotle, *On Man in the Universe*, trans. Butcher, 426–27, and 436. Also, see Abrams, *Glossary of Literary Terms*, 33; Frye, *Harper Handbook to Literature*, 13. Cf. Gowler, *Host, Guest, Enemy*, 30; Shepherd, *Narrative Function*, 51–67, esp. 66.

24. On the intricacies of character development see Wallace, *Recent Theories*, 116; Resseguie, *Narrative Criticism of the New Testament*, 128.

25. See Prince, *Narratology*, 71–72.

26. Aristotle, *Poet.* 6.7–21; Aristotle, *On Man in the Universe*, trans. Butcher, 426–27, 436. Cf. Hochman, *Character in Literature*, 8, 37, 41, 49–58; Chatman, *Story and Discourse*, 119–45, esp. 121, 126–31; Harvey, *Character and the Novel*, 31–33, 56–57. Garvey, "Characterization in Narrative," 63, 66–68. Also, see Abrams, *Glossary of Literary Terms*, 33–35.

literature and in life."[27] Other literary critics, such as John Harvey and Seymour Chatman, also support this view of character in literature. In *Character in the Novel*, Harvey argues, "The process of retrieving character from fiction involves acts of reconstruction on the part of the audience and that reconstruction draws on the reader's own experience not only on people and language in which we talk about people but of themselves."[28]

Chatman follows a similar path by insisting "that character is retrieved from texts as a cumulative image that is consciously or unconsciously extrapolated and then rationalized as a paradigm of traits belonging to the character."[29] Hochman extends this connection to religious communities by stating,

> We need only look at the Alexandrian commentaries on Homer or at the rabbinic and patristic commentaries on the Bible to see the extent to which human behavior, as reported in the sacred texts, was seen to invite interpretation and understanding on common-sense as well as theological grounds.[30]

Consequently, the audience envisions a character from the substance of their own experiences not, as some might suppose, by imposing themselves into the story but by recognizing the characters as sharing something similar to their own experiences.[31] In this sense, in literature just as in life, the image or conceptualization of the character takes on an existence of its own.[32] Since Luke's characters also invite "interpretation and understanding on common-sense as well as theological grounds" for his audience, we argue he intends his characters to be mimetic (like real people) rather than semiotic (signs represented as words in the text).[33] By portraying the community as a character in Acts as mimetic, we argue the audience is able to imagine the community engaging in theological creativity as if they too were part of it.

---

27. Hochman, *Character in Literature*, 36.

28. Harvey, *Character in the Novel*, 57, 73, 111.

29. Chatman, *Story and Discourse*, 118–19.

30. Hochman, *Character in Literature*, 28–29.

31. Harvey, *Character in the Novel*, 54. Cf. Hochman, *Character in Literature*, 39.

32. Chatman, *Story and Discourse*, 118–27; Hochman, *Character in Literature*, 36.

33. For differences concerning mimetic vs. semiotic characters see Rimmon-Kenan, *Narrative Fiction*, 33; Harvey, "Characterization in Narrative," 11–13.

Characterization is the author's technique of developing characters in a story through a process of *showing* and *telling*.[34] In the act of showing, the author reports what characters say and do, including what they may think and feel, leaving it to the reader or audience to discern the motives or meaning behind what is said, done, thought, or felt. In the act of telling, the author directly reveals the motives or meaning behind what is said, done, thought, or felt.[35] Examples of telling include revealing meaning-laden names and personal information.[36] As we will see, Luke's characterization of the community of believers in theological creativity involves the process of showing and telling.[37]

Throughout this study, we will see Luke characterize the community in Acts in such a manner so that his audience is able to identify with it as if they were (individually or corporately) part of the first-century community in his story. By shaping and supporting the first-century community of believers as a character within the story, Luke provides his audience a character with which to identify. In so doing, Luke's story functions as a window for his audience to look through to observe the behavior of community and as a mirror in which they might see themselves functioning in a similar manner.[38]

We will begin with the assumption that in Luke's Gospel Jesus is the central character, protagonist, and interpreter for the disciples on issues of theological creativity.[39] However, we will maintain that in Acts a major

34. See Resseguie, *Narrative Criticism*, 121–23, 126–30; Garvey, "Characterization in Narrative," 63–78, esp. 63. Cf. Bennema, *Encountering Jesus*, 37. For Bennema's' treatment of *crowd*, see Bennema, "The Crowd," 201–12. Cf. Abrams, *Glossary of Literary Terms*, 34.

35. For support, see Garvey, "Characterization in Narrative," 66–68; Alter, *Art of Biblical Narrative*, 116–17; Resseguie, *Narrative Criticism*, 126–30; Abrams, *Glossary of Literary Terms*, 34.

36. For example, family history, emotional disposition, physical characteristics, etc. For support see Garvey, "Characterization in Narrative," 68–69.

37. For a similar study involving showing and telling of a group of people as a "theological entity" see Cousland, *Crowds in the Gospel of Matthew*, 1–9.

38. Cf. Harvey, *Character in the Novel*, 110; Chatman, *Story and Discourse*, 118–19; Hochman, *Character in Literature*, 39. For the use of window and mirror as metaphor in literary analysis, see Krieger, *Window to Criticism*, 3–70. For a direct application in hermeneutical studies, see Osborne, *Hermeneutical Spiral*, 203; Pratt, "Pictures, Windows, and Mirrors," 156–67; Culpepper, *Anatomy of the Fourth Gospel*, 3–4.

39. Examples in Luke's Gospel concerning the centrality of Jesus' character as protagonist include 1:35; 2:10–11, 24, 38, 46–47; 3:21–22, 23a; 4:1–2, 14–15, 20–22, 31–32, 40, 42; 5:1–11, 13–14, 20, 24, 27, 32–35; 6:2–3, 8–10, 12–16, 20–49; 7:6–9, 13–16, 21–28,

shift in characterization occurs after his ascension in chapter 1. With the community's return from the Mount of Olives to Jerusalem, Luke's view of the first-century community of believers changes from passive (in the Gospel) to active (in Acts).[40] As we will see, although Jesus remains an active and important character in Acts, Luke transfers the role of protagonist and interpreter from Jesus to the community of believers.[41]

Some argue Jesus remains the central character and protagonist throughout Acts.[42] However, there are numerous examples in Acts 1–4 to support our claim that the role of protagonist is shifted to the community, both corporately and among individuals within it.[43] Apart from the ascension account (Acts 1:1–8) and vision-episodes (7:55–56; 9:3–7), Jesus does not direct action in Acts in the same manner as in Luke's Gospel. Although the community and its members speak of Jesus and act on behalf of Jesus, he is not present. Peter makes a similar observation when he states in Acts 3:21, "Jesus, *who must remain in heaven* until the time of universal restoration" (emphasis mine). Consequently, we maintain that the community acts on its own behalf and functions as the protagonist in Acts following the ascension story.

Review of Literature

While no one has focused on the community as a character in Acts, the role of community in hermeneutics as well as characterization in Luke's writings have been important topics of discussion. This is particularly true in renewal studies.

36–50; 8:1, 9–10, 19–21, 22–25, 32–33, 38–39, 48, 50, 54–56, etc. Each scene is focused on Jesus, and he directs the action. Even issues concerning John the Baptist and his family (1:13–17; 3:3–4; 7:27), Mary and Joseph (2:1–24, 41–52), Simeon (2:25–35), and Anna (2:36–38) narratively place Jesus as the center of action.

40. In contrast to our argument here, Twelftree attributes this transition to Pentecost rather than as a result of the ascension. But we will demonstrate this to be inaccurate since Luke shows this role reversal already in progress in the replacement of Judas. See Twelftree, *People of the Spirit*, 28, also 36–38. Cf. Gaventa, *Acts*, 40.

41. Alternatively, Shepherd and Koch hold that the Holy Spirit is the main protagonist in Acts. Shepherd, *Narrative Function of the Holy Spirit*, 40–41; Koch, "Spirit," *Encyclopedia of Biblical Theology*, 3:888.

42. Such as Gaventa, *Acts*, 27, 31–35; Twelftree, *People of the Spirit*, 23, 30, 43.

43. Examples of the community and its members as protagonist see Acts 1:12–14, 15, 23, 26; 2:14, 22, 29, 37–42, 43–47; 3:1, 3–7, 11–12, 17–21; 4:1–4, 8–10, 19–20, 23–31; and 32–37.

The Community of Believers as an Interpretive Community

Prior to 1990s, nearly all classical Pentecostal research adopted an evangelical hermeneutical strategy that ties biblical meaning to authorial intent.[44] Taking up such an approach seemed appropriate for the traditional "high view" of Scripture typically held among Pentecostal scholars.[45] In an effort to address theological problems associated with a Pentecostal view of experience, Gordon Fee advocated a strong delineation between didactic and historical portions of Scripture. For Fee *"descriptive history* of the primitive church must not be translated into *normative experience* for the ongoing church."[46] For support, Fee drew upon the work of numerous prominent evangelical scholars.[47]

The dominance of evangelical hermeneutical principles gained further impetus among Pentecostals following an article by Robert Johnston published in *Pneuma: Journal for the Society of Pentecostal Studies* in 1984. In it he calls for Pentecostal scholars to root their hermeneutical efforts within the "evangelical wing of the church," despite initial evangelical reticence to include Pentecostals in the National Association of Evangelicals.[48] While praising Fee for modeling how Pentecostals ought to frame their hermeneutical discussions within the broader evangelical tradition, Johnston

44. For examples of evangelical hermeneutics, see Kaiser, *Classical Evangelical Essays*; Hirsch, *Aims of Interpretation*; Kaiser and Silva, *Introduction to Biblical Hermeneutics*; Grenz, *Theology for the Community*, esp. 380–82, 397–404; Grenz, *Renewing the Center*, esp. 92; Packer, "Bible in Use," esp. 62, 68. For Vanhoozer's "revised" understanding of authorial intention see Vanhoozer, *Is There a Meaning*, 26, 201–80. Concerning an affinity for evangelical theological method among Pentecostals, see Cross, "Proposal," 46–47, also 46, n. 3–4; Phillips and Okholm, *Family of Faith*, 254; Archer, *Pentecostal Hermeneutic*, 148–54. Cf. Dayton, "Some Doubts," 251.

45. For supportive assessments see Oliverio, *Theological Hermeneutics*, 83–88, 133–35; Cargal, "Beyond the Fundamentalist-Modernist Controversy," 168–71; R. Johnston, "Pentecostalism and Theological Hermeneutics," 55–56. Cf. Fee, "Hermeneutics and Historical Precedent," 124–27.

46. Fee, "Hermeneutics and Historical Precedent," 121 (italics original). Cf. Pinnock, "Truce Proposal," 6–9. For a more recent (and supportive) analysis of Fee's contribution in this regard see Oliverio, *Theological Hermeneutics*, 167–77. Concerning reluctant acceptance into the NAE, see Johnston, "Pentecostalism and Theological Hermeneutics," 55.

47. See Fee, "Hermeneutics and Historical Precedent," 119–23. Fee's dialogue partners include John Stott (1964), Paul Weiland (1965), Grant R. Osborne (1971), Walter J. Hollenweger (1972), Anthony Hoekema (1972), and Clark Pinnock (1976).

48. Johnston, "Pentecostalism and Theological Hermeneutics," 52–56. His article also provides a synopsis of his book *The Use of the Bible in Theology*.

speaks critically of so called "neo-Pentecostal hermeneutical strategies," such as those by Michael Harper, because they base their doctrines on the community's (their) experience rather than "upon careful study of the bible."[49] Consequently, evangelical concerns—such as inerrancy of Scripture and efforts to locate Spirit baptism within the *ordo salutis*—shaped the emergence of Pentecostal concerns within the scholarly community while subsequently curtailing discussion concerning the value of experience or the community's role in the interpretative process.[50]

For example, Pinnock, whose publications frequently engaged Pentecostals, consistently maintained that interpretation must be rooted in authorial intent.[51] For Pinnock, the "danger of unbridled reader interest transforming the text" is always a threat. Consequently, for him, a community of tradition must serve as a guide in order to remaining consistent with the "intended meanings."[52] Nevertheless, he does concede that a community of faith is needed and provides the best context for understanding Scripture because individual Christians "exist in a network . . . of committed others."[53] While Pinnock contends that the community is an important part of the hermeneutical process, his view of community is often couched within a larger discussion concerning commitment to the text of Scripture.[54] However, issues raised among "Postliberal" scholars in the 1980s, such as Hans Frei, opened new avenues of hermeneutical discussion for Pentecostals by emphasizing postmodern concerns, literary critical approaches (i.e., narrative criticism), and a renewed emphasis on the Christian community's use of Scripture.[55]

49. Johnston, "Pentecostalism and Theological Hermeneutics," 52, also 51–54; Harper, *New Way of Living*, 12, 20–21. Other Pentecostals sited by Johnston as forging the way in evangelical hermeneutics include George Montague, Russell Spittler, and Gerald Sheppard. For comments concerning a low view of Pentecostal and Charismatic scholarship among evangelicals, see Cross, "Proposal," 46.

50. For support see Oliverio, *Theological Hermeneutics*, 83–88, esp. 85 and 87. Cargal attributes this to the lack of Pentecostal institutions offering advanced theological degrees, which meant Pentecostals, if they wanted an advanced degree, attended evangelical institutions. See Cargal, "Beyond the Fundamentalist-Modernist Controversy," 163–87, esp. 169. For an extensive review of evangelical/Pentecostal debates, see Archer, *Pentecostal Hermeneutic*, 125–48.

51. Pinnock, "Work of the Holy Spirit," esp., 9, 16; Pinnock, "Role of the Spirit," 494.

52. Pinnock, "Role of the Spirit," 494–95.

53. See Pinnock, "Work of the Holy Spirit," 17.

54. For an example of his methodological argument see Pinnock, "Truce Proposal," 8.

55. Postliberalism encompasses a theological outlook that emerged in the 1970s and

In the wake of these new areas of hermeneutical inquiry came publications focused on the issue of genre at the forefront.[56] For example, Robert C. Tannehill's narrative commentary was one of many literary treatments of Acts, specifically as a form of ancient novel or biography.[57] Other studies, aligned more closely to our inquiry concerning the community's role in theological creativity, addressing decision-making in the early church include works by Luke Timothy Johnson and Jeff Brown.[58] Johnson's study focuses on the role of individual leaders rather than on the community as a whole. In our view his goal is to use apostolic actions in Acts as a springboard from which to address larger social concerns affecting the contemporary church.[59] His challenge for more research concerning "the active role of the assembly and not just leaders" is addressed in this study.[60] Brown also addresses episodes in Acts similar to our study. However, his method is more canonical in nature, drawing on both New Testament and patristic writings with an emphasis on church order and polity.[61] While the writings of Luke are integral to both Johnson and Brown, neither limits their inquiry

---

80s and is generally associated with a community of scholars from Yale University and often referred to as "the Yale school." Postliberals recognize a shift in the thinking process of those living in the "after-effects" of the Enlightenment—the modern era—to a postmodern thinking process generally shaped by language, culture, and practice. For examples, see Frei, "'Literal Reading' of Biblical Narrative," 36–77; Tanner, "Theology and the Plain Sense," 59–78; Lindbeck, *Nature of Doctrine*, 15–29. Also consider the works of Frei, *The Eclipse of Biblical Narrative*; Frei, *The Identity of Jesus Christ*.

56. For support see the work of Pervo, *Profit with Delight*. For an extensive review and analysis of other publications, see Penner, "Madness in the Method?," 223–93, esp. 226–51.

57. Tannehill, *Narrative Unity of Luke-Acts*. For examples of subsequent works using literary analysis, see L. Johnson, *Acts*; Kurz, *Reading Luke-Acts*; Parsons and Pervo, *Rethinking the Unity of Luke and Acts*; Dunn, *Acts*; Kee, *To Every Nation*; Spencer, *Acts*; Talbert, *Reading Acts*; Gaventa, *Acts*.

58. See Johnson, *Scripture and Discernment*; Brown, *Corporate Decision-Making*.

59. See chapters 5 and 7 respectively in Johnson, *Scripture and Discernment*. In chapter 7, Johnson directly addresses the role of women in the church, the hermeneutical challenge of homosexuality and the Christian community, and the sharing of possessions among the body of believers. See Johnson, *Scripture and Discernment*, 108, 139–51.

60. Johnson, *Scripture and Discernment*, 108. We will address the "active role of the community" in chapters 1–5.

61. Brown's work assumes general continuity across the spectrum of these writings and concludes, "The Bible supplies more than sufficient instruction to churches on how to structure and conduct church order (187)." Brown, *Corporate Decision-Making*, 4–5, 172–87.

to Luke's portrayal of the first-century community of believers engaging in theological creativity.

"The Community" in Renewal Studies

Attempts to explain the role of the community in the interpretive or hermeneutical process by renewal scholars was sparse prior to the 1990s.[62] However, that changed with a challenge by Rickie D. Moore. He is one of the earliest Pentecostals to engage in conversation concerning the cooperative nature of Spirit–Community–Scripture, what he described as "the text, the community, and also the ongoing voice of the Holy Spirit," and its importance in hermeneutical discussion.[63] Moore challenged his peers to avoid, "the liberal-critical tradition and the conservative Evangelical tradition," by concluding both extremes approach interpretation as a matter "essentially limited to the reader and the text."[64] For Moore, limiting the interpretive process to reader and text (Community–Scripture) leaves engagement with the Spirit out of the process.

Within a few years, many scholars engaged Moore's challenge. For example, John Christopher Thomas sought to illustrate the community's role in theological creativity through an exegesis of Acts 15.[65] Here, Thomas describes how the Apostles wrangle over the inclusion of non-Jewish converts into full fellowship. He concludes that the interpretive method employed is one that moves from context to text and one in which "the experience of the Spirit in the community helped the church make its way through this hermeneutical maze."[66] For him, the way the community begins its deliberations with the believing community's perception of the Spirit's work (e.g., Peter's vision and encounter with Cornelius), followed by the testimony of Paul and Barnabas and, finally, James' use of Scripture, serves as evidence

---

62. Again, in the context of this research, the term renewal refers to Christian traditions that emphasize the work of the Holy Spirit within creation in general and in the life of the Christian community in particular. Generally speaking, these include Pentecostal and Charismatic traditions.

63. R. Moore, "Canon and Charisma," 75–92, esp. 75 n. 1. Earlier hints of his position are recognizable in a 1987 student-led publication, see Moore, "Pentecostal Approach to Scripture," 4–5, 11.

64. Moore, "Canon and Charisma," 75 n. 1.

65. J. Thomas, "Women, Pentecostals," 41–56, esp. 44–49.

66. Thomas, "Women, Pentecostals," 50.

for his claim. We find his view of Spirit–Community–Scripture compelling and will engage him more directly in chapter 4.

Other voices around this same time include French Arrington, who also uses the council of Acts 15 to demonstrate a "biblical model for interpretation," that includes Scripture, experience, tradition, and reason, and to describe the Pentecostal community of faith as those bound together "by the bond of love, interdependence and accountability."[67] One final example includes Mark Stibbe, who addresses the role of community in the context of defending his own theological method, one he sees as unhinged from evangelical constraints of authorial intent.[68] For him, genuine Charismatic community occurs within the fellowship of believers who exercise the charisma of prophecy and enjoy a "shared experience" while also providing an environment of checks and balances.[69] Generally speaking, these views subordinate the community's role to Spirit and Scripture as if one or the other "tells" the community what to do without explaining adequately how the community adjudicates either. Consequently, we find these views inadequate to explain a harmonious and cooperative triadic view of Spirit–Community–Scripture.

In the early 2000s, three Pentecostals scholars published books that offer a sustained argument for (or a view of) a cooperative triadic notion of Spirit–Community–Scripture. These voices include Amos Yong (2002), Kenneth J. Archer (2004), and Simon Chan (2006). We have selected their works because they are diverse in perspective[70] and because, as we will show, their studies can benefit from a sustained inquiry of Luke's portrayal of the first-century community of believers engaged in theological creativity. After a cursory review below, we will revisit their assumptions in our

67. Arrington, "Use of the Bible," 106.

68. Stibbe, "This Is That," 185.

69. Stibbe, "This Is That," 186. "It is the 'fellowship of the Holy Spirit' enjoyed by all those who have been baptized in the Spirit, going right back to the book of Acts (and even further back, to the charismatic history of ancient Israel)." In a rejoinder, Lyons challenges Stibbe's notion of community as a locus of accountability and calls it "problematic." See Lyons, "Fourth Wave," 170, 175.

70. We will consider their works in order of publication date. Yong's (*Spirit–Word–Community*) view of community is philosophical in nature. Archer's (*Pentecostal Hermeneutic*) bases his view of community on a modern cultural heritage of north-American early twentieth-century Pentecostal experience. Chan (*Liturgical Theology*) links his view of community to historic Christian tradition.

conclusion and offer specific ways in which our study compliments, clarifies, or refutes their findings.[71]

Amos Yong

Philosophically, Yong defines the Christian community or church as "an organic, dynamic and eschatological people of God called after the name of Jesus and constituted in the fellowship of the Holy Spirit."[72] For Yong, a Christian community finds expression in a local church or fellowship of churches (denomination).[73] Yong identifies the Pentecostal community in its most basic terms, as those who have experienced Spirit baptism, without necessarily linking it to a specific dogma. His challenge is for the Pentecostal church to be adaptive in light of the contemporary workings of the Holy Spirit through discernment and an ever-emerging understanding of Scripture through theological reflection.[74]

As the Pentecostal church moves into the twenty-first century and past its fourth generation, Yong argues issues once taken for granted, such as "what is the church?," or even "who are the Pentecostals?," have led many theologians and church leaders to reexamine the nature and function of the church.[75] Yong's particular challenge to the Pentecostal community is to reflect on what it means to be part of historic Christianity—specifically, to identify the defining marks of the Church throughout the ages—from a Pneumatological perspective so as to retrieve these qualities not only for the present time but also in order to clarify the "church's self-definition."[76] Moreover, in *The Spirit Poured Out on All Flesh*, Yong addresses the growing need of Pentecostals to develop a more adequate ecclesiology.[77] According to him, Pentecostals tend to be highly individualist in nature and generally resistant to hierarchical structures (at least beyond a charismatic figure, preacher, or prophet) while their ecclesiological understanding tends to be

71. See chapter 6.

72. Yong, *Spirit Poured Out*, 122.

73. Yong, *Spirit-Word-Community*, 17.

74. For his nuanced definitions of Pentecostal, Pentecostals, pentecostal, and pentecostalism see Yong, *Spirit Poured Out*, 18–22.

75. For examples, see Yong, *Spirit Poured Out*, 122–24, 131–34.

76. Yong, *Spirit Poured Out*, 133.

77. See Yong, *Spirit Poured Out*, 121–66. Matters of ecclesiology are taken up in greater detail by Chan, *Liturgical Theology*.

a matter relegated to common sense—that is, one not requiring an elaborate dogmatic delineation.[78]

Finally, Yong argues that a legitimate discussion of the community's role in the interpretive or hermeneutical process must take into consideration the impact external aspects—such as ecological factors, nature, culture, gender, geo-political, socio-economic, and intellectual factors—have on a community of believers.[79] All such matters become important theological concerns for the church if it is to understand itself as a responsible community who interprets sacred Scripture and discerns the present-day workings of the Holy Spirit.[80] Unfortunately, Yong does not identify how this interaction might, so to say, "work" specifically in daily experience beyond suggesting that it could not happen apart from its interaction in and among a wider society. We will engage these issues directly in light of our findings in the final chapter.

Kenneth Archer

For Archer, community is identified by a group's "story."[81] He contends that the Pentecostals' story, or narrative tradition, gave rise to what he calls the Central Narrative Convictions (CNCs) of the early twentieth-century north-American Pentecostal community. The convictions that emerged from their encounter with Spirit baptism functioned as the primary interpretive lens for the early Pentecostals' reading of Scripture and self-understanding of the Spirit's work.[82] For Archer, these convictions are crystallized in the motifs of the "latter rain" and "primitivism" and he claims that these

78. See Yong, *Spirit Poured Out*, 122–24, 131–34. "The implicit response is that one asserts but does not define what seems self-evident" (132).

79. According to Yong, such theological considerations are also crucial for the development of a historic and contemporary Pentecostal ecclesiology. Yong, *Spirit–Word–Community*, 297–310.

80. See Yong, *Spirit–Word–Community*, 282–86, 297; Yong, *Spirit Poured Out*, 122–34.

81. See Archer, *Pentecostal Hermeneutic*, 94–126, esp. 95–114. Aside from identifying North American early twentieth-century Pentecostalism as the context for his study, Archer does not specifically identify who the Pentecostal community is or how the community functions in the interpretive process beyond an anecdotal level. For Archer, in its most basic sense, a community of believers is the church where one attends or the ministerial fellowship where one is credentialed.

82. Archer, *Pentecostal Hermeneutic*, 114–18. For a revised version of chapter 4, see Archer, "Pentecostal Story."

motifs are so crucial to Pentecostal identity that there could be no Pentecostal story without it.[83] He argues the Pentecostals of the early twentieth century made use of these two motifs to explain their encounter with Spirit baptism as the promised "latter rain" of the Holy Spirit and to justify their general disdain for church history in favor of a return to early apostolic living.

In a follow-up article, Archer describes how the kernel of Pentecostal experience and the emerging convictions of the day were collapsed into a "revised Pentecostal story," a homogenization of latter rain and primitivism teaching.[84] Later, Archer enlarges on his concept of the Pentecostal story by explaining how the narrative of a community functions to provide a "coherent and cohesive structure for articulating Pentecostal identity."[85] Here, he identifies the "Five-fold" gospel as the primary central narrative conviction (CNC) by which Pentecostals approach biblical interpretation and that this conviction encompasses the "doxological testimonies" that shape Pentecostal community.[86] Consequently, he concludes that the Pentecostal story (narrative tradition) is the lens through which Scripture is read.[87]

Archer claims that a "hermeneutical community," is an "important and necessary component of the hermeneutical strategy" if it is to function interdependently in the triadic notion of "Scripture, Spirit, and community."[88] Any such strategy for Pentecostals should include the following aspects. First, a narrative strategy that embraces a dialectical negotiation for meaning between text and reader since all written communication is "underdeterminate" and "needs" the reader to complete the communicative event.[89] Second, a Pentecostal strategy must incorporate a text-centered and

83. See Archer, "Pentecostal Story," 47. For a succinct description of the "Latter Rain" and "Primitivism" motifs see Archer, "Pentecostal Story," 45–54.

84. For a fuller definition of "Classic Pentecostalism," see Archer, "Pentecostal Story," 57–59. See also Archer, *Pentecostal Hermeneutic*, 117–18.

85. See Archer, "Pentecostal Way," 310–14.

86. Archer states, "The proclamation of the Full Gospel is the declaration of the redemptive activity of God in Christ Jesus and the Holy Spirit to the community. . . . Thus the Five-fold Gospel is not a set of quaint platitudes but deep-seated affectionate affirmations flowing from our worship of the living God who has transformed our lives." Archer, "Pentecostal Way," 312.

87. Archer develops this argument in *Pentecostal Hermeneutic*, 94–126, esp. 98–99.

88. Archer, *Pentecostal Hermeneutic*, 158, 164. Concerning a philosophical view of the "hermeneutical community," see Israel, Albrecht, and McNally, "Pentecostals and Hermeneutics," 160–61.

89. Archer, *Pentecostal Hermeneutic*, 157, 175.

reader-oriented interpretive method.[90] He maintains that reading Scripture as a literary whole, allowing one passage to inform another, is essential to a Pentecostal reading of Scripture.[91] Third, the Pentecostal strategy must embrace a "hermeneutic of suspicion" and a "hermeneutic of retrieval."[92] Archer has raised several important aspects relevant to our study and we will revisit these aspects in light of our findings in the final chapter.

Simon Chan

Simon Chan approaches Christian community from a different perspective than Archer's direct connection to classical Pentecostalism and one more akin to Yong's philosophical approach with a call for a more robust ecclesiological formation. For Chan, the Christian community is first and foremost one that identifies itself with ancient Israel and apostolic experience. He states, "To call the church the people of God is to recognize that it exists in continuity with the ancient covenant people of God . . . even those . . . who continue to be addressed in the New Testament as the people of God."[93]

Second, the community of believers must acknowledge itself as a people "with a history—a history of ups and downs, of successes and failures."[94] Conceiving of identity in this regard requires continual reevaluation and an eschatological view of life. In regard to this eschatological dimension, Chan states, "The church is constantly on the move, in need of being transformed by the Spirit until it is completely restored at the consummation of the age."[95] Since the contemporary Christian community is not the "ideal" community, the community must continually see itself moving towards the ideal community in Christ just as every generation of believers has had to do from the patriarchs to the present age.

90. Archer, *Pentecostal Hermeneutic*, 157.

91. Archer, *Pentecostal Hermeneutic*, 163–64. For Archer, the Pentecostal strategy should seek to "capture the inner texture of the text and interpret Scripture with Scripture," what he refers to as the "Bible Reading Method" (163).

92. Suspicion (i.e., willingness to suspect). Retrieval (i.e., willingness to listen). Archer, *Pentecostal Hermeneutic*, 158. See also Ricoeur, *Freud and Philosophy*, 27.

93. Chan, *Liturgical Theology*, 24. The church community does not replace ancient Israel or the apostolic community, rather it is adopted into the same family.

94. Chan, *Liturgical Theology*, 26.

95. Chan, *Liturgical Theology*, 32. In other words, the community envisions itself as a group that is not already "there" but "going there."

Third, Chan describes the community as a peculiar people. As such, the community adheres to certain "core practices." He states,

> These marks are variously conceived. For John Calvin, the marks of the church are Word and sacrament. For Luther, they are the Word of God, baptism, Holy Communion, church discipline, church office, worship and discipleship. In sum, the people of God are distinguished by their faith in Jesus Christ, and the unique quality of their community by faithfulness to that gospel.[96]

However the markers are defined, the community's ethos is defined by specific rituals and doctrines the make them into a community that is in the world but not of the world—as a "community of character."[97]

Fourth, in order for a community to function in cooperative sense, it cannot deny that it too is part of history, part of an ongoing tradition. Chan argues that a popular conception of *sola Scriptura* takes an "ahistorical view of the church supported by an ahistorical view of Scripture, cut off from tradition."[98] Consequently the community dislodges the biblical text from any former living community, even possibly that of the first-century apostles, and forces the text to function as a series of propositional truth claims, as if those principles had never been lived-out before. While he maintains the essentiality of Scripture for the believing community he does not define community by its commitment to Scripture alone.

Finally, for Chan, the basic identity of Christian community is not "found in what it *does* but in what it *is*."[99] Chan draws upon Sergius Bulgakov's conception of "divine-humanity" to describe a church community as the body of Christ with Christ as its head.[100] From this position, the church community is revealed by its spiritual-ontological existence rather than from any sociological structure.[101] As we will see, Chan's five descriptors of the community of believers find concrete expression in our study. We will address these issues in light of our findings in the final chapter.

---

96. Chan, *Liturgical Theology*, 26, 27. Bloesch refers to these core practices as "the marks of the church." See Bloesch, *Church*, 174.

97. Chan, *Liturgical Theology*, 27. Also see Bloesch, *Church*, 133.

98. Chan, *Liturgical Theology*, 30.

99. Chan, *Liturgical Theology*, 23 (italics original).

100. For more detail of Bulgakov's understanding of divine-humanity, see Bulgakov, *Comforter*, 355–58.

101. Chan, *Liturgical Theology*, 24–39, esp. 29.

Studies on Characterization in Luke-Acts

In this final section, we will draw attention to the methods utilized by Robert Brawely (1990), David B. Gowler (1991), John Darr (1992), and William Shepherd Jr. (1994) because their works focus on characterization in Luke's writings and because of the way in which their methodologically approach is helpful to our inquiry.[102]

Robert Brawley defines characters in literature as a "product of combinations—combinations of semes."[103] His work draws heavily on literary notions popularized by Roland Barthes. For Barthes, semes are essential signs or clues provided by the author such as emotions, personal traits, thoughts, and actions united under a proper name or assigned to an entity within the story.[104] Brawley further-develops Barthes' notion by exploring how the reader, or recipient, becomes aware of and gives meaning to narrative characters as a unified whole and by using the clues provided in Luke-Acts.[105] Like Henry James, Brawley maintains that plot is dependent on characters and characters are dependent on plot.[106] Brawley applies these two aspects from Barthes and James in an attempt to demonstrate God as a character in the writings of Luke.[107] Unlike our study, he views characters as semiotic (as signs) rather than mimetic (as real people). Nevertheless, his effort to assign the role of character to an entity does parallel our own effort to assign character to the community, especially in chapters 1 and 4.

For David Gowler, debates concerning character and characterization in literature revolve around two primary concerns: (1) whether characters should be viewed as mimetic (as real persons) or as semiotic (as words/signs on a page) and (2) the relationship of characters to plot.[108] His socio-

102. For a thorough review of earlier redactional and text-critical studies on characters in Luke-Acts, see E. J. Richard, "Luke: Writer, Theologian, Historian," 3–15; Darr, *Herod the Fox*, 65 n. 2.

103. Brawley, *Centering on God*, 107.

104. See Barthes et al., *S/Z*, 67; Barthes, *Semiotic Challenge*, 234–35.

105. Brawley, *Centering on God*, 107.

106. Brawley, *Centering on God*, 108. As James states, "What is character but the determination of incident? What is incident but the illustration of character?" James, "Art of Fiction," 302.

107. Brawley, *Centering on God*, 111–24. In subsequent works he applies his method to characterize Jesus, Paul, and Peter.

108. "Theories that lean to the side of mimesis argue that characters are like real people, whereas semiotic theories dissolve characters into textuality." Gowler, *Host*, 29. Cf. Rimmon-Kenan, *Narrative Fiction*, 33. Cf. Harvey, *Character and the Novel*, 11–13.

narratological approach is in large part drawn from the work of Shlomith Rimmon-Kenan and argues characters are both mimetic and semiotic as well as subordinate or superior to the plot and dependent on the genre of literature.[109] Methodologically, Gowler evaluates characters on a "scale of descending reliability and explicitness."[110] When reliability and explicitness are low, the reader must consider "cultural scripts" and ancient literary (era) norms in order to fill in the gaps.[111]

Moreover, Gowler maintains both reliability and explicitness are expressed in narrative by either direct definition or indirect presentation.[112] For Gowler, direct definition guides the readers to a conclusion whereas indirect presentation requires the readers to draw their own conclusions. A summary of his socio-narratological approach is as follows:

1. Direct Definition: the most explicit form of characterization, requiring evaluation on a descending scale of reliability (dependent on who is speaking). Narrators and characters have varying degrees of reliability and explicitness.

2. Indirect Presentation: displays rather than overtly announces character traits and activities. The reader must determine the inference and value to the overall plot as well as apply varying degrees of reliability and explicitness. The following are examples:

   a. Speech—what the narrator and characters state, including internal thoughts. Less explicit than direct definition and subject to reliability;

   b. Action—by characters, including acts of commission, omission, or even those contemplated;

Harvey uses the terms mimesis (this is category he favors) and autonomy. Mimesis "affirms the root proposition that 'Art imitates Nature'" and autonomy indicates a "created *thing*, a self-sufficient artefact containing its meaning and value within itself." Harvey, *Character and the Novel*, 11–12 (italics original).

109. Gowler, *Host*, 70–71, 73. Cf. Rimmon-Kenan, *Narrative Fiction*, esp. 29–42.

110. Gowler, *Host*, 55, esp. 55 n. 88, where Gowler states, "Reliability is the measure of what extent a speaker's veracity may be trusted. Explicitness refers to the clarity of the message."

111. Gowler argues, "Cultural scripts vary from age to age and culture to culture, but every text is a socially symbolic act and assumes certain cultural norms." Gowler, *Host*, 73–74.

112. Gowler, *Host*, 55–75, esp. 61. Direct definition (information from the narrator) is explicit. Indirect presentation highlights qualities and traits of characters or locations requiring the reader/audience to draw conclusions from the inferences.

c. Appearance—how the character appears;

d. Environment—including geography, social status, and personal or family background;

e. Comparison/Contrast—may be explicit or implicit.[113]

Gowler's application of direct definition and indirect presentation will help us identify the community as a character, particularly in chapters 2, 3, 4, and 6.

John Darr's approach to characterization in Luke-Acts begins with the reader's response in the process of reading.[114] He follows the literary theories of Stanley Fish and Wolfgang Iser in this regard.[115] Darr defines character as "any figure or group in a literary work" and characterization as "the process by which characters are formulated, depicted and developed."[116] He states,

> A pragmatic approach to characterization requires that the critic be especially sensitive to narrative sequence. The goal is not to arrive at a static conception of a character (the author's mental image of the character, for example), but, rather, to trace the reader's successive construction and assessment of a character during the dynamic process of actualizing the text (i.e. reading it). Character is cumulative and the manner, means, and timing of its accumulation is hermeneutically significant.[117]

Just as narrative sequence and timing are hermeneutically important for Darr, so it is in chapters 4 and 5 of our study. As we will see in these chapters, issues of sequence and timing are important to understanding why the first-century community of believers in Luke's story respond as it does at various moments in theological creativity. Consequently, we will argue

---

113. Gowler, *Host*, 72–73. For analysis and evaluation of Gowler's method, see W. Shepherd, *Narrative Function*, 87–89.

114. Darr, *On Character Building*, 11.

115. For example, see Fish, *Is There a Text*, 7–17, esp. 10–11, 15–16. For an analysis of Fish's influence, see Porter, "Why Hasn't Reader-Response," 278–92. Cf. Iser, *Act of Reading*, 35–36, 107; Iser, *Implied Reader*, 34–35. For an analysis of Iser's influence see Aichele, *Postmodern Bible*, 31, 41–51; Archer, *Pentecostal Hermeneutic*, 179–80.

116. Darr, *On Character Building*, 11, 173 n. 1.

117. Darr, *Herod the Fox*, 73, also 73 n. 29. Cf. Springer, *A Rhetoric of Literary Character*, 17, 178–79. Despite Springer's support for the "successive construction and assessment of character" advocated by Darr (*Herod the Fox*, 73), she is opposed to the use of highly subjective reader-response analysis.

that failing to appreciate the narrative sequence in Acts leads to a misunderstanding of the community's actions and confusion concerning Luke's overall plot.[118]

Lastly, William Shepherd Jr. presents Acts as novel-like in nature with a focus on the character and characterization of the Holy Spirit. His treatment offers a compelling amalgamation of both Gowler's and Hochman's method for evaluating characters and characterization in Luke's presentation of theological development in the early church.[119] For example, he uses of Hochman's character categories of action and conflict as evidence for justifying the Holy Spirit as a character within Luke's writings.[120] Furthermore, he applies Gowler's methodology for evaluating reliability and explicitness using direct definition and indirect presentation. Shepherd's methodology is similar to ours in that we too use the character categories of action and conflict throughout our study while applying the method of direct definition and indirect presentation to identify the community as a character in Luke's narrative.

Methodology

We will begin our study with the assumption that Acts is a narrative tale written by Luke with an emphasis on how he portrays the first-century community of believers as an integral character in his story. We will take for granted that Luke is writing about an historical people while characterizing the events and characters for his own narrative purpose. As noted earlier, to characterize is to give someone or something in a story substance (e.g., traits), which ultimately moves the story forward in grand and minute ways.[121] Moreover, characterization involves the author's technique of developing characters in a story.[122] With these things in mind, we will follow a narrative-critical method that is sensitive to the conventions of first-century storytelling.

118. Cf. Darr, *Herod the Fox*, 74.

119. W. Shepherd, *Narrative Function*, 71–78, 87–89, 90–98. He provides detailed analysis in chapter 4, "Characterization of the Holy Spirit in Luke-Acts (II): The Acts of the Apostles," 153–243.

120. W. Shepherd, *Narrative Function*, 66.

121. Chatman, *Story and Discourse*, 119–45, esp. 126–31; Harvey, *Character and the Novel*, 31–33, 56–57.

122. Bennema, *Encountering Jesus*, 37.

In order to demonstrate the manner in which Luke characterizes the first-century community in his story as an essential element, we will utilize Hochman's categories of action and conflict as inherent motivating qualities to identify the community as a character in the story. We will then use direct definition and indirect presentation to identify its actions while paying close attention to narrative matters of sequence and time. Although this study addresses the triadic interplay between Spirit–Community–Scripture, our focus is limited to Luke's narrative use of the first-century community of believers as a character in theological creativity. Consequently, the role of the Spirit and Scripture, though important, will receive incidental consideration.

In chapter 1, we will examine Luke's portrayal of the community engaged in theological creativity in the days immediately following the ascension of Jesus (Acts 1:12–26). This chapter will demonstrate that, for Luke, the community is a distinct character in the narrative taking action in light of their theological beliefs concerning their role in the coming kingdom of Jesus. Specifically, we will see the community as a character decide on theological grounds to reestablish "The Twelve."

In chapter 2, we will examine the community's prayer in Acts 4:23–31 to see Luke's view of the community engaging in theological creativity following the apostles' first persecution in Jerusalem. The theological perspective idealized in the community's corporate prayer reveals the motivation for its decision to continue public preaching ministry despite threats from local authorities (4:16–21). We will explore how Luke reveals the identity of the community in and by the theological content contained in their prayer following the release of Peter and John. Furthermore, we will argue that the theological content of the prayer reveals Luke's characterization of the community and reveals what these early followers of Jesus believed concerning Jesus as Messiah.

In chapter 3, we will see how Luke describes the community engaging in theological creativity through the process of selecting and commissioning a new group of leaders in Acts 6:1–7. Here we will see Luke introduce a diverse community of believers as "groups within in a group," which he describes as disciples for the first time in Acts. Furthermore, we will see how Luke uses a social conflict between two previously unknown factions as the catalyst for a continually broadening leadership structure and expansion beyond the city of Jerusalem. By accentuating the diversity among the disciples as it deals with a social crisis in Jerusalem, Luke is able to demonstrate for his audience a theological explanation for continued growth among the disciples of Jesus.

In chapter 4, we will see that Luke's narrative, concerning the acceptance of the Gentiles into fellowship, offers a glimpse into the early efforts of the first-century community of believers to establish churches beyond Judea and into the surrounding territories. His episodic development of events concerning the evangelization of and fellowship with Gentiles culminates in a meeting of the "whole church" in Acts 15:1–31. We will argue that Luke's narrative development endeavors to demonstrate how the whole church, again, as groups within a group, manage to unite to resolve this crisis. Peter's vision and subsequent interaction with the house of Cornelius (Acts 10–11), the testimony of Paul and Barnabas (15:4, 12), along with James' interpretation of Scripture (15:15–18) enables the whole church to conclude that the missionary expansion of the gospel to the Gentiles is consistent with Scripture and a consequence of the Spirit's evidential work.

In chapter 5, we will demonstrate how Luke characterizes prophets and prophetic words as an influential factor for the first-century community of believers' engagement in theological creativity. In Acts 11:29–30, 13:1–4, and 21:4, 10–14 we will see the high regard Luke places on prophets and prophetic utterance. Moreover, we will demonstrate that the community, and not the prophet giving the prophetic utterance, is responsible for evaluating the purpose of the prophecy and deciding what course of action should be taken. As in previous chapters, the community will be presented as a central character who is active in recognizing and testifying of the Spirit's evidential work.

In our final chapter, we will bring together our findings from chapters two through five concerning Luke's portrayal of the first-century community of believers engaging in theological creativity. In light of our findings, we will reengage the works of Yong, Archer, and Chan concerning a cooperative triadic notion of Spirit–Community–Scripture in order to see how Luke's portrayal of the role of the first-century community of believers in theological creativity compliments, clarifies, and challenges their findings. In so doing, we will see how the community's role neither stands above nor is subordinate to Spirit or Scripture but rather functions cooperatively with both.

1

REESTABLISHING THE TWELVE
—ACTS 1:12–26

IN THIS CHAPTER, WE will examine Luke's narrative portrayal of the first-century community of believers engaged in theological creativity in the first few days following Jesus' ascension (Acts 1:9). Moreover, we will discover that, in Luke's view, the theological issues important to the first-century community require the reestablishment of the Twelve as its core leadership. The chapter will conclude by summarizing the main points and evidence to demonstrate Luke's view of the community as a character engaging in theological creativity.[1]

Identifying the Community

In order to identify Luke's view of the community in theological creativity in Acts 1:15–26, we must first examine the manner in which Luke characterizes and highlights the theological basis for the actions taken by that

---

1. Theological creativity is the act of reformulating formerly held theological interpretations in light of testimony concerning the Spirit's evidential work and an emerging understanding of applicable Scripture followed by commensurate action. The Spirit's evidential work is known only through the community's testimony. Therefore, theological creativity is the outcome of the interpretive process since it is theology in action, functional in nature, and situationally pragmatic in scope. Consequently, it involves the process of theological justification and action or reaction in light of current circumstances. In this sense, to be creative with theology is to take what is already a theological assumption and broaden or adapt it to current circumstances in light of the Spirit's evidential work and a consensus understanding of Scripture.

community. As we will see, the community of believers as a character is identifiable throughout Acts 1.

In this section, we will analyze the text with regard to the terms Luke uses to describe the community as well as the actions he ascribes to the community as a character. Utilizing Hochman's qualities of characterization in literature—specifically action, conflict, and need for resolution—identifying the community as a character in Luke's narrative becomes clear.[2]

Luke uses a variety of terms to describe the community and presents it as one motivated to specific actions. In so doing, he characterizes the community through a process of "showing and telling."[3] For example, immediately following the ascension of Jesus in Acts 1, Luke draws specific attention to the constituency and size of the group (Acts 1:12-15). Numbering one hundred and twenty (1:15), the community of believers includes eleven of the twelve disciples, whom Luke identifies as apostles (Luke 6:13), along with "certain other women," Jesus' mother, and brothers (siblings) of Jesus (Acts 1:14).

Much has been made of Luke's use of the number one hundred and twenty.[4] Johnson suggests Luke's use of it (and the number, twelve) is significant since the apostles see themselves as representative of the new twelve tribes of Israel (Luke 22:29-30).[5] For him, Luke draws on practices reminiscent of other first-century Jewish sects at Qumran. However, while evidence exists that one hundred twenty men are necessary to constitute a local Sanhedrin, it is unlikely that Luke's intention is to show continuity with Qumran for two reasons: (1) he includes women (Acts 1:14; D05 also includes "wives and children"), and (2) it is unproven whether anyone in Luke's audience would make such a connection.[6] Perhaps Luke's intention, in the most general sense, is to simply show that the community is large enough to require organization.[7] Whatever its numeric purpose, it is im-

---

2. Hochman demonstrates the function of characters within narratives and the manner in which they move the story forward. See Hochman, *Character in Literature*, 49–51, 138–40.

3. For an explanation of "showing and telling," see the introduction.

4. Grabbe, *Introduction to Second Temple Judaism*, 80, 135; Johnson, *Acts*, 34; Twelftree, *People of the Spirit*, 15.

5. L. Johnson, *Acts*, 39.

6. Comparisons between the early church and Qumran are generally unhelpful. For support see Conzelmann, *Acts*, 10; Haenchen, *Acts*, 164; Fitzmyer, "Jewish Christianity in Acts," 239; Rengstorf, "Election of Matthias," 182.

7. Marshal, *Acts*, 64.

portant to keep in mind that foremost in the agenda of the believers is the restoration of the "kingdom to Israel" (Acts 1:6) and the selection of Judas' replacement as one of the Twelve (1:15–26).[8]

In a further example of showing and telling, Luke narratively reveals the community's theological interests through the way they question Jesus and through their ensuing course of action to replace Judas (1:6–7, 15–26). Both their question and action possess eschatological expectations. While first-century Jewish expectations concerning the Messiah is beyond the scope of this study, how Luke characterizes these early believers' messianic expectations is certainly relevant. Marion L. Soards identifies four characteristics applicable to religiously sectarian Jews at the time of Luke's writing:

1. *monotheism*, i.e., the belief in the God of Abraham;

2. *nationalism*, i.e., a conviction that the God of Abraham gave to Abraham's heirs the "promised land;"

3. *concern for the Law*, i.e., belief that part of God's covenant with Israel was the giving of the Law as the standard for life in the context of the covenant; and,

4. *an apocalyptic perspective on the world*, i.e., a conviction that the world was set in opposition to God and that God was about to intervene [on] behalf of God's rightful lordship and in redemption of God's chosen people.[9]

Soards admits these are common assumptions among New Testament studies and highly debated in the wider field of first-century Jewish studies.[10] Notwithstanding, whether or not the average religiously minded first-century Jew held eschatological or apocalyptic views, it seems apparent in Luke's story that the community in Acts 1 did (Acts 1:.6, 21; Luke

---

8. For example, Dunn argues, "It was a matter of theological principle for the first Christians to be able to speak of an unbroken group of 'the twelve' as a fundamental factor in Christian beginnings (1 Cor 15:5; Rev 21:14)." Dunn, *Acts*, 4. Tannehill states, "the expressions of disappointment and revived hope in Luke 24:21 and Acts 1:6 serve to remind us of the importance of this hope for Israel." See Tannehill, *Narrative Unity of Luke-Acts*, 15.

9. Soards, "Historical and Cultural Setting," 37–38, also 166 n. 11 (italics original). For a similar list, minus the "apocalyptic perspective on the world," see W. Davies, "Contemporary Jewish Religion," 706–8.

10. Soards, "Historical and Cultural Setting," 166 n. 11. Also see Grabbe, *Introduction to Second Temple Judaism*, 80; Davies, "Contemporary Jewish Religion," 706.

22:28–30).[11] In light of this, we argue that what seems important to this earliest community of believers in Acts 1 is driven by a theological understanding of their importance as participants in the coming kingdom of Jesus (Luke 22:28–30) and of an expectation of the restoration of national sovereignty (Acts 1:6).[12]

In a final example, Luke narratively reveals that a sense of conflict with and a need for closure on the matter of Judas Iscariot weighs heavily on the apostles in two ways. First, given the nature of the *analepsis* found in Acts 1:18–19, it is narratively apparent that the community also felt public pressure to reinstate their number to twelve and put behind them the scandal produced by Judas' defection.[13] We see this in the background information useful for Luke's Greek-speaking audience (Acts 1:18–19).[14] In so doing Luke highlights the attention Judas' death and ensuing events had garnered.[15] By revealing their final question to Jesus (1:6) as well as news concerning the perception of a public scandal (1:19) Luke is able to demonstrate that the community of believers is motivated by at least three factors:

1. An eschatological perception that Jesus would restore Israel's independence (Acts 1:6);

2. Local perception (known to all the residents) concerning the treachery of Judas' betrayal, death, and publicity garnered over the purchase of *Hakeldama* (field of blood, 1:19);[16] and

11. Despite the existence of messianic expectations among first-century Jewish sects, research available today makes it clear that a variety of views existed concerning messianic expectations. As Grabbe notes, there is no "single 'Jewish messianic expectation' in the late second-temple period." Grabbe, *Introduction to Second Temple Judaism*, 80, 135. For an extended analysis of Luke's eschatological views see Keener, *Acts*, 1:682–88; E. Sanders, *Jesus and Judaism*, 95–106.

12. Clearly, Luke characterizes the apostles seeing themselves as a continuation of Jewish tradition. For support see Jeremias, *New Testament Theology*, 234; E. Sanders, *The Historical Figure of Jesus*, 120, 185; McKnight, "Jesus and the Twelve," 223–28.

13. An *analepsis* in narrative is the addition of information occurring earlier in the timeline of the story but withheld until the current text-time (a flashback). See Rimmon-Kenan, *Narrative Fiction*, 46–51.

14. Acts 1:18–19, "Now this man acquired a field with the reward of his wickedness; and falling headlong, he burst open in the middle and all his bowels gushed out. This became known to all the residents of Jerusalem, so that the field was called in their language Hakeldama, that is, Field of Blood." For general views on suicide in antiquity, see Keener, *Acts*, 3:2498–507, esp. 2505–6.

15. Fitzmyer refers to Luke's sources as "folkloric." Fitzmyer, *Acts*, 224.

16. Luke does not indicate the fate of Judas in his Gospel. A comparison between

3. A group-perceived need to refill the twelfth position in light of Jesus' declaration that " . . . you will sit on thrones judging the twelve tribes of Israel" (Luke 22:30; Acts 1:17, 22).

Second, we see the conflict with and need for closure revealed when Peter states, "One of these [men] must become a witness with us" (Acts 1:22). Luke's use of the word δεῖ (must) signals their sense of the divine will.[17] He presents a community working to put the scandal of Judas behind them. In Luke's story, the only way forward from the community's perspective is to replace Judas and prepare for the restoration of the kingdom (Acts 1:6). These Jewish followers of Jesus in Jerusalem corporately possess a theological need to fill the twelfth position vacated by Judas Iscariot. In light of his defection, Luke characterizes the reestablishment of the Twelve as a matter of utmost importance to the nascent community. For Johnson, this is a problem "left over from the Gospel."[18] The betrayal and suicide of Judas breaks the circle of the Twelve "whom he [Jesus] also designated apostles" (Luke 6:13).

In addition to showing and telling, Luke addresses or describes the community in Acts 1 as *apostles* (1:2, 26),[19] *brothers* (1:15), and as *believers*.[20] As we will see, the latter two (brothers, believers) overlap in use and meaning allowing Luke to narratively address the community on two distinct levels. The first identifiable group is the apostles, who number eleven. The second identifiable group are the brothers/believers, who number one hundred twenty and include the eleven apostles. Thus, Luke's primary terms for the community include apostles and believers.[21]

---

the Judas traditions in Luke 22:3–5; Acts 1:18–19; and Matt 27:3–10 leave the matter somewhat ambiguous as to Judas' state of mind, the circumstances of his death, and the purchase of the field.

17. Danker indicates Luke's uses δεῖ "to indicate that something that happened should by all means have happened, lit. 'had to' in Luke 15:32; 22:7; 24:26; Acts 1:16; 17:3." See BDAG, "δεῖ," 213–14, esp. 2c. Also see Grundmann, "δεῖ," *TDNT*, 2:21–25, esp. 22–23; Reasoner, "Theme of Acts," 637–38, 652–53; Schnabel, *Jesus and the Twelve*, vol. 1 of *Early Christian Mission*, 393; Johnson, *Acts*, 35.

18. Johnson, *Acts*, 38.

19. Which also includes various pronouns and descriptors: "apostles" (1:2, 26); "them" (1:3, 4, 10, 26); "you" (corporate sense, 1:4, 7, 8, 11); "they" (1:6, 9, 10, 11, 12, 13, 23, 24, 26); "their" (1:9); "these" (1:14); "themselves" (1:14); "this ministry" (1:17, 25); and "this apostleship" (1:25).

20. Which also includes various: "brothers" (1:14); "believers" (lit. brothers; 1:15); "crowd" (1:15); "friends" (1:16); "us" (1:17, 21, and 22).

21. For a conflation of brothers and believers, see below.

Apostles

With his use of the term apostle (Gr. ἀπόστολος, *apostolos*) in Acts 1:2, Luke presents the calling of the apostles as an integral experience for the early community and as a work of the Spirit.[22] He uses the term thirty-four times in his Gospel and Acts and generally focuses on the message (or work) rather than specific persons.[23] Consequently, as Karl Rengstorf argues, the word apostle in the New Testament contains "no trace of the common non-biblical use for the act of sending" but rather always "denotes bearers of the NT message" with emphasis on the message or work.[24] As such, Luke uses the term as a commission rather than an office.[25] In support of this, Rengstorf states,

> The fact that there is no office is also brought out by the obvious conclusion of the task with the return to Jesus. In Lk. 9:49 f. and par. the band of disciples is not at work, because it is with Jesus. We never hear of any activity of the disciples in His immediate presence. They are always "sent out" by Him. When they are with

22. The placement of the modifier "through the Holy Spirit" is awkward in most Greek texts, leaving it unclear whether it modifies Jesus' post-resurrection teaching or his selection of the apostles. Although it is not apparent in the NRSV rendering of Acts 1:2, Codex Bezae indicates that Luke views the selection of the original apostles (Luke 6:13) as a work of the Spirit who guided Jesus in the process. For general discussion, see Metzger, *Textual Commentary*, 236–41. Culy and Parsons argue the prepositional phrase, as found in the UBS text, must modify the post-resurrection commands of Jesus (ἐντειλάμενος) rather than the selection of the apostles (ἐξελέξατο). However, they suggest it should likely follow the relative pronoun οὓς and modify the selection of the apostles. "While this proposition is unusual, it is consistent with Luke's theme of God's servants being empowered by the Holy Spirit." Culy and Parsons, *Acts*, 3. Haenchen is emphatic that "διὰ πνεύματος ἁγίου relates to the succeeding phrase, the choice of the Apostles." Haenchen, *Acts*, 139. John J. Kilgallen concludes, "The most fitting sense" for 1:2 is "until the day when, having given orders to his apostles whom he had chosen because of the Holy Spirit, he was taken up." Kilgallen, "Apostles Whom He Chose," 417. Pervo translates verse 2 as, "until that day when he was taken up after instructing the apostles whom he had been inspired to choose." Pervo, *Acts*, 31, 36 n. 41. Johnson translates verse 2 as " . . . up to the day he was lifted up. Through the Holy Spirit, he commissioned the apostles whom he had selected." Johnson, *Acts*, 23, 24 n. 2. Some favoring the traditional reading "having given orders through the Spirit" including Bruce, *Acts*, 99; Dunn, *Acts*, 6; Barrett, *Critical and Exegetical Commentary on Acts*, 1:69.

23. For example, Luke 6:12–13; 9:1–2, 10. For support see Karl Rengstorf, "ἀπόστολος," *TDNT*, 1:407–447, esp. 420–445; BDAG, "ἀπόστολος," 122.

24. Rengstorf, *TDNT*, 1:421, 422.

25. Cf. Agnew, "Origin of the NT Apostle-Concept," 75–96, esp., 84; Meier, "Circle of the Twelve," 639–40; Rengstorf, *TDNT*, 1:426–27; Pervo, *Acts*, 48–49.

Him, it is as hearers and ministers, after the manner of the pupils of the rabbis. This is of decisive importance in relation to the early Christian view of the apostle. . . . It should be obvious that the apostolate as such has no religious character, but is simply a form. These apostles receive their religious impress from the One who gives them their commission, and always in such a way that the commission itself is the main thing and the apostles are only its bearers.[26]

However, exceptions to this claim are found in Luke's use of the term in his gospel (Luke 22:14; 24:10) and early in Acts to describe a fixed group of twelve leading disciples in Jerusalem (eleven plus one, Acts 1:26; 6:3).[27]

Luke's interest in twelve apostles, as an entity, has been the topic of much discussion primarily from an historical point of view.[28] Such historical matters are not of concern here. However, Luke's use of twelve apostles in the plot of Acts is of considerable importance in order to see their role and theological influence within the larger community of believers. He lists them by name in Luke 6:13 and Acts 1:13.[29] Although the other Synoptic writers also list the twelve by name (Matt 10:1–4; Mark 3:13–19), Luke alone adds "whom he also designated apostles" (Luke 6:13). His reference to the apostles as a fixed group of twelve effectively ties each together in his Gospel and Acts.[30] However, whereas Peter's criteria for apostleship limits

26. Rengstorf, *TDNT*, 1:427.

27. For example, Acts 1:2, 26; 4:33, 35–37; 5:12; 6:6; 8:1, 14; 11:1; and 15:1, 6, 22. According to Culy and Parsons, the term apostle(s) in Acts applies only to the Twelve (Luke 6:13) with the exception of 14:4 and 14:14. Culy and Parsons, *Acts Handbook*, 3. Also see Haenchen, *Acts*, 139 n. 3.

28. See Meier, "Circle of the Twelve," esp. 648; McKnight, "Jesus and the Twelve"; Schnabel, *Jesus and the Twelve*, 263–65; Haenchen, *Acts*, 122–24; In favor of the early existence of the Twelve, see Sanders, *Jesus and Judaism*, 61–119, esp. 98–106; McKnight, "Jesus and the Twelve," 206–11. For sustained arguments against such a group see Crossan, *Who Killed Jesus*, 75; Funk, ed., *Acts of Jesus*, 71.

29. The primary difference between Luke and the other Synoptic writers entails the substitution of Judas the son of James (Luke/Acts) for Thaddaeus (Matt/Mark). Fitzmyer suggests differences between the various Synoptic and Acts manuscripts may indicate the early church no longer accurately preserved the names of the Twelve and that they became insignificant "even to the extent that people no longer could recall who once constituted the Twelve." Fitzmyer, *Gospel According to Luke I-IX*, 620. For further text-critical analysis on this issue, see Lindars, "Matthew, Levi, Lebbaeus, 220–22. Also see Sanders, *Historical Figure of Jesus*, 120–22; McKnight, "Jesus and the Twelve," 203–4 and n. 2.

30. Luke 8:1; 9:1; 9:10 in conjunction with 9:12; 22:3, 47; Acts 6:2. For corroboration see Meier, "Circle of the Twelve," 638, also n. 7; Fitzmyer, *Gospel According to Luke I-IX*,

future appointees (Acts 1:21–22), Luke's later use is more generalized since the designation of apostle extends beyond a group limited to twelve as the story proceeds (14:4, 6).[31] This exception, along with Luke's general use of the term in his gospel as well as the declining use of the term as a fixed group, reveals a demarcation between the community's use of the term in Acts 1 and Luke's use as the plot develops.[32]

Believers

Luke first uses the familial term brother (Gr. ἀδελφός, adelphos) in reference to the brothers of Jesus (Acts 1:14).[33] He then uses it in 1:15, which the NRSV generically translates as believers since Luke excludes gender distinction with the inclusion of women (1:14).[34] D05 (Codex Bezae) attempts

---

254.

31. Note the transition in Luke's description of the leadership in Jerusalem from the "apostles," to the "Twelve," to the "apostles and elders" (15:2, 4, 6, 22–23; 16:4 adds " . . . who were in Jerusalem"), and finally to "elders" in 21:18, where he omits "apostles" and only retains "elders." Dunn states, "Of the three most prominent and influential people in the subsequent narrative (Peter, James brother of Jesus, and Paul), only one met the qualifications to become one of the 'the apostles'!" Dunn, *Acts*, xx, 21. On the expansion of the apostolate by Luke see Meier, "Circle of the Twelve," 640; Rengstorf, *TDNT*, 1:426–27; Twelftree, *People of the Spirit*, 25–28.

32. Concerning Luke's declining use of the Twelve, see McKnight, "Jesus and the Twelve," 209–10. As we will see in later chapters, Luke's use of a fixed group of apostles decreases, becomes less defined, and finally ends altogether as his story moves beyond his Jewish source in Acts 1–8 and broadens to include others engaged in preaching the gospel message (Acts 14:4).

33. ἀδελφος (brother) and its cognates occur thirty-three times in Acts. 1:14, 15, 16; 2:29, 37; 3:17, 22; 6:3; 7:13, 26, 37; 10:23; 11:29; 12:17; 13:15, 26, 38; 14:2; 15:3, 7, 13, 22, 23;, 33, 40; 16:2; 18:18; 21:17; 23:1, 5, 6; 28:17, 21. For supports see Soden, "ἀδελφός," *TDNT*, 1:144–46; BDAG, "ἀδελφός," xxviii, 18–19. Culy and Parsons translate literally as "siblings." Culy and Parsons, *Acts Handbook*, 13. Cf. Fitzmyer and Barrett suggest "relatives." Fitzmyer, *Acts*, 216–17; Barrett, *Acts*, 1:90.

34. In the front material of BDAG (3rd ed.), Danker states, "There is no longer any doubt in my mind that ἀδελφος can mean 'brothers and sisters' in any number. There are passages that scarcely permit any other interpretation (xxviii)." See also Culy and Parsons, *Acts Handbook*, 13–14; Pervo, *Acts*, 49; Keener, *Acts*, 1:756. However, Luke's primary word for describing the act of believing (or those who believed) is πιστεύω (e.g., Acts 2:44; 4:4, 32; 5:14; 8:12, 13; 9:42; 10:45; 11:21; 13:12; etc.). Usually, his use signals an action taken (i.e., believers were added, they believed, many believed, all that believed, etc.) rather than a title for the community (i.e., the believers).

to correct this confusion by substituting *mathētēs* (Gr. μαθητής, disciple).[35] Finally, Luke uses brothers in 1:16, which the NRSV translates as friends. Granted, context is critical to translation and interpretation, and it is not always clear when Luke intends men only (i.e., only the men in the assembly or only the apostles or leading elders) or a larger group of believers (i.e., the believers not restricted by gender or leadership). However, since Luke goes to the trouble of distinguishing the presence of Jesus' brothers, includes women, describes the one hundred twenty as a crowd (1:15),[36] and includes the presence of Joseph Barsabbas and Matthias, we argue that the narrative clues strongly favor Peter addressing the whole community of believers (one hundred twenty) and not only the apostles or only the men. Luke's use of familial language narratively creates a sense of affection within the community and draws the audience into the story as if they too are family.

The believers serve as the primary or active character in Acts 1 with the Apostle Peter serving as the moderator (Acts 1:15–17, 20–22). While Luke initially begins by narrating the encounter of the apostles with Jesus and two angels (1:2–11), followed by the identification of Peter as the moderator, he ultimately shifts the audience's attention to the believers as a unified group.[37]

Competing Agendas

In Acts 1, we maintain that Luke does not endeavor to distinguish the actions of the apostles from that of the community of believers. As a community, the brothers/believers join together to pray (1:14), to come to a resolution concerning Judas' betrayal, to propose potential candidates, and to witness the casting of lots. In Luke's story, the community of believers listens to Peter's speech and participates in the selection of Judas' replacement. As a plot device, the apostles and the believers function in tandem and they act as a unified character.

35. For more discussion on Luke's use of μαθητής see Ch. 3, "The Disciples," esp. notes 6–7. Cf. Johnson, *Acts*, 34; Rius-Camps and Read-Heimerdinger, *Message of Acts*, 1:116; Epp, *Theological Tendency*, 159. According to Metzger, the scribe of the Bodmer Papyrus of Acts substitutes ἀποστόλων in an effort to also avoid confusion with the aforementioned brothers of Jesus. Metzger, *Textual Commentary*, 247.

36. Only on this occasion does Luke use ὄχλος to describe community of believers. For analysis see Meyer and Katz, "ὄχλος," *TDNT*, 5:582–90, esp. 586–88; BDAG, "ὄχλος," 745–46, esp. 745 1bβ.

37. Acts 1:16, 17, 21, 22, 23, 24, 26.

Furthermore, in characterizing the believers in Acts 1, Luke distinguishes between Jesus' agenda (particularly his mandate and vision, Acts 1:3–5, 7–8), and the agenda of his followers (1:6, 15–26). This conflict is evident in their immediate actions following Jesus' ascension. By accentuating the conflicting agendas between Jesus' mandate and that of the pre-Pentecost community in Acts 1, Luke can show that the theological creativity of the community is rooted in their theological understanding of their nation and the importance of twelve apostles in the coming kingdom of Jesus.

The Agenda of Jesus

Jesus orders the disciples to wait in Jerusalem for the "promise of the Father" (Acts 1:4), which in Luke's narrative is to be "baptized with the Holy Spirit" (1:5, 8) and fulfilled at Pentecost (2:1–4). Luke shows that it is important to Jesus that the community receive the Holy Spirit so that they might expand their witness beyond Jerusalem into the surrounding regions (1:8).[38] For Luke, the agenda of Jesus is global in nature and his plot bears this out as the story proceeds.[39] However, in Jesus' absence, Luke shows which character now determines the direction of the story.[40] As noted earlier, the role of protagonist and interpreter shifts to the community of believers following Jesus' ascension.[41]

The Agenda of the Community of Believers

The mandate of Jesus to his followers seems to elude this early community of believers. In Acts 1, Luke's audience receives no indication that the believers understand the significance of waiting for the promise of the Father (1:4–5) but instead envision the kingdom of Israel (1:6) in nationalistic or geopolitical terms.[42] It is as if, as Chrysostom states, "They had no clear

---

38. Marshal, *Acts*, 60–61; Twelftree, *People of the Spirit*, 76.

39. As we see in Luke 24:47; Acts 1:8; 2:39; 8:1, 4, 26, 40; 9:1–2, 10, 31, 32, 35, 36; 10:1, 23, 27–29, 44–48; 11:17–18, 19–22; 13:1–4; 15:11, 19, 23, 28, 30–31, 36, 39–40; 16:1, 6–11; 17:1, 10, 16; 18:1; 19:1; 23:11; 28:30–31.

40. Cf. Rius-Camps and Read-Heimerdinger, *Message of Acts*, 1:6.

41. Compare with Luke 24:44–49.

42. Marshal, *Acts*, 60. Cf. Jervell, *Unknown Paul*, 98–99.

notion of the nature of [the] kingdom," to which Jesus spoke.[43] Consequently, they organize in a manner consistent with the conventions of the
day.[44] As we have seen, Luke introduces these conventions by indicating the
size of the group and by revealing their theological concerns.

Summary

So far, we have analyzed the community as a character introduced by Luke
in the wake of Jesus' ascension but prior to Pentecost. Hochman's qualities
of characterization in literature—specifically action, conflict, and need for
resolution—enable us to identify the community as a character in Luke's
story. Although Peter is often regarded as the prominent single character,
we have demonstrated that it is the community of believers functioning as
a group that takes center stage in Luke's narrative in the following ways.
First, we see the community of believers listening to Peter, agreeing, praying, proposing, and casting lots. Second, Luke describes the community in
familial language that has broad applicability by not limiting the group to
the apostles or according to gender and by drawing the audience into the
story. Third, Luke presents the apostles and believers of Acts 1 function
harmoniously as the central character in the narrative who engage in theological creativity by replacing Judas and reestablishing the Twelve.

Moreover, the contrast between Jesus' mandate and concerns of the
pre-Pentecost community is stark. In Luke's story, the mission for Jesus in
Acts 1 is global and universal in nature and beyond nationalistic concerns.
Rather than follow the Jesus-character as the main protagonist at this point
of the story, Luke establishes the community as the protagonist by revealing their theological understanding and interests. By doing this, we see the
community existing as an independent character in the story.

In the following section, we will show the community's role in theological creativity concerning the necessity for reestablishing the Twelve. By
highlighting the differences between the agenda of Jesus and the community in Acts 1, we will see that the actions of the community are rooted in
a theological understanding of both their nation and the importance of
twelve apostles.

43. John Chrysostom, *Hom. Acts* 2.

44. Jacob Jervell disagrees with this assessment on historical grounds. But through
indirect presentation Luke indicates these conventions and the community's theological
concerns. Cf. Jervell, *Unknown Paul*, 98.

The Community in Theological Creativity

Having evaluated the narrative of Acts 1 and the way Luke establishes the community as a character in the story, we will now examine the relevant theological issues of importance to the community and see how they engage in theological creativity.

Scripture as an Explanation for Experience

The community of Acts 1 possesses a theological concern for the continuation of the Twelve, consistent with their original call by Jesus (Luke 6:13–16), so that they might fulfil his mandate to sit on "thrones judging the twelve tribes of Israel" (Luke 22:30).[45] In story form, Luke reveals that their need to reestablish the Twelve is an act of theological necessity. As noted earlier, the experience of the remaining apostles and their belief in the significance of twelve members, along with the public scandal Luke includes as an *analepsis* (Acts 1:18-19), motivates the community to replace Judas.[46] According to Luke, Peter draws inspiration to replace Judas from his understanding of Ps 69:25 and 109:8.[47] Clearly, Ps 109:8 serves as justification for the election of a new member to the Twelve.[48]

45. For support see Fitzmyer, *Gospel According to Luke I-IX*, 253; Rengstorf states, "*Die synoptische Überlieferung ist darin ganz einheitlich, daß sie ihn durch Jesus selbst begründet sein läßt.*" ["The synoptic tradition is consistent [that] Jesus himself established {the Twelve}."] Rengstorf, "Zumwahl des Matthias," 45; Meier, "Circle of the Twelve," 657 n. 56. For a sustained argument against the Twelve originating with Jesus, see Schmithals, *Office of Apostle*, 67-71; Klein, *Zwölf Apostel*, 213-16. Pervo concludes, "Klein's claim that Luke invented the identification of 'the Twelve' with 'the apostles' is an exaggeration." Pervo, *Acts*, 54 n. 44. Cf. Haenchen, *Acts*, 122-29.

46. *Analepsis* is a "flashback" to earlier events.

47. (1) Ps 68:25 LXX, "ἐκχεον ἐπ᾽ αὐτοὺς τὴν ὀργήν σου, καὶ ὁ θυμὸς τῆς ὀργῆς σου καταλάβοι αὐτούς" (Let their habitation be made desolate; and let there be no inhabitant in their tents). Compare with Ps 69:25 NRSV, "May their camp be desolation; let no one live in their tents." (2) Ps 108:8 LXX, "γενηθήτωσαν αἱ ἡμέραι αὐτοῦ ὀλίγαι, καὶ τὴν ἐπισκοπὴν αὐτοῦ λάβοι ἕτερος" (Let his days be few; and let another take his office of overseer). Compare with Ps 109:8 NRSV, "May another seize his position." For Luke's general characterization of Scripture in Acts see Arnold, "Luke's Characterizing Use," 300-23.

48. However, it is possible that Peter needed no justification if Luke's inclusion of Judas son of James (Acts 1:13) rather than Thaddaeus (Luke 6:13-16) as one of the Twelve indicates that a member had already been replaced during Jesus' ministry. If this is the case, then a precedent for replacing departed members of the Twelve already existed. For support and analysis see Novick, "Succeeding Judas," 796; Zwiep, *Judas and the Choice of Matthias*, 23-27, 93-94.

Views on the use of Ps 69:25 may be divided broadly along two lines. On the one hand, the character Peter construes Ps 69:25 as a reference to the property acquired in the aftermath of Judas' betrayal.[49] On the other hand, the citation refers to Judas' ministry or position within the Twelve and the vacancy created by his apostasy.[50] As Johnson notes, "Luke characteristically uses the impersonal verb *dei* ('it must') in such statements about the inexorability of the divine will (see Luke 9:22; 17:25; 24:7, 26, 44; Acts 3:21; 9:16; 14:22), and especially in connection with the fulfillment of scriptural passages (Luke 22:37; 24:26, 44; Acts 1:21; 17:3)."[51] From the first citation, Peter concludes that what happened to Judas was a fulfillment (past tense) of Scripture.[52] And from the second citation, replacing Judas also fulfills (present tense) Scripture.

Consequently, we argue the implication of Acts 1:21–22 is that, in light of Ps 109:8, it is theologically necessary that someone take Judas' place. Furthermore, since their understanding of Scripture is justifying their experiential need to replace Judas, it is reasonable to conclude their method for selecting his successor should also follow a theological precedent from Scripture, the use of lots. Consequently, we argue that the first-century community of believers engages in theological creativity by linking their theological understanding of a restored-nation of Israel with Jesus' selection of twelve apostles.

Selecting a Successor

In ancient Israel, drawing or casting lots was utilized for distributing land inheritances, for arriving at a variety of decisions, and for divvying up various daily priestly and custodial duties particularly during Second Temple Judaism.[53] In Acts 1, the community of believers draw on a culturally fa-

---

49. Novick, "Succeeding Judas," 797–99. Also see Talbert, *Reading Acts*, 14; Conzelmann, *Acts*, 12.

50. See Haenchen, *Acts*, 161; Fitzmyer, *Acts*, 220–21; Marshal, *Acts*, 65.

51. Johnson, *Acts*, 35.

52. The Do5 does not use the past tense of δει. Conzelmann argues, "The use of the present tense (δει) by the Western text means the scribes misunderstood the passage and related the necessity to the selection of a replacement rather than to the destiny of the traitor." Conzelmann, *Acts*, 10.

53. Lev 16:8; Josh 7:10–21; 1 Sam 14:40–42; 1 Chr 25:8; 26:12–13; Josephus, *Ant.* 7.366–367. Cf. Brown, *Corporate Decision-Making*, 104. On this issue, Brown relies heavily on Strack and Billerbeck, *Kommentar zum Neuen Testament*, 2:596–97.

miliar method with theological implications for deciding between candidates. Notwithstanding, William Beardslee contests the notion that Luke is drawing on ancient Israel's past and its connection to the replacement of Judas.[54] He maintains that Luke's use of lots in the selection of Matthias is metaphorical and similar to that in use at Qumran during the first century CE and means "a decision by the community, reflecting God's decision."[55] For Beardslee, "casting lots" is an idiom for "making a decision."[56] However, he offers no explanation for how the community of believers accomplished this task or why physically casting lots could not be an option.

Arie W. Zwiep draws attention to the odd manner in Luke's expression, "and they cast lots for them."[57] He states,

> The normal way to describe the procedure would be καὶ ἔ βαλον κλήρους "and they cast lots," as for example in Jonah 1:7. Luke, however, has δίδωμι instead of βάλλω and adds a rather ambiguous dative (αὐτοῖς "to them/for them"). In the Septuagint we find the expressions δίδωμι τι τινι ἐν κλήρῳ, which means "to give something to someone for a possession" (e.g., Ex 6:8; Num 18:21, 24, etc.). But this meaning does not fit the present context. Δίδωμι κλήρους τινι, is a correct translation of לדון נתן ל/על "cast a lot for/over" (Lev 16:8, also in plural, etc.). It seems that Luke or his source has given us an ultra-literal translation of a Semitic construct, perhaps to give it an air of (biblical) antiquity.[58]

Zwiep concludes the Semitic background of the expression "may also be of help to find out who exactly are in view with *autois.*"[59] A number of proposals for Luke's intent have been offered. First, Matthew Black suggests *autois* (they) represents the Aramaic ethical dative: "they (the apostles) gave themselves lots."[60] Later, Fitzmyer argues it should be taken as a *dativus commodi* (action for or against someone) and renders the passage, "They gave lots for them (for Barsabbas and Matthias)," as rendered in the NRSV.[61] More

54. Beardslee, "Casting of Lots," 245–52, esp. 245, 249–50.

55. Beardslee, "Casting of Lots," 250.

56. For a similar conclusion, see Rius-Camps and Read-Heimerdinger, *Message of Acts*, 1:133–36.

57. Acts 1:26, "And they cast for them (NRSV)." NA28 "καὶ ἔδωκαν κλήρους αὐτοῖς."

58. Zwiep, *Judas and the Choice of Matthias*, 170–71.

59. Zwiep, *Judas and the Choice of Matthias*, 171.

60. Black, *Aramaic Approach to the Gospels and Acts*, 104.

61. Fitzmyer, *Acts*, 228. Also Lohfink, "Bemerkungen zur neuen Einheitsübersetzung der Bibel: Übersetzungsfehler in der Apostelgeschichte" (Comments on the New Bible

recently Zwiep indicates *autois* could be taken as an indirect object: "they gave lots *to them* (to Barsabbas and Matthias)."[62] Of these three, Zwiep's conclusion seems most likely in light of Luke's narrative description, "and they cast lots" (Acts 1:26). The community provided Barsabbas and Matthias with lots (e.g., markers or chips), who then placed their lots into some kind of vessel that was then shook in some manner (e.g., shaken out or drawn out). The first marker to exit the vessel from the shaking process belonged to Matthias.

Whether the lots were shaken out or drawn out is theologically significant to this discussion. Research by Anne Marie Kitz concerning "lot casting" within an ancient Near Eastern context notes a sharp contrast between the two methods.[63] While acknowledging a variety of methods in the use of lots in decision-making, she maintains all methods fall roughly under two categories. First, "lot casting" implies the need for divine guidance. Through some process of shaking, the lot falls from the vessel to the ground, thus revealing a divine answer or direction. Second, "lot drawing" indicates no need for divine direction. The candidate places their lot or marker into the container, and then one lot is drawn out by a designated official.[64] In the first instance, the outcome is accepted as a divine response. In the second, the outcome is essentially one of happenstance.

Luke's narrative directly indicates that the community was seeking a divine response and consequently "cast" lots (Acts 1:24). Therefore, we argue that Luke's story suggests the community chose their method on theological grounds and for theological reasons. For them, the outcome served to authenticate the Divine will, "Lord . . . show us which one of these two you have chosen."[65] Thus, the first-century community of believers engage in theological creativity by drawing on an ancient custom from Scripture to identify the replacement for Judas.

Translation: Misunderstandings in the Acts of the Apostles), 244–46, esp. 245; Schneider, *Apostelgeschichte*, 1:220.

62. Zwiep, *Judas and the Choice of Matthias*, 171.

63. Kitz, "Hebrew Terminology of Lot Casting."

64. Kitz, "Hebrew Terminology of Lot Casting," 208 n. 3, 214.

65. As the story proceeds, the use of lots is abandoned and the Divine will is discerned in light of the Spirit's evidential work. We revisit this discussion in chapter 3, "The Laying on of Hands."

Summary and Conclusions

Early in the narrative of Acts, Luke develops the community as a character and as a functioning entity within his story. In doing so he portrays a dynamic group acting and reacting to its own experience.[66] We have argued that the first-century community of believers engage in theological creativity by linking their theological understanding of a restored-nation of Israel with Jesus' selection of twelve apostles and by drawing on an ancient custom from Scripture to identify the replacement for Judas.

Peter's use of Scripture validates the community's experiential need to replace Judas, and the election of Matthias brings it to resolution. The narrative evidence indicates that Luke includes the story of reestablishing the Twelve because he (Peter) considered it theological necessary. Jesus "chose twelve of them, whom he also named apostles" (Luke 6:13) to "sit on thrones" (Luke 22:30). Luke uses that necessity, in conjunction with the public scandal concerning Judas' public betrayal and death, as motivation for their action and reestablishment of the Twelve.

Thus, Luke's subplot in Acts 1:16-26 begins and ends with resolving the vacancy of Judas. Furthermore, we see his portrayal of the earliest believing community reestablishing the Twelve on theological grounds using Scripture to justify their actions and the casting of lots to reveal the divine choice. Consequently, Luke's view of the first-century community of believers portrays the community's role within an interpretive process involving Spirit–Community–Scripture.

66. Utilizing Hochman's qualities of characterization in literature—specifically action, conflict, and need for resolution—identifying the community as a character in Luke's narrative is clear. Hochman demonstrates the function of characters within narratives and the manner in which they move the story forward. See Hochman, *Character in Literature*, 51, 138–40.

2

Revealing Jesus as Servant and Son—Acts 4:23–31

In this chapter, we will consider Luke's depiction of the first-century community of believers engaging in theological creativity following the apostles' first persecution Acts 4:23–31.[1] Once again, we find Luke "showing and telling" in order to characterize the community. In order to describe this process, we will first explore how Luke identifies and characterizes the community. From that we will be able to see the theological issues important in his story. Since we will argue that Luke characterizes the community through the content of a prayer that he incorporates into his story, we will analyze each aspect of the prayer with attention to its tradition, structure, and theological content.

As we highlight theological aspects that Luke presents in the community's corporate prayer, we will see (1) a theological foundation for their belief in Jesus as Messiah (4:16–21) and (2) what motivates the characters' continued preaching despite threats from local authorities. We will

---

1. Theological creativity is the act of reformulating formerly held theological interpretations in light of testimony concerning the Spirit's evidential work and an emerging understanding of applicable Scripture followed by commensurate action. The Spirit's evidential work is known only through the community's testimony. Therefore, theological creativity is the outcome of the interpretive process since it is theology in action, functional in nature, and situationally pragmatic in scope. Consequently, it involves the process of theological justification and action or reaction in light of current circumstances. In this sense, to be creative with theology is to take what is already a theological assumption and broaden or adapt it to current circumstances in light of the Spirit's evidential work and a consensus understanding of Scripture.

conclude with a summary of the main points and evidence to demonstrate Luke's portrayal of the community as a character engaging in theological creativity.

Identifying the Community

Since identifying the community of believers in this passage is crucial to our study, it will be important to consider the narrative clues present in Luke's story. This includes both his use of the Servant/Son motif to describe Jesus as Messiah and the grammatical structure of the prayer.

Which Community?

Immediately after the first recorded persecution of the apostles, Peter and John return to their companions (Acts 4: 23).[2] According to Luke, the church has expanded to five thousand men in a relatively short time span (4:4).[3] Although Luke records a massive increase in the number of believers, the context limits the size of the group to the Twelve or possibly a representative group similar to the one hundred and twenty envisioned in Acts 1:12. Given the narrative circumstances and their recent release by the

2. Gr. πρὸς τοὺς ἰδίους, "to their own."

3. See Acts 1:15; 2:41; 4:4; 21:20. For remarks signaling exponential growth in and around Jerusalem, see 5:14; 6:1, 7. Luke is the only New Testament writer to provide numerical data for the first-century church in Jerusalem, and only in its earliest days. Josephus notes the number of Pharisee men of his day at about six thousand (*Ant.* 17.41–42) and Essence men at about four thousand (*Ant.* 18.18–20), however, he includes no numbers when writing of Christians (*Ant.* 18.63–64; 20.200). Whether Luke's conversion numbers (Acts 2:41; 4:4) include both local residents and pilgrim travelers (who presumably return to their home afterward) is anyone's guess. Jeremias and Reinhardt estimate the population of Jerusalem in the mid-first century at not less than sixty thousand. During festival times, the population may have increased to over two hundred thousand. For support, see Jeremias, *Jerusalem in the time of Jesus*, 83 n. 24. In a subsequent revision, Jeremias amends his estimation of Jerusalem downward to twenty-five to thirty thousand. Reinhardt, "Population Size of Jerusalem," 237–65. For general comments concerning growth beyond Jerusalem, see Acts 9:31; 11:21, 24; 12:24; 14:1, 19:20. For views positive to Luke drawing on a known tradition for the size of the Jerusalem church, see Marshal, *Acts*, 82, 99; Dunn, *Acts*, 34. Dunn, while recognizing ancient historians tend to inflate their numbers, maintains Luke's intention is to show "a large initial movement of successful recruitment by the new sect." Dunn, *Acts*, 34. For views that Luke invents the number of Christian adherents, see Haenchen, *Acts*, 188–89; Pervo, *Acts*, 86–87, also n. 115–17; Twelftree, *People of the Spirit*, 66.

Jerusalem authorities (4:23), it is unlikely Peter and John return to a place with a large crowd present. Consequently, we argue that the community of Acts 4:23 is likely limited to the apostles (with perhaps a few others) and is the central character in Luke's story.[4]

Once again, conflict brings this character to the forefront.[5] Beginning in Acts 4:23, Peter and John fade from center stage and we see this community of believers as a single character unified in belief and in speech. They hear the report of Peter and John (Acts 4:23), raise their voice (4:24), corporately experience the shaking of the building and the infilling the Holy Spirit (4:31), feel emboldened to proclaim the word of God (4:31), are of "one heart and soul" (4:32), share possessions for the common good of all (4:32, 34–35), and (along with the rest) witness the great power of God (4:33).

Following a long description of events (Acts 3:1–4:22), Luke brings the matter to a head in a "choral finale" followed by a second summary of events (4:32–35).[6] Peter and John return to their friends who, upon hearing the report of the two, lifted "their voices together to God and said" (4:23–24, emphasis mine).[7] The ensuing prayer is the longest corporate prayer in Acts.[8]

A Praying Community

Important to Luke's characterization of the first-century community of believers in Acts 4:23–31 is how he structures the prayer within the narrative and what it reveals about the community. Demonstrating Luke's

4. Although Irenaeus envisions a "metropolis of the citizens of the new covenant," from the context it seems more likely this group, although significant, is representative of the whole community of believers. See Irenaeus, *Haer.* 3.12.5. Johnson limits the group to the apostles rather than the community as a whole. Johnson, *Acts*, 83, 90. Cf. Plymale, *Prayer Texts of Luke-Acts*, 81; Haenchen, *Acts*, 226; Conzelmann, *Acts*, 34.

5. For the role of conflict in characterization see Hochman, *Character in Literature*, 51, 138–40; S. Moore, *Literary Criticism and the Gospels*, 15.

6. Dunn, *Acts*, 55.

7. For ancient literary examples of a group speaking as one voice, see Virgil: "Then Drances, an elder, replied in turn . . . He spoke, and they all murmured assent with one voice" (*Aen.* 11.122–3); Apuleius: "They stretched their arms towards heaven, and clearly, with one voice, bore witness to her wondrous beneficence" (*Metam.* 11.13). Cf. Keener, *Acts*, 2:1166, also 2:1166 n. 1213; Gaventa, "To Speak thy Word," 76–82, esp. 76–77.

8. Wahlde, "Acts 4:24–31," 238. Also see Plymale, *Prayer Texts of Luke-Acts*, 78–88.

characterization of the community through the community's prayer will require consideration of its tradition, structure, and narrated outcome. First, consideration of the structure and their theological interpretation will aid our awareness of this community's theological view of Jesus. Second, we will take into consideration the community's request and God's response for Luke's most striking characteristic of this unified character. Through this process we will see that Luke reveals the character of the community directly through its prayer (Acts 4:24b–30) and only indirectly through a report of action (4:31c).

It seems unlikely Luke recorded a first-hand account of a prayer offered by everyone in unison. If so, it would certainly represent an extraordinary "miracle of choral speaking."[9] Even I. Howard Marshal insists, "The view that the Spirit inspired each member to say exactly the same words reflects an impossibly mechanical view of the Spirit's working."[10] Most scholars agree that Luke fabricates the prayer-speech for rhetorical effect.[11] Notwithstanding, Moule and a few others conclude Luke is following a reliable source in this community prayer.[12] The most practical plain-sense reading of the text suggests Luke envisions the community either (1) selecting representatives to pray of which this particular prayer is preserved or (2) selecting one member to pray on behalf of the whole group thus forming the basis of the tradition.

9. Hamm, "Acts 4:23–31, 227. Cf. Dunn, *Acts*, 55.

10. Marshal, *Acts*, 108.

11. See Haenchen, *Acts*, 185, 228. Even Richard Bauckham concludes, "The sermons in Acts are not, of course, really sermons: They are literary representations of sermons." Bauckham, "Kerygmatic Summaries," 185–217, esp. 216. For general treatment regarding speeches in Acts, see Dibelius, *Acts*, 49–86. Cf. Munck, *Acts*, xliii–xlv.

12. Moule, "Christology of Acts," 172. Cf. Marshal, *Acts*, 108; Gallagher, "From 'Doingness' to 'Beingness,'" 47; Hengel, *Acts and the History of Earliest Christianity*, 104; Fornara, *Nature of History*, 154–55; Witherington states, "The idea that there was a historical convention of composing speeches for historical narratives is a modern myth. That 'appropriate' speeches were sometimes created out of thin air and put on characters' lips in ancient works is certainly true; that there was a historical convention encouraging such a practice, much less that Thucydides encouraged such a practice, is untrue." Witherington, *Acts*, 455–56; also see Witherington, *History, Literature, and Society*, 23–32. For statistical data supporting this claim, see R. Martin, "Syntactical Evidence of Aramaic Sources," 38–59, esp. 54, 59. Dunn agrees the prayer includes themes consistent with "Jewish confession and worship of the one God, creator of all" but stops short of assigning the tradition to a recognizable source. Dunn, *Acts*, 57.

Prayer Structure

The community's prayer in Acts 4:24–30 presents a contemporary interpretation of Psalm 2:1–2 using a style consistent with a chiasm.[13] The word *chiasm* (chiasmus) is based on the Greek letter *chi* (χ) and refers to the inverted parallelism of words or concepts in a literary unit utilizing inversion and balance.[14] Presenting the tradition in this manner suggests the importance both the passage and its interpretation had for the community.

In 4:24–28, the chiasmus begins with a quotation from Psalm 2 (LXX) and then proceeds to connect the relevant events from Jesus' encounter with the ruling powers and mob in Jerusalem as outlined below.

Acts 4:24–28 chiasm

A–Why did the Gentiles rage and the people imagine vain things?
  B–The kings of the earth took their stand and the rulers have gathered together
    C–Against the Lord and against his Messiah
    C–Against your holy servant Jesus, whom you anointed.
  B–For in this city, in fact, both Herod and Pontius Pilate
A–With the Gentiles and the peoples of Israel, gathered together against your holy servant Jesus, whom you anointed, to do whatever your hand and your plan had predestined to take place.

Retaining the tradition in this manner makes it easy to remember and rehearse and for Luke to include in his story with minimal explanation.

---

13. "Contemporary" within the story. For studies on chiasmus in biblical antiquity see Stock, "Chiastic Awareness and Education," 23–27; Welch, *Chiasmus in Antiquity*, 9–16.

14. For example, if a unit consists of four phrases or sentences, the first phrase (A) corresponds to the last phrase (A). The second phrase (B) corresponds to the third phrase (B). The resulting structure would be A, B, B, A. See Wahlde, "Problems of Acts 4:25a," 43; Lund, *Chiasmus in the New Testament*, vii. Lund does not include Acts 4:24–30 as an example of chiasm in his study. See also Resseguie, *Narrative Criticism*, 281.

Evidence of Pesher

Acts 4:27–28 provides an interpretation of Ps 2:1–2, commonly referred to as *pesher*, by drawing on contemporary events.[15] Thus, the prayer links the Gentiles with the Roman executioners, "peoples" with the nation of Israel (viz., Sanhedrin), Herod Antipas with "the kings of the earth," and Pilate with the "rulers." Such an interpretation is not without its problems, but it supports our claim that Luke has included both a tradition and an interpretation in his narrative tale.

The evidence for this claim is twofold. First, it is not readily apparent why Luke uses *laós* (Gr. λαός, peoples) to describe Gentile masses in Luke 2:31 (who are either in need or are simply bystanders) only to later use it as a reference for hostile Israel in Acts 4.[16] For the most part, Luke tends to de-emphasize the participation of the crowd or mob in his passion narrative.[17] Clearly, Luke uses *laós* (people*)* and *laois* (Gr. λαοῖς, *peoples*) differently in Acts 4. As Kilpatrick notes,

> Most commentators are agreed in taking λαοὶ in Acts iv.25 and λαοῖς in verse 27 as referring to Israel. When we turn to the other example of the plural in Luke-Acts, Luke ii.31, the commentators are as much agreed that λαοὶ *is the Gentiles. Nowhere else in Luke-Acts is* λαός *used of the Gentiles and in the one other example of the plural in Acts iv above it is clearly Israel. We must allow for the possibility that he intended a difference in meaning.*[18]

Consequently, we argue the narrative use of "people" in Acts 4:25 and "peoples" in 4:27 as Jewish masses indicates Luke is using the term as intended by the community of believers in the story; that is, he is drawing the

---

15. *Pesher* (Aram. interpretation). Johnson, *Acts*, 84; Twelftree, *People of the Spirit*, 133. This type of *pesher* is most common among the community of Qumran. Consider 1QpHab, 4QpNah, 4QpPs37, and 4Q171, 173. For a more extensive review of *pesher*, see T. Lim, *Pesharim*; Brooke, "Qumran Pesher," 483–503. For Luke's characterization of Scripture in Acts see Arnold, "Luke's Characterizing Use," 300–23, esp. 310–11.

16. Gottfried Schille argues equating "peoples" with Israel is not characteristic of the OT in general or Luke's writings in particular. See Schille, *Apostelgeschichte des Lukas*, 141. However, for examples of "peoples" in pre-Christian Jewish sources where "peoples" refers to both Jewish and Gentile hostiles, see Pss. Sol. 17:22–29; 4QFlor, frg. 1. Cf. Keener, *Acts*, 2:1168–69, as well as n. 1234 and n. 1236.

17. Consider Luke 23:13–25, 35–38.

18. Kilpatrick, "ΛΑΟΙ at Luke 2.31 and Acts 4.25–27," 127. Cf. R. Meyer and Strathmann, "λαος," *TDNT*, 4:29–57, esp. 50–57; BDAG, "λαος," 586–87.

received tradition and one that is different from his own use earlier in his Gospel.

Second, Luke presents both Herod Antipas and Pilate more favorably in his Gospel than the *pesher* conveys in Acts 4:27.[19] Only Luke records Jesus' appearance before Antipas (Luke 23:6–12). According to his Gospel, Antipas plays little, if any, role in the direct trial or execution of Jesus.[20] Aside from a bit of mockery, Antipas is disposed to send Jesus back to Pilate without recommendation (23:11b). Consistent throughout his Gospel, Luke, so to say, "sticks to the facts" regarding Antipas and leaves (whether intentional or not) the more negative commentary to the other Gospel writers.[21] In the prayer, Antipas is clearly culpable in Jesus' suffering and death and suggests a view of the king that is harsher than what Luke presents in his Gospel.

Moreover, Luke also portrays Jesus' trial before Pilate in a more favorable light by showing Roman reticence to convict.[22] Despite Luke's earlier portrayal, the community's prayer (4:27–28) implicates Pilate directly as a co-conspirator in Jesus' persecution and death (4:27). This subtle observation, in which Luke presents Pilate in his Gospel in one manner and presents him in another manner in the community's prayer in Acts 4, also supports our claim that Luke has included a tradition consistent with the community's view and not his own.

---

19. For analysis of Antipas in Lukan writings, see Stenschke, *Luke's Portrait of Gentiles*, 126–44. Antipas was one of the sons of Herod the Great. Upon the death of Herod in 4 BCE, Antipas was named tetrarch over the region of Galilee and Peraea (Transjordan) until 39 CE. Luke simply refers to Antipas as Herod, ruler over Galilee (Luke 3:1; 23:6–7). Compare Mark 6:14–29 and Luke's much-abbreviated version in Luke 9:7–9. Also, Josephus, *Ant.* 17:188; 18:36–38, 109–19. Antipas is best remembered for his scandalous marriage to Herodias (niece of one brother and former wife of another brother) and his role in the beheading of John the Baptist.

20. See Luke 23:6–15, esp. 13–15. Tyson and Bates argue Luke conceals or "codes" his rancor for Antipas for his own sociopolitical reasons. Tyson, "Jesus and Herod Antipas," 239, 245; Bates, "Cryptic Codes," 74–93, esp. 75, 92.

21. Cf. Matt 14:1–12; Mark 6:14–24; 8:14–15. An exception to this argument may appear in Luke's reference to Antipas as "that fox" (Luke 13:31–33).

22. For example, Luke 23:4, 13–25, esp. 13–16; Acts 3:13; 13:28. Compare with Matt 27:1–26, 57; Mark 15:1–15, 42–45; John 18:28—19:16. Moreover, Luke maintains similar reticence in subsequent trial proceedings. See Acts 16:38–40; 18:14–16; 22:23–30; 23:16–35; 24:22–27; 25:11–27; 26:24–32; 27:43; 28:16, 18, 30.

The Community's Request and God's Approval

Critical to Luke's presentation are the differences in which the ancient community in the Psalm and the community of believers in Acts identify with and apply Psalm 2:1-2. In Psalm 2, the psalmist calls for their bonds to be broken and cast away (v. 3), for the Lord's voice to terrify their enemies by declaring his possession of Zion (vv. 4-6), for the nations to be broken in pieces (v. 9), and for all to serve the Lord under penalty of God's wrath (v. 11a). The psalmist ends with an afterthought of sorts, a blessing for all who take refuge in the Lord (v. 11b).

However, the community in Acts 4 seeks no vindication, no summary judgment, no consequence for its persecutors, and no afterthought of protection or blessing for itself. Instead, the community calls on the sovereign Lord (Acts 4:24) for boldness in speech and miraculous signs to authenticate its course of action (4:29-30). Moreover, they decide to proclaim the message of Jesus no matter the consequence—a decision that is theologically motivated by at least two factors: (1) the connection it makes between the sufferings and rejection of Jesus and its own persecution and (2) the community's view of Jesus' relationship to God as God's Servant.

Therefore, the primary contrast between those praying in Psalm 2 and those praying in Acts 4 is in the requested outcome. In Psalm 2, the request is for deliverance from and for the destruction of their enemies. In Acts 4, the request is for bold speech despite the Sanhedrin's prohibition (Acts 4:29). Rather than retribution against its tormentors, this community seeks "healings, and signs and wonders" in the name of Jesus (4:18, 30).

At the end of the prayer, Luke narrates that the building is shaken and that everyone involved was filled with the Holy Spirit (Acts 4:31). Luke uses the phenomena as evidence that the community's prayer was heard.[23] After the sign of God's presence and response, Luke concludes the episode with a second summary (Acts 4:32-35) which further functions as indirect evidence that God answered the community's request for boldness and miraculous signs (4:29-30).

---

23. For a similar encounter see 2 Esd 6: 17-18, 29-32a. Also, "The trembling of the place in answer to a prayer is described . . . by Ovid (*Metam.* XV. 669-72) and Virgil (*Aen.* III. 88-91)." Haenchen, *Acts*, 228, also n. 2.

SUMMARY

As we have seen, the inclination of the text limits the size of Peter's and John's companions to the Twelve or possibly a representative group like the one hundred twenty envisioned in Acts 1:12. On this occasion Luke characterizes the community of believers as a unified body in and through the theological content contained in their prayer.

At this point in our analysis of the community's prayer, we may conclude that the way Luke inserts the prayer into the story as an early tradition in the form of Jewish *pesher*, highlights three primary characteristics of the Jerusalem community: (1) it considers the sufferings of Jesus equal to the prophetic sufferings of the Messiah, (2) it feels a connection between Jesus' sufferings and its own, and (3) it reveals the community's non-violent nature and hope for its neighbors. In the following section, we will show specific areas in which this community of believers engages in theological creativity.

The Community in Theological Creativity

In Acts 4:23–31, Luke reveals a community engaged in theological creativity through a prayer that expresses how they see Jesus in relationship to the sovereign Lord and how they see themselves in relationship to Jesus. As we will see, it is significant that the prayer is addressed to the sovereign Lord and not addressed to either Jesus or the Spirit. Despite the absence of any direct use of the title or concept "Son of God," the sovereign Master, Jesus, and Spirit are present in 4:24–31.[24] The community expresses its theological belief concerning Jesus' relationship to God using a type (David) and an anti-type (Messiah) as both Servant and Son of God. As we will see, this Servant/Son motif is of great interest to the community depicted in Acts 1–4.[25]

---

24. Cf. Hengel, *Acts and the History*, 104.

25. See Acts 1:16; 2:25; 2:34; 4:25. For a review of rabbinic tradition concerning David and Messiah, see Fitzmyer, "David, 'Being Therefore a Prophet,'" 332–39, esp. 333 n. 4. For a review of the Davidic Messiah in Luke-Acts see Strauss, *Davidic Messiah in Luke-Acts*, 15–30.

Theological Use of Servant/Son Motif

King David, as a type, serves as a primary source of inspiration in the first part of Acts and is set forth as a model for Jesus (as) Messiah, the anti-type.[26] Evidence of the early community's identification of King David as the prototype of Jesus as Messiah is prominent in the apostles' preaching.[27] For example, Peter establishes the connection between David and Jesus by using Ps 16:8–11 in Acts 2:25–33 and Ps 110:1 in Acts 2:34–35. In his sermon, Peter concludes that David proclaimed these words of himself as "the favorite one" (2:27).[28] For Peter, Jesus is the fulfilment of the prophetic voice of David (2:29–33, 36). The community begins its prayer with this pattern, and its connection has firm roots in apostolic tradition.

Significant discussion has ensued concerning the somewhat incoherent grammatical construction of Acts 4:25a.[29] Bruce refers to it as "a translator's crux,"[30] and argues the only way to translate the passage with any hope of clarity is "to take David as the mouth (i.e., mouthpiece) of the Holy Spirit."[31] In light of the difficulties, we suggest two possible translations for Acts 4:25a: (1) "who said by the Holy Spirit through the mouth of our father your servant David" or (2) "it is you, our Father, who said

26. See Acts 1:16; 2:25; 2:34; 4:25. Concerning Luke's use of David see Strauss, *Davidic Messiah in Luke-Acts*, 76–129; Bovon, *Luke the Theologian*, 103–6; Schweizer, "Concept of the Davidic 'Son of God' in Acts," 186–93.

27. See Acts 1:16–17, 20; 2:25–36; 4:11, 25.

28. Heb. *hāsîd*, Gk. ὅσιόν, usually translated "Holy One." Kaiser argues the proper translation should be "favorite one." Kaiser, "Promise to David in Psalm 16," 219–229, esp. 224–26.

29. Haenchen proposes both τοῦ πατρὸς ἡμῶν (of our father) and διὰ πνεύματος ἁγίου (by [the] Holy Spirit) were inserted during later textual transmission. Haenchen, *Acts*, 226, esp. n. 3. Conzelmann agrees the text is corrupt. Conzelmann, *Acts*, 34. Also see Torrey, *Composition and Date of Acts*, 16–17; C. F. D. Moule, "H. W. Moule on Acts 4:25," 220–21; Wahlde, "Problems of Acts 4:25a," 265. Cf. Foakes-Jackson, *Acts*, 168; Keener, *Acts*, 1:643.

30. Bruce, *Acts*, 156.

31. Bruce, *Acts*, 105 n. 29. He further states (without citation) that Westcott and Hort refer to "the extreme difficulty of text, which doubtless contains a primitive error." Bruce, *Acts*, 105 n. 29. Nestle-Aland (NA28) has adopted the following: "ὁ τοῦ πατρὸς ἡμῶν διὰ πνεύματος ἁγίου στόματος Δαυὶδ παιδός σου εἰπών." From this, the NRSV translates, "It is you who said by the Holy Spirit through our ancestor David, your servant." In light of this textual construction, Metzger includes the following note: "Recognizing that the reading of p74 ℵ A B E *et al* is unsatisfactory, the Committee nevertheless considered it to be closer to what the author wrote originally than any of the other extant forms of text." Metzger, *Textual Commentary*, 281.

by the Holy Spirit through the mouth of your servant David." The latter translation fits the opening address to the Sovereign God most directly and presents the Father (as Master), Messiah (David-type), and the Spirit at work in revealing Jesus as the antitype to David. While not satisfying every concern, both translations adequately capture the essence of the available textual evidence.[32]

Critical to our theological claim is Luke's use the word *país* (Gr. παῖς, servant/son). He uses it four times, twice in Peter's sermon at Solomon's Porch (Acts 3:13, 26) and twice in the community's prayer (4:27, 30). Aside from its use in Matthew 12:18 (which is a quotation from Isaiah 42:1–4), Luke's use of *país* in relationship to Jesus constitutes its primary usage in the New Testament.[33] The question of importance to this discussion is, "What did Luke mean when using *país*?"[34]

In Luke 2:43, he uses the term to refer to the "child" Jesus. However, later in 7:7, he uses the same term to refer to a centurion's "slave or servant"

32. Passages of this nature—that is, OT allusion with contemporary application—are less frequent as the narrative proceeds, suggesting Luke's reliance on a Palestinian source for relevant information and inspiration concerning his characterization of the Jerusalem community of believers. Of the eighty-four citations of and allusions to Old Testament Scripture in Acts, only five occur after Acts 15. Thirty-two references occur between Acts 1:20—4:26 (38 percent). Of the remaining, twenty-seven citations or allusions occur during Stephen's sermon (Acts 7); thirteen occur during Paul's first missionary experience among diaspora Jews (Acts 13–14); five occur during the Jerusalem Council (Acts 15). Luke's heavy use of Scripture early in Acts favors a Palestinian or Jewish source to which reliance on Scripture would be more important. As his sources change, so does his use of Scripture. For statistical analysis of Luke's use of OT Scripture, see Meek, *Gentile Mission*, 17–23, 137–44; Witherington, *Acts*, 123–27. For support concerning Luke's general reliance on Palestinian/Aramaic sources more so in the first half of Acts, see Twelftree, *People of the Spirit*, 69; T. Smith, "Sources of Acts," 55–75; Hemer, *Acts*, 335–64. For a more cautious approach, see Keener, *Acts*, 1:176–83, 642–45.

33. For analysis see Oepke, "παῖς," *TDNT*, 5:636–54, esp. 637–39, 652–54. For Danker, παῖς addresses "Christ in his relation to God . . . it has the meaning of servant because of the identification of the 'servant of God' of certain OT passages." However, he goes on to concede, "In the case of [Acts 3:13, 26; 4:27, 30] it is hardly possible to decide which meaning is better . . . and could suggest the translation son." BDAG, "παῖς, παιδός" 750–51. Outside the NT, παῖς also appears in such early Christian writings as Did. 9:2; 10:2 (servant); 1 Clem. 59:2, 4 (servant or son); Barn. 6:1; 9:2 (servant); and in the Mart. Pol. 14:1; 20:2 (son). Translations from Lightfoot and Harmer, *Apostolic Fathers*.

34. According to Jeremias, παῖς θεοῦ is rare in Judaism after 100 BCE and means either *child* or *servant* of God depending on context. Jeremias, "παῖς θεοῦ," *TDNT*, 5:664–717, esp. 5:678–79. Cf. BDAG, "παῖς, παιδός" 750–51. Fitzmyer and Ménard concede its use is considerably argued. Fitzmyer, *Gospel According to Luke I–IX*, 211; Ménard, "PAIS THEOU as Messianic Title," 92.

in a social sense (i.e., a favored or highly regarded servant). What we find is that the meaning is dependent on context and subject to the author's intention.³⁵ The difficulty, of course, is in determining either context or intention. So, what does the context in Acts 3–4 reveal concerning Luke's intention in using *país*? Luke provides an interpretive clue for his usage in the opening salutation (Acts 4:24b-25); first by addressing the sovereign Lord (Acts 4:24b) and then second by addressing the Holy Spirit (4:25).

First, we see that with one voice the community addresses the Sovereign Lord, *despotés* (Gr. δέσποτης, Master).³⁶ As in Luke 2:29, the prayer of Acts 4:24-27 addresses the sovereign Lord who is master over all. Second, Luke identifies the Holy Spirit as the active agent in the lives of God's servants—namely, David and his holy servant, Jesus Messiah.³⁷

The majority of English translations render *país* as "servant" for all four instances in Acts (3:13, 3:26, 4:27, and 4:30), often providing a footnote indicating the alternative "child or son."³⁸ For the most part, its association with "Sovereign Lord," *despotés* (Master), suggests that *país* should be rendered servant. Nevertheless, Fitzmyer remarks,

> The question is complicated by the use of *pais* in Greek literature and in the Hellenistic world of the time. There it was used in a religious sense, to express a special relationship to a god. *Kronou pais*, "a child of Cronus," is found in *The Iliad* 2. 205. Similarly in Greek

35. Cadbury, "Titles of Jesus in Acts," 365; Jeremias, "παῖς θεοῦ," *TDNT*, 5:700-705.

36. The Gr. δέσποτής in the LXX is used by Abraham (Gen 15:2, 8), Joshua (Josh 5:14), Judith (Jdt 9:12), Raguel (Tob 8:17), Judas Maccabeus (2 Macc 15:22), Jonah (Jonah 4:10), Jeremiah (Jer 1:6; 4:10; 15:11), and Daniel (Dan 9:8, 15-17, 19). However, in the New Testament, aside from Acts 4:24, δέσποτής is used by Luke in Luke 2:29 (the Nunc Dimittis). The Song of Simeon (Luke 2:29-32) is often referred to as the Nunc Dimittis because of its first phrase in Latin, "now you dismiss"; Latin translation: "*Nunc dimittis servum tuum, Domine*," of which the NRSV translates, "Master, now you are dismissing your servant in peace." Codex Bezae (D05) adds ὁ θεός and reads, "Master you are the God who made . . . " See Rius-Camps and Read-Heimerdinger, *Message of Acts*, 1:270, 273-74. Danker describes δέσποτής as one who has legal control and authority over subjects, such as a "Ruler of a city." BDAG, "δέσποτης, δέσποτα," 220.

37. Lit., χριστοῦ αὐτοῦ, "his Christ." See Acts 4:25, 27b, 30b.

38. English translations choosing "servant" include: NIV, NLT, ESV, NASB, NKJV, CEV, HCSB, ISV, JB Phillips, NET, GOD'S WORD, ASV, Darby, ERV, TLB, Weymouth NT, and WEB. Translations choosing "son" or "child" include: KJV, Aramaic Bible in Plain English, Jubilee 2000, Douay-Rheims, WBT, WYC, and Young's. The Amplified Bible contains, "servant and son." Danker states, "In the case of [4:27, 30] it is hardly possible to decide which meaning is better . . . and could suggest the translation son." BDAG, "παῖς, παιδός," 750.

OT writings, the righteous Jew is called *paida kyriou*, "a child of the Lord," where this meaning is certain because of the later use of *huios theou* of the same person (Wis 2:13, 18). From this variety of usages arises the hesitation about the sense of the term in Acts.[39]

Given this evidence, the word *país* could and likely would be interpreted differently depending on who is using it and who is hearing it. In other words, the word *país* would depend on who is saying it (e.g., Luke's Palestinian source) and who is hearing it (e.g., Luke's Greek audience). From this, we conclude that the evidence found in its usage here suggests that the cultural or literary uses of *país* for Luke, who is writing in Greek, and his audience, who are largely non-Jews, would envision Jesus as God's Son more readily than as God's servant.[40] At the same time, we maintain that a Jewish audience would envision Jesus as God's Servant more readily than God's Son.

Since Luke has already broached the subject of the relationship between David and the Messiah (Luke 20:41–44), he is likely aware of the coterminous usage. The prayer of Acts 4:24–30 reveals how this first-century community of believers theologically expressed Jesus as Messiah, in terms coterminous with King David, and demonstrates their engagement in theological creativity.[41] Furthermore, the prayer expresses how they theologically understood Jesus as "Son of God."[42] Jesus is God's servant as David is God's servant. Jesus is God's son as David is God's son. King David and Jesus Messiah are both servant and son.

Belief in the Sovereignty of God Leads to Action

A theological understanding of God's sovereignty is important in the context of the disciples' prayer (Acts 4:24, 28). For us to see how, it will prove helpful to dividing the prayer into two parts: (1) the situation (Acts 4:24–28) and (2) the community's resolution and request (4:29–30). The first part begins and ends with reference to God's foreordaining power.

39. Fitzmyer, *Gospel According to Luke (I-IX)*, 211.

40. Ménard, "PAIS THEOU," 92.

41. Cf. Dunn, *Acts*, 56–57; Carpenter, *Primitive Christian Application*, 59–60; Conzelmann, *Acts*, 28. In opposition see Haenchen, *Acts*, 185, 205, esp. n. 4.

42. Concerning the blend of Jesus as Servant/Son see Harnack, "Bezechnung Jesu als 'Knecht Gottes,'" 212; Cadbury, "Titles of Jesus in Acts," 5:367; Hamm, "Acts 4:23–31," 229.

Calling on the sovereign Lord (4:24) and acknowledging how events had transpired at the behest of God and according to God's plan (4:28), the disciples, so to say, "sandwich" their experience of persecution within the purview of divine will.[43]

In the second part, the community, at great risk, takes solace in the providence of God (Acts 4:29-30).[44] If the persecution of King David and Jesus the Messiah are subject to the jurisprudence of the Sovereign Lord, then the persecution of Peter and John (4:1-22), as well as others in the community of faith, are also under the umbrella of divine providence. As Jesus Messiah faced hardship, so they too must suffer. Rather than seek retribution for suffering, the community calls for boldness despite its suffering (4:29). The community calls on God for an outpouring of healing and miraculous power to authenticate its calling and embolden its ongoing commitment to preaching (4:30).

Summary and Conclusions

In Acts 4:23-31, we see Luke portraying his characters' theological understanding of and identification with Jesus as Messiah. In his story, despite persecution from the authorities, the community of believers gather together to pray to the sovereign Lord for perseverance and for a manifestation of God's power. Luke begins with Peter and John returning from persecution. However, he quickly replaces Peter and John with a group of believers as the central and only character in the narrative. We have argued that the nature of the story limits the body of believers to a distinct group (viz., a group within a group) rather than a massive crowd like those envisioned in Acts 2:41 and 4:4. By excluding individual characters from the narrative, Luke is able to present to his audience a unified character who is active in theological creativity.

The prayer Luke incorporates portrays the community engaging in theological creativity by connecting their beliefs in both God's sovereign protection and in the Messiah as His Servant to both Jesus and themselves. We have argued that Luke does this by characterizing this community of believers as possessing a theological understanding that associates Jesus with both King David and the Messiah of Psalm 2 in the following manner.

43. Cf. Wahlde, "Acts 4:24-31," 240.
44. Cf. Plymale, *Prayer Texts of Luke-Acts*, 81.

First, Jesus is God's Servant/Son. Luke describes the community's understanding of Jesus as the Servant and Son of God as inextricably linked to its understanding of David as God's servant and son. Second, he characterizes the community connecting its own persecution and suffering with the sufferings and persecution of Jesus. Since Jesus suffered unjustly, and within the providence of the divine will, so will the community. Using Psalm 2 as a guide, the community of believers recognize the prophetic nature of their circumstance and refuse to relent in the face of cruel treatment. Rather than retribution against its enemies, they seek boldness to continue preaching and request a manifestation of God's miraculous power. As a result, they resolve to preach despite persecution.

In light of our analysis of the community's prayer, we conclude that the manner in which Luke inserts the prayer into the story as an early tradition in the form of Jewish *pesher*, highlights three primary characteristics of the Jerusalem community: (1) it considers the sufferings of Jesus equal to the prophetic sufferings of the Messiah, (2) it feels a connection between Jesus' sufferings and its own, and (3) it possesses a non-violent nature and hope for its neighbors.

Moreover, it also reveals two instances in which the community engages in theological creativity: (1) belief in Jesus as God's Servant/Son motivates it to keep preaching, and (2) trust in the sovereignty of God is foundational to its resolve. As we have seen, Luke portrays this claim by juxtaposing the community of Psalm 2 with the community of Acts 4. Thus, we conclude that Luke's use of the prayer presents his character's role in an interpretive process involving Spirit–Community–Scripture.

3

Selecting the Seven—Acts 6:1–7

According to Luke's story, the church is experiencing rapid growth and is committed to the welfare of his members.[1] To meet the social demands inherent within an increasingly diverse and dynamic group of believers committed to the social welfare of all, Luke portrays a community broadening its recognized leadership structure. He presents the followers of Jesus, who originally form under the egis of the Twelve, embracing a new tier of leadership known as the Seven.[2] Unique in Luke's story is the way he describes selecting and commissioning of the Seven from among a previously unidentified group within the Jerusalem church. In this chapter, we will see Luke's portrayal of a community of believers engaging and participating in the process of selecting and commissioning a new group of leaders in Acts 6:1–7.

Luke describes the community's role in theological creativity by identifying the community as a body of believers, referred to for the first time in Acts as disciples.[3] Furthermore, he introduces two distinguishable fac-

1. See Acts 1:15; 2:41–47; 4:4, 32–34; 5:12–16; 6:1–7. For later indications of growth and care among the disciples also see 8:4–8, 40; 9:31; 11:18–21, 24b, 29–30; 12:24; 14:1; 21:20.

2. Concerning the Twelve see Acts 1:12–13, 26; 2:14, 42; concerning the Seven see 6:3, 5; 21:8.

3. Theological creativity is the act of reformulating formerly held theological interpretations in light of testimony concerning the Spirit's evidential work and an emerging understanding of applicable Scripture followed by commensurate action. The Spirit's evidential work is known only through the community's testimony. Therefore, theological creativity is the outcome of the interpretive process since it is theology in action,

tions, one of whose social need serves as the catalyst for action in the story. By accentuating the diversity of the disciples in Jerusalem, Luke can offer his audience a theological explanation for continued growth among the disciples of Jesus.

In order to describe Luke's view of the community engaging in theological creativity in Acts 6:1–7, we must first consider how Luke characterizes the community as, so to say, "groups within a group" as well as the central social issue significant to the plot. After that we will analyze the theological implications implicit in broadening the leadership of the early church to include the Seven, especially in the need *for* and commissioning *of* new leaders through the "the laying on of hands" (6:6). The chapter will end with a summary of the main points and evidence to demonstrate Luke's portrayal of the first-century community of believers engaging in theological creativity.

Identifying the Community

Luke begins this episode with the phrase, "Now during those days" (Acts 6:1). His opening signals not only an indeterminate transition of time in the narrative but also a shift in focus since the latest persecution of the apostles (Acts 5:17–42).[4] In the context of Acts 6, Luke's characters include (1) the disciples, (2) the Hellenists and Hebrews, (3) widows, (4) the Twelve, and (5) the Seven as subgroups within the community of believers—that is, as groups within a group. Moreover, he informs his audience that the central issue in his story concerns a social conflict between Hebrew and Hellenist inhabitants of Jerusalem concerning the care and welfare of Hellenist widows (6:1).[5]

---

functional in nature, and situationally pragmatic in scope. Consequently, it involves the process of theological justification and action or reaction in light of current circumstances. In this sense, to be creative with theology is to take what is already a theological assumption and broaden or adapt it to current circumstances in light of the Spirit's evidential work and a consensus understanding of Scripture.

4. Furthermore, as Bruce concludes, Luke's use of the phrase "now during those days" (Ἐν δὲ ταῖς ἡμέραις ταύταις) may also indicate a change in source. Bruce, *Acts*, 180. Also see Dunn, *Acts*, 242–44; Barrett, *Acts*, 1:307. Dunn thinks the source is from the church in Antioch, Syria, and is recounting to Luke what they consider its origins. Dunn, *Acts*, 79. Cf. Simon, "St. Stephen and the Jerusalem Temple," 140; Haenchen, *Acts*, 260 n. 1.

5. We will argue that Luke's opening statement in 6:1 narratively implies that this is active issue pervasive among all Jews in Jerusalem. See conclusions in this chapter.

To fully appreciate the disciples as a unified character in the story, we must analyze the various sub-groups (groups within a group) from which Luke constructs the community of disciples. Doing so will help us see how Luke brings each group together into one unified character. The following progression is by order of appearance in Luke's story.

The Disciples

In Acts 6:1, Luke refers to the community formally as *mathētēs* (disciples).[6] From this point forward in the narrative his use of the term encompasses all the followers of Jesus, is not limited to a specific group or location, and becomes his default word for identifying the followers of Jesus.[7] In Luke's story, the disciples (as a group) are a conflation of culturally diverse and ideologically disparate groups of Jesus' followers coexisting under a common banner and sharing a common commitment to each other.[8]

Hellenist and Hebrew Factions

In Acts 1–5, the apostles and their earliest followers are the central focus of the narrative.[9] However, in chapter 6 Luke introduces nomenclature for two previously unspecified subgroups among the community of disciples.

6. Earliest use of μαθητής include Herodotus, *Hist.* 4.77, where Anacharsis is described as a "student" of Hellas and in in P.Oxy. IV, 725.15 as an "apprentice." For an extensive review of the concept in antiquity see Rengstorf, "μαθητής," *TDNT*, 4:416–23. In Luke's Gospel μαθητής (disciple, student, follower) and its derivatives are limited to Jesus' closest followers (the apostles) and include: Luke 5:30, 33; 6:1, 13, 17, 20, 40; 7:11, 18, 19; 8:9, 22; 9:14, 16, 18, 40, 43, 54; 10:23; 11:1; 12:1, 22; 14:26, 27, 33;16:1; 17:1, 22; 18:15; 19:29, 37, 39; 20:45; 22:11, 39, 45. After Luke 22:45, Luke discontinues the use of μαθητής until it reemerges in Acts 6:1 where it includes all the disciples of Jesus everywhere. See Acts 6:1, 2, 7; 9:1, 10, 19, 21, 25, 26, 36, 38; 11:26, 29; 13:52; 14:20, 22, 28; 15:10; 16:1; 18:23, 27; 19:1, 9, 30; 20:1, 30; 21:4, 16.

7. See Rengstorf, "μαθητής," *TDNT*, 4:390–461, esp. 457–59; Danker states, "Acts uses μαθητής almost exclusively to denote the members of the new community of believers . . . so that it almost equals *Christian* (compare 11:26); Acts 6:1, 7; 9:19; 11:26, 29, 13:52; 15:10." BDAG, "μαθητής," 609–10. Cf. Lienhard, "Acts 6:1–6," 229, 231; Haenchen, *Acts,* 260 n. 1.

8. Notice how its usage escalates following Stephen's death. See 9:1, 10, 19, 21, 25, 26, 36, 38; 11:26, 29; 13:52; 14:20, 22, 28; 15:10; 16:1; 18:23, 27; 19:1, 9, 30; 20:1, 30; 21:4, 16. It may also more broadly define all those who flee Jerusalem following Stephen's death (Acts 8:1).

9. Walton, "How Mighty a Minority," 305–327, esp. 305; Barrett, *Acts,* 1:307.

First, Luke introduces the Hellenists, a faction whose scope and influence later most broadens the circle of believers (Acts 8:1; 11:19–21). His use of the term as a title constitutes its first in the available literature making its origins and meaning somewhat of a mystery.[10] Luke identifies the second faction as Hebrews. The lack of any further description makes its use even more enigmatic. A considerable body of literature has been written concerning the identity of the Hellenists and Hebrews in Acts 6:1.[11] Since Luke's use of the terms as proper names of groups (nouns) is unique to his writings, making his meaning obscure,[12] issues concerning the identification of the Hellenist and Hebrew factions are complicated and largely unresolved.[13]

For example, Haenchen and others view the primary distinction between the two groups to be (a) Greek-speaking Jewish disciples from the Diaspora (who include the Seven and their respective house-churches) and (b) Aramaic-speaking Jewish disciples (who include the apostles and church core).[14] For Haenchen, like Baur before him, Luke is writing of two specific groups among the disciples with distinct and opposing theological perspectives, an "us and them" scenario.[15] However, since Luke does

10. See Stanton, "Hellenism," *DNTB*, 464; Bruce, *Acts*, 181; there is no earlier use as a noun in *TLG*. For additional analysis see Windisch, "Ἑλληνιστής," *TDNT*, 2:504–16, esp. 507–12; For Danker, it refers to "a Greek-speaking Israelite in contrast to one speaking a Semitic language." BDAG, "Ἑλληνιστής," 319.

11. For examples, see Walton, "How Mighty a Minority," 305–327; Stanton, "Hellenism," *DNTB*, 464–73; Hill, "Acts 6:1—8:4," 129–53; Brehm, "Meaning of Ἑλληνιστής in Acts," 180–99; Tyson, "Acts 6:1–7 and Dietary Regulations," 145–61; Kraft, "Multiform Jewish Heritage," 174–199; Windisch, "Ἑλληνιστής," *TDNT*, 2:504–16; C. Moule, "Once more," 100–102; Cadbury, "The Hellenists," 5:59–74. For extended treatment, consult Hengel, *Judaism and Hellenism*; Hill, *Hellenist and Hebrews* (1995); Mann, "Appendix VI: 'Hellenists' and 'Hebrews' in Acts vi 1," in Munck, *Acts*, 301.

12. Windisch, "Ἑλληνιστής," *TDNT*, 2:511. Cf. Bruce, *Acts*, 181; Dunn, *Acts*, 81–82. Mann adds, "Linguistically the verb *hellēnizein* as used by Plato meant 'to speak good Greek,' but it eventually came to mean 'to imitate Greek manners and customs,' and so acquired in some quarters a derogatory meaning." Mann, "Appendix VI," 301, in Munck, *Acts,* 301.

13. See Hemer, *Acts*, 175–76, also n. 31; Haenchen, *Acts*, 260 n. 3; Keener, *Acts*, 2:1253–59.

14. Haenchen, *Acts*, 260; Conzelmann, *Acts*, 47–61; Hengel, *Judaism and Hellenism*, 1:313–14; Hengel, *Acts and the History*, 71–75; Twelftree, *People of the Spirit*, 118; Dunn, *Acts*, 81.

15. Haenchen, *Acts*, 260–61, esp. n. 3. Also see Cullmann, "Significance of the Qumran Texts," 220–21. For Baur's influential argument that the early church was divided into two opposing factions, see Baur, "Christuspartei in der korinthischen Gemeinde"

not use such terminology to identify disciples in this manner on any other occasion, it is narratively reasonable to conclude his use in Acts 6:1 is not limited to disciples only.[16]

A few, beginning with Henry Cadbury in 1933, have argued that Luke intends his use of the terms to identify Jewish (Hebrew) and Gentile (Hellenist) disciples.[17] If this is the case, then Luke would be referring to a division between two ethnic groups among the disciples. But Luke's one-time use of the term Hebrews in this passage is insufficient narrative evidence to distinguish Jew from Gentile.[18]

In an attempt to bolster Cadbury's claim concerning the presence of *Gentile* Christians as early as Acts 6, Tyson claims that "there are false starts in Acts."[19] He states,

> Although dietary regulations are rejected in Acts 10–11, some are reintroduced in chapter 15. Three times Paul says that he will no longer go to Jews but to Gentiles (13:46; 18:6; 28:28). There is no clear rejection of Jews and a consequent embrace of Gentiles after either 13:46 or 18:6. Both should be regarded as anticipations of the outcome that does not arrive until 28:28.[20]

Tyson argues that Luke includes Gentiles as part of the Jerusalem church in Acts 6:1 ("a false start") even though Luke does not introduce the circumstances for their inclusion until later in the story. For him, Luke is not violating his own literary structure. However, his argument is not convincing for the following reasons.

First, if Hebrew and Hellenist are Jewish and Gentile believers respectively, then Luke has introduced a factor that undermines the need for events occurring in Acts 10–15, thus sabotaging his own narrative plot.[21]

(The Christ-party in the Corinthian community, the opposition of Petrine and Pauline Christianity in the early church, and the Apostle Peter in Rome), 61–206.

16. See Acts 6:9; 9:29; 11:20. Still, Haenchen concludes Luke's emphasis of the terms Hebrew/Hellenist limits the groups to the church and not the broader Jerusalem community. Haenchen, *Acts*, 265–69. In opposition to Haenchen see Hill, *Hellenists and Hebrews*, 22–24.

17. Cf. Cadbury, "Hellenists," 5:59–74; Tyson, "Acts 6:1–7," 157–58.

18. For support see Windisch, "Ἑλληνιστής," *TDNT*, 2:512; Marshal, "Palestinian and Hellenistic Christianity," 277.

19. Tyson, "Acts 6:1–7," 158.

20. Tyson, "Acts 6:1–7," 158.

21. In support, see Windisch, "Ἑλληνιστής," *TDNT*, 2:512. Below, we will make an argument supporting events recorded out of sequence. But doing so does not disrupt or

If non-proselytized Gentile disciples already existed within the Jerusalem community in Acts 6 as claimed, then Luke's painstaking description of Peter's experience at Cornelius' home (Acts 10–11) and the conflict surrounding the admission of non-proselytized Gentiles into the community of faith (13–15) are anticlimactic thereby foiling the plot.[22]

Second, Paul's claim that he will go "to the Gentiles" is stated to Jews living in different cities and regions.[23] Making such a declaration to various groups in diverse locations does not preclude him from proclaiming the gospel to Jews in a new region. Rather, we argue that Luke's story merely shows Paul is finished with that particular group of Jews and moving on. Consequently, since Luke does not use the term Hebrew as a blanket term to describe Jews anywhere else and since introducing Gentile disciples into the story at this point undermines his plot development, we argue Luke does not use Hebrew and Hellenist to distinguish between Jewish and Gentile disciples.

One final example includes Abram Spiro and William Albright, who argue Luke's "Hebrews" are Samaritan disciples living in Jerusalem and suggest the term best describes a growing Samaritan faction within the larger community of believers, which includes Stephen and Philip.[24] Albright justifies his claim by citing similarities between Stephen's sermon in Acts 7 with the Samaritan Pentateuch (SP) as evidence. Their argument is narratively compelling for the following reasons: (1) in that Luke does have Stephen "at odds" with a *Hellenist* synagogue (Acts 6:9); (2) in the manner in which Stephen's sermon is favorable to the tabernacle staying in ancient Ephraim with Joshua and negative to a permanent temple structure in Jerusalem (7:44–50); and (3) in light of Philip's success among the *Samaritans* in the wake of Stephen's death (8:4–25).

However, Earl Richard demonstrates convincingly any similarities between Acts 7 and the Samaritan Pentateuch (SP) may be explained on

---

spoil the plot as Tyson claims.

22. We will address Tyson's issue concerning dietary issues below.

23. Acts 13:46–52; 18:6–8; 28:25–28.

24. Albright argues, "This testimony is confirmed from all branches of Samaritan literature where the self-designation "Hebrews" appears scores of times. It may also be inferred from Jewish literature." Albright, "Appendix V," in Munck, *Acts*, 285–300, esp. 292. Presumably, they claim, the conflict is between Samaritan disciples and Greek-speaking Jewish disciples from the Diaspora. For other support hinting at a similar conclusion see Josephus, *Ant.* XI, viii, 6; Bruce, *Acts*, 181. For extended analysis see Hill, *Hellenist and Hebrews*, 44–49.

textual, rather than "biographical, historical, or theological" grounds.[25] Moreover, he argues that any similarities one might see between Stephen's defense and the Samaritan text may also be explained from a variety of other translations.[26] Consequently, in order to conclude that the Hebrews of Acts 6 in general or Stephen (let alone Philip) in particular are Samaritan in heritage, one must seek evidence on grounds other than similarities with the SP. At this point, evidence for such a claim is insufficient. Which brings us back to where we started, that identifying the Hellenists and the Hebrews in Acts 6 is complicated and largely unresolved. So, where does this leave us?

Narratively speaking, it is reasonable to assume Luke indicates a recognizable distinction between factions within the Jerusalem church despite Dunn's assertion that to speak of the Hellenists as a party or faction goes beyond the evidence.[27] However, that being said, it seems apparent that the divisions raised by Luke are not, so to say, "hard and fast." Despite the implication of segregation in Luke's account, the apostles address those embroiled in the conflict in familial terms as brothers (pl, form of *adelphos*), which the NRSV translates as "friends" since women are not only included but who are positioned at the center of the story.

Given the consensus that Palestinian Judaism in the first century CE was pluralistic in nature, it is safe to assume most if not all sects within Judaism were influenced by Greek culture to one degree or another making such a demarcation, such as ideological or theological difference, difficult to identify.[28] More aptly, it is, as Craig Hill states, "The earliest church was untidily diverse, not neatly divided."[29] Luke's lack of description concerning

25. Richard, "Acts 7," esp. 202, 204, 207 n. 70. He concludes Luke's source is drawing on an early Greek *Vorlage* of the LXX and that "such a reading . . . as indicated by the Samaritan texts, had its roots in a Hebrew recension" (199). Kahle confirms that many of the similarities between Acts 7 and the SP are also found in the proto-Palestinian texts used in the development of the LXX. Kahle, *Cairo Geniza*, 144–49.

26. Richard, "Acts 7," 200, 205, 207; Mare, "Acts 7," 1–21, esp. 8–11.

27. See Dunn, *Acts*, 82. Yet, earlier he indicates using the term disciples 6:1 may suggest the term disciples originates with the Hellenist community as its own unique self-description. Dunn, *Acts*, 81. Cf. Marshal, "Palestinian and Hellenistic Christianity," 271–87, esp. 277.

28. For support, see Hill, *Hellenists and Hebrews*, 2. See also Hengel, *Between Jesus and Paul*, xiv; Smith, "Palestinian Judaism in the First Century," 67–81, esp. 81; Mann, "Appendix VI," in Munck, *Acts*, 302; Brehm, "The Role of the 'Hellenists' in Christian Origins," 6–8; Brehm, "The Meaning of Ἑλληνιστής," 185–92.

29. Hill, *Hellenist and Hebrews*, 4. See also Hill, "Acts 6:1—8:4," esp. 130–31; Marshal,

chiding factions supports Hill's assessment. Moreover, even though numerous scholars rightly argue that it is no longer legitimate to separate Palestinian Judaism from Hellenistic Judaism rigidly as opposing factions,[30] especially on theological grounds, it is narratively apparent that Luke intends to identify a division of some sort (Acts 6:1).[31]

Consequently, in light of Luke's singular undefined use of the term Hebrews in Acts 6:1 and his use of Hellenist in the remainder of his story (who are not disciples, 6:9; 9:29; 11:20), we conclude the nomenclature Hebrew and Hellenist in Acts 6:1 is applied by Luke as a general division among all Jews in and around Jerusalem, some of whom are part of the community of believers.[32] We will offer more evidence to support this claim below but concede this view is not widely held.

Furthermore, given the preceding discussion, we conclude Luke does not use the term Hebrews to describe either Jewish or Samaritan disciples but rather generational inhabitants of Jerusalem, whose mother tongue is Semitic. Moreover, even if Greek-speaking Jewish disciples were regarded as Hellenists they do not necessarily represent non-Jewish disciples in

---

"Palestinian and Hellenistic Christianity," 278–79; Simon, "St. Stephen and the Jerusalem Temple," 141.

30. Davies, *Paul and Rabbinic Judaism*, xxiii; Nickelsburg, *Early Judaism and Its Modern Interpreters*, 11. Cf. Hill, *Hellenists and Hebrews*, 1–4; Hengel, *Between Jesus and Paul*, 12; Hengel, *Acts and the History*, 101; Marshal, "Palestinian and Hellenistic Christianity," 274–75. For other works concerning the diversity of first-century Judaism, see Kraabel, "The Roman Diaspora: Six Questionable Assumptions," 445–464; Kraft, "The Multiform Jewish Heritage of Early Christianity," 174–199; Porton, "Diversity in Postbiblical Judaism," 57–80.

31. Nickelsburg considers this longstanding assumption to be "one of the most damaging oversimplifications of earlier scholarship." Nickelsburg, *Early Judaism*, 11. However, in Luke's narrative, we maintain that Hellenists and Hebrews are distinguishable. Charles Moule's 1958 claim seems to account for differences in ideology or theology by narrowing the distinction between Hellenist and Hebrew on linguistic terms rather than as opposing groups, between those who spoke only Greek (the Hellenists) and those able to speak Greek but whose native tongue was Semitic (the Hebrews). See Moule, "Once more," 100. While Windisch generally agrees, he does point out that there is no compelling reason why Hellenist should indicate Greek-speaking and Hebrew indicate Hebrew-speaking. Windisch, "Ἑλληνιστής," *TDNT* 2:512.

32. Such a premise best explains why the Apostles (the Twelve) are never identified as Hebrews and the only other references to Hellenists in Acts (directly or indirectly) do not include disciples (Acts 6:9; 9:29; 11:20). It may also provide a reasonable explanation as to why some of the disciples are expelled from Jerusalem while the Apostles (and possibly other disciples) are allowed to remain (Acts 8:1–4).

general since all other references to Hellenists in Acts have no apparent association with the disciples (Acts 6:9; 9:29; 11:20). [33]

As we have shown, both the evidence available concerning the terminology and Luke's use elsewhere in Acts suggest Hellenists are Diaspora Jews whose first language is Greek and who have immigrated to Palestine from areas influenced by Greek culture.[34] Thus, in the narrowest sense, we acknowledge both Hebrew and Hellenist among the disciples. However, in the broadest sense, we conclude that Luke's use addresses the general population of Jerusalem and not simply the community of disciples.

The Widows of Acts 6

The widows in Luke's story are characterized in the most basic (flat) terms.[35] Beyond the possible ethnic and cultural conclusions drawn from being described as Hellenist or Hebrew, the reader is provided surprisingly little information about these widows. Generally speaking, widow-accounts in Luke feature women in a positive manner who are often destitute, dependent, vulnerable to exploitation, or in need of economic and social support.[36] However, in Acts 6, Luke provides nothing specific beyond the mention of their possible affiliation and need.

So, what conclusions may be drawn from Luke's writings concerning widows in first-century Jerusalem? Consistent with Luke's view in his Gospel and Acts, it is reasonable to conclude both Hellenist and Hebrew widows are unable to provide their own sustenance and, as such, are in need of a social support system.[37] Since we conclude Luke's use of Hellenist and

33. Some argue the Hellenists described by Luke in Acts 6 are Greek-speaking converts who remain in Jerusalem following the events of Pentecost (2:8–11). See Mann, "Appendix VI," in Munck, *Acts*, 302.

34. Windisch indicates Hellenist Judaism did make a distinction when appropriating Greek values by rejection the mythology, cultus, and immoral aspects of Hellenes while drawing various aspects from their language, philosophy and culture. Windisch, "Ἑλληνιστής," *TDNT*, 2:506. Cf. Bruce, *Acts*, 181; Haenchen, *Acts*, 266–67.

35. Spencer, "Neglected Widows in Acts 6:1–7," 727–28.

36. For example, in Luke's Gospel, stories featuring widows include (1) Anna in the temple (Lk 2:36–38); (2) the widow of Nain (7:11–17); (3) the persistent widow (18:1–8); and finally (4) the poor widow (21:1–4).

37. For support, see Hiebert, "When Shall Help Come," 125–41, esp. 137. In opposition to the claim that the widows of Acts 6 are "destitute," see Schüssler Fiorenza, *In Memory of Her*, 162–68.

Hebrews is general in nature and not limited to the disciples, we also maintain that the conflict concerning widows was not unique to the disciples but rather something common among all Jews living within the region. As a generalized problem for Jews in and around Jerusalem, the disciples are indiscriminately affected by a regional problem.[38]

The Twelve

As the conflict concerning the care and provision of widows grows among the Hellenist and Hebrew factions, the Twelve call the whole community of believers together to seek a remedy. This is the only occasion in Acts where Luke refers to the apostles as the Twelve (6:2). He revisits a theme initiated and directly stated in his Gospel—namely, the Twelve as a corporate entity.[39]

Luke indicates it is the Twelve who take the initiative by calling the "whole community of the disciples" together to find a resolution (Acts 6:2).[40] In this episode, the Twelve function as arbiters over issues affecting the community of disciples (6:3). However, Luke also characterizes the Twelve as those who see their primary commitment to prayer and preaching (6:4).[41] Their solution is to find additional leaders who might oversee daily or routine responsibilities (6:3). It is unclear who oversaw the administration of funds and goods on previous occasions (2:45; 4:34–35).

Whatever role the Twelve may have had concerning the general welfare of the community on earlier occasions, administrative care for the widows' distribution was something they were unwilling to engage (6:2b).[42] Consequently, the Twelve entrust the community with selecting seven men to oversee this task (6:3, 6). Despite F. Scott Spencer's sharp critique of the decision made by the Twelve to delegate the matter to others,[43] functionally

---

38. For support, see Rius-Camps and Read-Heimerdinger, *Message of Acts*, 2:12, esp. n. 2.

39. Luke 6:13; 8:1; 9:1, 12; 18:31; 22:3, 30, 47. For extended discussion, see chapter 1.

40. Luke indirectly alludes to the Twelve in Acts 1:17, 22, and 26.

41. Their role as preachers and teachers and their commitment to prayer is emphasized in Acts 2:42; 4:20, 29, 33; 5:12, 20–21, 25, 28–29, 42.

42. This action is heavily criticized by some. For example, see Spencer, "Neglected Widows," 715–33.

43. Spencer, "Neglected Widows," 729.

speaking, the Seven serve as extensions of the Twelve given their commission to serve (6:6).[44]

The Seven

Luke does not identify those selected to oversee the widow distribution as "the Seven" in Acts 6. However, he does identify this group as such in 21:8 when Philip is reintroducing into the plot. What we learn of this group in Acts 6 is that seven were selected by the community as men in good standing who were full of the Spirit and wisdom (6:3).

The consensus that the Seven are Hellenists is based on each having a Greek name (with the possible exception of Philip).[45] As Marshal concludes, "It seems probable that the men appointed were drawn from the Greek-speaking part of the church that had raised the original complaint."[46] But Greek names were common throughout the region and across the Roman Empire, even among Jews.[47] Consequently, simply possessing a Greek name is not sufficient evidence for identifying a person's origin as some have supposed.[48] The only biographical information provided by Luke is that Nicolaus was a proselyte from Antioch (Acts 6:5).

Much has been made of the "table-waiting" function of the Seven.[49] However, as is evident from the subsequent preaching ministry of Stephen

44. We will offer evidence of this on theological grounds later in this chapter. For the suggestion that they are the leaders of seven Hellenist house-churches and essentially pastors, who not only administrate the daily distribution of food to their own widows but also engage in preaching ministry, see Dunn, *Beginning from Jerusalem*, 255.

45. Cf. Bruce, *Acts*, 129, 142; Marshal, *Acts*, 124, 127; Dunn, *Acts*, 83.

46. Marshal, *Acts*, 124, 127. Also see Hill, *Hellenists and Hebrews*, 24–28; Polhill, "Hellenist Breakthrough," 475–86, esp. 476.

47. Ferguson, "Hellenist in the Book of Acts," 166–67. Cf. Keener, *Acts*, 2:1280–88.

48. Dunn concedes, "The deduction is by no means certain." Dunn, *Acts*, 83. Cf. Barrett, *Acts*, 1:314. As indicated earlier, Spiro and Albright maintain that Stephen, one of the Seven, is a member of the Hebrew (Samaritan) faction. See Albright, "Appendix V," in Munck, *Acts*, 285. For a myriad of proposals see Simon, "St. Stephen and the Jerusalem Temple," 127–42; Manson, *Epistle to the Hebrews*, 25–46; Simon, *St. Stephen and the Hellenists*, 1–19.

49. In Luke 17:8, διακόνει μοι ἕως φάγω καὶ πίω, "wait on/serve me while I eat and drink" (NRSV). For ancient usage see Philo, "to serve" *Contempl.* 70; Josephus, "to wait at table," *Ant.* 6.52; 11.163; 11.166, 188; "to serve/obey," *Ant.* 9.25. For extended discussion see Beyer, "διακονέω," *TDNT*, 2:89–93; Schnabel, *Jesus and the Twelve*, 428–30; Witherington, *Acts*, 249–50; Fitzmyer, *Acts*, 348; Pao, "Waiters or Preachers," 127–44.

and Philip, it is unlikely the Twelve view the Seven as table-waiters in any conventional sense. Clearly Luke uses *diakonéō* (Gr. διαχονέω, to serve) to describe the need at hand (Acts 6:2).[50] However, it is likely a convenient play on words and not a description of the Seven's scope of ministry or necessarily the origins of the ministry of deacons.[51] After all, Luke uses *diakonía* and its various derivatives for the administration of the common fund, service in general, and for preaching ministry.[52] At this point and consistent with the narrative, what seems apparent is the introduction of a new level of leadership within a specific subgroup.

Summary

Through Luke's narrative tale the audience receives insight concerning the growing body of believers known as disciples. In Luke's Gospel, the disciples are the most immediate followers of Jesus (the Twelve) but from this point forward in the narrative the term includes all the believers in every place.

After introducing the community of believers as disciples in Acts 6:1, Luke's story appears to fracture them into various sub-groups in such a way making it difficult to view them as a single group (Acts 6:1). However, as the story concludes, the audience sees the community as a single character, coexisting under a common banner and sharing a common commitment to each other (6:7). This new moniker for the community of believers encompasses the various subgroups (groups within a group) under the umbrella of one name, disciples.

Luke manages this task through the introduction of a crisis in the form of a wider social concern, which provides him with a story plot

50. For support see Beyer, "διαχονεῖν," *TDNT*, 2:84.

51. For support see Beyer, "διαχονέω," *TDNT*, 2:81–89, esp. 84–85; and "Deacon as a Church Official," 2:89–93; Danker states, "Acts 6:2 possesses a special problem: *care for, take care of*. The term διαχονία (v. 1) more probably refers to administrative responsibility, one of whose aspects is concern for widows without specifying the kind of assistance that is allotted. V. 2 may contain wordplay involving the phrase τὸν λόγον τοῦ θεοῦ with λόγος designating a ledger entry, in which case τράπεζα, which is also a banker's term, may here denote *accounts*." BDAG, "διαχονέω," 229–30, esp. 230.

52. For the common fund, see Luke 8:3; for service in general, see Luke 4:39; 10:40; 12:26, 27, 37; 17:8; 22:27; Acts 6:4; 11:29–30; for preaching ministry, see Acts 6:2; 19:22. Cf. Dunn, *Acts*, 83. In support, Beyer states, "In the secular world *diákonos* could be used to describe such varied people as messengers, stewards, bakers, assistant helmsmen, and even statesmen." Beyer, "διαχονέω," *TDNT*, 2:89.

capable of bringing the community together as one character committed to a common cause. Although the disciples experience labeling by social classifications (Hebrews and Hellenists) as well as unequal treatment (Hebrew widows vs. Hellenist widows), Luke brings them all back into this one new classification, the disciples. He demonstrates this by referring to the "whole community" together on two occasions (Acts 6:2, 5).[53] According to Luke, everyone involved in the conflict is involved in the solution.

Under the guidance of the Twelve, the community of disciples select the Seven to manage the mundane affairs inherent in a growing and diverse community. Although some find fault with the Twelve for refusing to oversee the care of the widows and choosing instead to relegate the matter to others, the manner in which Luke crafts the story indicates something far nobler. As we will see below, the act of devising a plan to remedy a common problem between local (Hebrew) and immigrant (Hellenist) Jews demonstrates this community's engagement in theological creativity.

The Community in Theological Creativity

Having considered Luke's characterization of the disciples as groups within a group and in the way they all work together to solve a critical social need, we will now consider how Luke demonstrates the community engaging in theological creativity. The consequences for the community's decisions are far-reaching in nature and demonstrate:

1. The way leaders receive appointment and how the commissioning process evolved;

2. How experiences in a growing community broadened the community's understanding of ministry leadership; and even

3. How these decisions possessed unforeseen consequences given Jesus' mandate for the community to expand beyond the region of Jerusalem (Acts 1:8).[54]

---

53. Consult NA28 for Acts 6:2: "τὸ πλῆθος τῶν μαθητῶν" (lit. "the community [crowd or multitude] of disciples"); 6:5, "παντὸς τοῦ πλήθους" (lit. "the whole community [crowd or multitude]").

54. As discussed in chapter 1.

The Laying on of Hands

Unique in the selection of the Seven is in the way they become nominees and then receive commission. According to Luke, the "whole community of disciples" participates in the selection process (Acts 6:5). Unfortunately, this aspect of the process is not otherwise described. The Twelve provide criteria for candidacy (6:3). Each nominee must be (1) of good standing (i.e., good reputation), and (2) full of the (Holy) Spirit and wisdom. Beyond this criterion, Luke provides no details concerning the actual process. However, as we will see, he does provide details concerning their commissioning (6:6).

The first instance of "the laying on of hands" as an act of commissioning in Acts occurs in conjunction with the selection of the Seven (Acts 6:6).[55] To this point, Luke limits the ritual act to healing episodes and to the impartation of the Holy Spirit.[56] Since his use of the ritual involves a point of contact or transference of power it is ironic that Luke does not include it when Jesus commissions the Twelve (6:12–16) or the Seventy (10:1–24) for itinerate ministry.[57] Nevertheless, given the importance of the ritual act as a symbol in ancient Israel and its uniqueness in application in Acts 6:6, the question remains: Why was it used on this occasion and how was it implemented? The text of Acts 6:6 is somewhat unclear when it comes to informing the reader who lays hands on whom. Was it the Twelve or the community who laid hands on the Seven?[58]

55. Other instances of commissioning include the missionary call of Barnabas and Saul (Acts 13:1–3) and possibly Saul's calling (9:11–18, although the direct application is healing and baptism in the Holy Spirit).

56. For acts of healing see Luke 4:40; 13:13; Acts 9:12, 18; 28:8; also possibly 3:7; 19:11–12; 20:10. For the impartation of the Holy Spirit see Acts 8:17–19; 9:17; 19:6. For direct acts of commissioning see Acts 6:6; 13:3.

57. For manuscript analysis, see Schnabel, *Jesus and the Twelve*, 316–20.

58. The Greek sentence structure is unclear on this issue since the subject and consequential action is separated by considerable distance. Acts 6:5–6, "καὶ ἤρεσεν ὁ λόγος ἐνώπιον παντὸς τοῦ πλήθους καὶ ἐξελέξαντο Στέφανον, ἄνδρα πλήρης πίστεως καὶ πνεύματος ἁγίου, καὶ Φίλιππον καὶ Πρόχορον καὶ Νικάνορα καὶ Τίμωνα καὶ Παρμενᾶν καὶ Νικόλαον προσήλυτον Ἀντιοχέα, οὓς ἔστησαν ἐνώπιον τῶν ἀποστόλων, καὶ προσευξάμενοι ἐπέθηκαν αὐτοῖς τὰς χεῖρας" (NA28). The subject, παντὸς τοῦ πλήθους, "the whole community" chose [the seven] (v. 5), put them before the Apostles, "and [who] prayed and laid their hands on them" (v.6). In light of the syntax, we argue that since the subject is the "whole community" in v.5 the "who" (v. 6) refers back to the community. For support see Barrett, *Acts*, 1: 315. For text-critical analysis and support see Culy and Parsons, *Acts Handbook*, 110; Rius-Camps and Read-Heimerdinger, *Message of Acts*, 2:17, 25–26.

Most commentators press for a commonsense approach to the ritual's application and, as in the Moses/Joshua tradition (Num 27:18–23; Deut 34:9), conclude it is the Twelve who lay their hands on the Seven in a symbolic act of transference.[59] In the commissioning of Joshua, Moses alone lays his hand on Joshua while standing in front of the "whole congregation" (Num 27:22–23). It is reasonable to conclude that Luke is aware of its use in ancient Israel during the commissioning of Joshua as successor to Moses. If this be the case, then the implication is for the Twelve to lay their hands on the Seven.

However, it is just as likely that Luke is also aware of the commissioning of the Levites (Num 8:5–10). During the commissioning of the Levites, the "whole congregation of the Israelites . . . shall lay their hands" on the candidates for commission (Num 8:9–10). If the tradition concerning the Levites is of influence in Acts 6, then it is the disciples who perform the ritual of commissioning and lay their hands on the Seven. As we will see, the answer to this dilemma lies in the manner in which Luke presents the candidates for recognition.

As noted earlier in Acts 1, Luke depicts the early community facing a choice between *two* qualified candidates. As we concluded in chapter 1, the believers provided the candidates for Judas' replacement with lots (e.g., markers or chips), who then placed their lots into a vessel or jar. Through some process of shaking, the lot fell from the vessel to the ground and thus revealed a divine answer or direction. Luke's narrative in Acts 1 suggests the Twelve were seeking a divine response and consequently cast lots to determine the outcome. The first marker out was the divine choice. Thus, what Luke reveals is that lots were cast for *two* candidates chosen from among the one hundred twenty and the "lot fell on Matthias," revealing the divine will.[60]

However, in Acts 6, Luke indicates that the Twelve instruct the disciples to select seven men for this task. The Twelve are not facing a choice between candidates.[61] The community of disciples select the Seven who will do the job. Comparing Luke's story in Acts 1 with that in Acts 6 enables us to see the community engaging in theological creativity because they select the Seven based upon their own evaluation of those who meet the Twelve's

59. For example, Fitzmyer, *Acts*, 351; Johnson, *Acts*, 111; Johnson, *Scripture and Discernment*, 87; Dunn, *Acts*, 84.

60. Acts 1:26a, "καὶ ἔδωκαν κλήρους αὐτοῖς καὶ ἔπεσεν ὁ κλῆρος ἐπὶ Μαθθίαν" (NA28).

61. For additional support see Brown, *Corporate Decision-Making*, 114, n. 139.

criterion. In light of the community's role in selecting the Seven (and the structure of Acts 6:5–6[62]), we argue the authorization or commissioning for local ministry stems from the body of disciples and not from an oligarchy of leaders.

Moreover, the role of the disciples in commissioning the Seven indicates a remarkable evolution in Luke's story.[63] The empowerment of the "whole community of the disciples" to "select seven men of good standing, full of the Spirit and of wisdom, whom we may appoint to this task" demonstrates a partnership in which both the Twelve and disciples participate while also serving as evidence of their engagement in theological creativity. Therefore, we conclude that the Twelve join with the disciples in "laying their hands" on the Seven as one unified community of believers.

The Need for Localized Leadership

The neglect of the Hellenist widows in the region and in the church demonstrates to the Twelve the need for localized (grassroots) leadership.[64] For all their zeal and ability in overseeing the large numeric growth Luke reports, the Twelve are now reported as unable to manage the culturally diverse and complex social nature of the growing movement. Rather than reorganizing their own leadership duties, the Twelve opt for a new venture by sharing oversight of the community with others who are more closely associated with those in need. Luke resolves both the crisis of division (Hellenist vs. Hebrews) and need (widows' distribution) by having the whole community of disciples (Twelve and all) functioning as a unified character (Acts 6:2, 5).

The selection of the Seven is based on theological grounds since the Twelve must be devoted to prayer and preaching ministry (Acts 6:2, 4) and

---

62. As noted above and repeated here: Acts 6:5–6, "καὶ ἤρεσεν ὁ λόγος ἐνώπιον παντὸς τοῦ πλήθους καὶ ἐξελέξαντο Στέφανον, ἄνδρα πλήρης πίστεως καὶ πνεύματος ἁγίου, καὶ Φίλιππον καὶ Πρόχορον καὶ Νικάνορα καὶ Τίμωνα καὶ Παρμενᾶν καὶ Νικόλαον προσήλυτον Ἀντιοχέα, οὓς ἔστησαν ἐνώπιον τῶν ἀποστόλων, καὶ προσευξάμενοι ἐπέθηκαν αὐτοῖς τὰς χεῖρας" (NA28). The subject, παντὸς τοῦ πλήθους, "the whole community" chose [the seven] (v. 5), put them before the Apostles, "and [who] prayed and laid their hands on them" (v.6). Considering the syntax, we argue that the subject is the "whole community," the "who" (v. 6) refers back to the community.

63. Cf. Brown, *Corporate Decision-Making*, 116; Garrett, "Congregation-Led Church," 319–21, n. 52; Beyer, "*diákonos*," "Deacon as a Church Official," *TDNT*, 2:605.

64. By localized we mean of a local area, grassroots, or oriented close to or originating within the area needing leadership.

the Seven must be known for being full of the Spirit and wisdom (6:3, 5). The Twelve will share their oversight of the community with a new and more local level of leadership. As a ministerial group it acquires no formal name and future leadership expansions in Acts hardly resemble the process at work in Acts 6.[65] But one thing is apparent, in Luke's story grassroots issues require solutions with local leadership.

The meekness of the Twelve creates space and autonomy for local leadership in closer proximity to the problem resulting in exponential growth for the church in Jerusalem (Acts 6:7). The disciples draw on their theological understanding of the transference of apostolic authority, considered once limited to the Twelve, to include the Seven and highlights their engagement in theological creativity. The evidence and witness of the Spirit in the lives of the Seven and the continued numeric growth of the community provide indirect evidence of divine approval.

Commitment to the Common Good of All

In his earlier summaries, Luke describes a society of mutual care and provision.[66] However, in Acts 6:1, Luke peers more directly inside the idyllic community of the early church in Jerusalem. While Luke has mentioned trouble in the past he has not mentioned social conflict within the body of disciples.[67] Now, in Acts 6, Luke provides a grassroots view of the complications inherent within a growing community of believers who are theologically invested and rooted in the idea of supporting the common good of all and not just their own.[68]

In the centuries following the Babylonian exile, many Jews immigrated to Jerusalem to live out their final years and be buried in or near the Holy City.[69] Lacking the social support system of extended family, first-century widows are dependent on public charity. The *Mishnah* mandates two methods for collecting alms for the poor, of which widows are

65. Consider Acts 11:22, 25, 30; 13:1-4; 15:2, 22.

66. See Acts 2:43-47; 4:32-35.

67. Such as the persecution of the Apostles in Acts 3-4 and the conflict involving Ananias and Sapphira in Acts 5. Cf. Dunn, *Acts*, 79.

68. From the time of Moses to the present narrative, the care of widows remained an important social obligation. See Exod 21:22; Deut 14:29; 16:11, 14; 24:17. See also Ps 68:5; 94:6; 146:9; Prov 15:25; Job 29:13; Isa 1:17; Mal 3:5.

69. See Josephus, *Ant.* 15.22, 34, 39; Keener, *Acts*, 2:1259; Haenchen, *Acts*, 261.

included.[70] Each Friday relief officers provide the local poor with funds to cover fourteen meals. Local residents contribute to the fund as an act of almsgiving. Relief officers go house to house gathering donations for the food tray and the transient poor may eat one meal from a food tray (three meals on *Shabbat*).[71]

Since Luke is writing a tale about a historical people-group, it is reasonable to conclude the disciples in his story possessed full knowledge of the local system of welfare. Having already supplemented the existing Jewish system of care to ensure the general welfare of their members (Acts 2:44–45; 4:32–35), we maintain that the whole community of believers now broaden their efforts to ensure the ongoing support and care of the Hellenist widows and demonstrates the first-century community of believers engaging in theological creativity.[72] Their action is an extension of their theological obligation to widows. The influx of a "great many priests" (6:7) serves as evidence that the disciples' supplemental care for Hellenist widows resonated deeply through the city. Here, Luke demonstrates the wisdom of the Twelve to see both their own limitation and humble need to share the responsibility for overseeing the ongoing social needs of the community by focusing on what follows: (1) on the impact of their decision on the city of Jerusalem (Acts 6:7) and then (2) on the ministerial effect and consequences of two of the Seven (6:8–8:40).

Summary and Conclusions

At some point, Hellenist widows find themselves unable to benefit from the general social system. As we have argued, Luke's initial reference addresses a widespread concern in Jerusalem among all Jews. The narrative of Acts 6:1–7 is best understood as a general problem within the region brought to the attention of the Twelve by the disciples for a solution. As a result, the whole community of believers work together to devise a solution to assist all Hellenist widows.

Though ironic, Luke provides no follow-up concerning the crisis among the widows. Instead, he narrates two unexpected outcomes. First,

70. M. *Peah* 1.1, 8.7. Also see Jeremias, *Jerusalem in the Time of Jesus*, 130–31.

71. Seccombe challenges the use of later *Mishnah* writings as evidence for organized charity in Jerusalem before 70 CE. See Seccombe, "Was There Organized Charity," 140–43. Cf. Fitzmyer, *Acts*, 348.

72. For textual support, see Acts 2:45; 4:34–35; 6:1–7. Cf. Haenchen, *Acts*, 262.

the care and concern for the weakest members of society touches a social nerve among the population of Jerusalem resulting in exponential growth. Moreover, any concern that the Twelve trivialize the widows by not handling their need is mitigated. Second, the implementation of a solution that successfully meets a societal woe of this magnitude in Jewish culture captures the attention of many within the priesthood and demonstrates the genuine nature of the Jerusalem disciples.

In sum, we see the community of disciples in Acts 6:1-6 as a unified character in Luke's story whose theological understanding *of* and necessity *for* caring for widows is met by broadening the leadership. We have argued that the disciples respond on theological grounds by first addressing a critical social need and then by ritually laying hands on those chosen for ministry, both of which are rooted in an awareness of their ancient past (Scripture). Their actions broaden their theological assumptions concerning the care for widows, the ministry focus of the Twelve, and their ritual use of the laying on of hands as an act of transference, thus demonstrating theological creativity. The selection of the Seven, who are full of the Spirit and wisdom, involves the community choosing its own leaders and then actively participating in their commissioning for service. Thus, we see Luke demonstrating the community's role in an interpretive process involving Spirit–Community–Scripture.

4

ACCEPTING THE GENTILES
—ACTS 15:1–35

IN THIS CHAPTER, WE will see how both prophetic vision and interpretation affect the community in its ongoing engagement in theological creativity.[1] Of particular significance to the community's action is the manner in which a heavenly vision alters their interpretation of Jewish custom and Scripture and how the community reevaluates Scripture in light of prophetic revelation. Peter's vision and the subsequent interaction with the house of Cornelius (Acts 10–11) along with James' prophetic interpretation of Scripture serve as evidence for the whole church (Acts 15) that the missionary expansion to the Gentiles is consistent with Scripture and evidence of Spirit's active presence.

Luke's episodic development of events demonstrates that the community's experience and decision concerning the salvation of and fellowship with Gentiles is founded on theological grounds and through the testimony of multiple witness concerning the evidential work of the

---

1. Theological creativity is the act of reformulating formerly held theological interpretations in light of testimony concerning the Spirit's evidential work and an emerging understanding of applicable Scripture followed by commensurate action. The Spirit's evidential work is known only through the community's testimony. Therefore, theological creativity is the outcome of the interpretive process since it is theology in action, functional in nature, and situationally pragmatic in scope. Consequently, it involves the process of theological justification and action or reaction in light of current circumstances. In this sense, to be creative with theology is to take what is already a theological assumption and broaden or adapt it to current circumstances in light of the Spirit's evidential work and a consensus understanding of Scripture.

Spirit. Consequently, after meeting and deliberating together as "the whole congregation," their declaration, "It seems good to us and the Holy Spirit" (15:28), summarizes the community's engagement in theological creativity.

Identifying the Community

Luke's narrative concerning the acceptance of the Gentiles into fellowship offers a glimpse into the early efforts of the first-century community of believers to establish churches in and beyond Judea and into the surrounding territories. The story arc in Acts 10–15 demonstrates the manner in which diverse believing communities engage and resolve the issue of admitting converts from non-Jewish ethnicities.[2] However, even though Luke's presentation is progressive in nature, we will argue that it is not sequential. Before he shows his audience a favorable outcome, he intentionally suspends his earlier method of linear storytelling (Act 1–8) in favor of one that brings to the forefront what he considers the most important pieces of the story. He does this by altering matters of sequence and time.

Supporting our claim will require analysis of Luke's writing technique concerning matters of sequence and time as well as a cursory consideration of Peter's mission to the house of Cornelius in Acts 10. Doing so will enable us to see how Luke's narrative style of storytelling affects the community's theological progress. With that foundation in place, we will then analyze Luke's characterization of various groups within the story and see the community of believers from Antioch and Jerusalem (as "groups within a group") function harmoniously as the whole church. We will conclude this chapter with a summary of the main points and evidence to demonstrate Luke's view of the community as a character engaging in theological creativity.

2. Concerning grammatical analysis of αλλοφυλος (foreigner, Gentile) in Acts 10:28, see Büchsel, "αλλοφυλος," *TDNT*, 1:264–67; BDAG, "αλλοφυλος," 48. Concerning ἔθνος (ethnic race, Gentile) in Acts 2:5; 4:25, 27; 7:7, 45; 8:9; 9:15; 10:22, 35, 45; 11:1, 18; 13:19, 46–48; 14:2, 5, 16, 27; 15:3, 7, 12, 14, 17, 19, 23; 17:26; 18:6; 21:11, 19, 21, 25; 22:21; 24:2, 10, 17; 26:4, 17, 20, 23; 28:19, and 28, see Bertram and Schmidt, "ἔθνος," *TDNT*, 2:364–72, esp. 2:369–70; BDAG, "ἔθνος," 276–77.

The Effect of Sequence and Time on Characterizing the Community

As argued earlier, characterization is both cumulative and the method and timing of its accumulation has hermeneutical implications.[3] At issue are not matters of historicity but rather understanding why the characters, in this case the first-century community of believers, theologically act and react as they do will aid our view of the community engaging in theological creativity. Identifying the schema of Luke's plot-development will help us see why this first-century community of believers respond the way they do at various points in the narrative.[4]

Since the sequence of events affects both the development of the plot and the characterization of the community, it will be helpful to understanding the manner in which Luke constructs his narrative tale. Through this process, we will be able to show that Luke is writing a story with aspects and events that, just like in all novels, are not always recorded in sequential order.[5]

For example, why does the Jerusalem community seem to accept Gentile conversions *following* the Cornelius event (11:18) but then send Barnabas to investigate rumors of Gentile conversions in Antioch (11:20–22)? Even more oddly, why do the Antioch prophets, missionaries, and delegation (13:1–3; 14:27–28; 15:2) seem unaware of the events concerning Cornelius until the meeting in Jerusalem (15:7–12)? The disjointed nature of the plot development makes the audience aware of "literary seams."[6] But

3. See Introduction, "Studies on Characterization in Luke-Acts" (John Darr). The audiences' development and analysis of character must refrain from jumping ahead. For support, see Darr, *Herod the Fox*, 73, also n. 29.

4. Examples: (1) Replacing a missing member of the Twelve is essential (1:15–26). But later, when James is killed, they do not replace him (12:1–2). (2) The gift of the Holy Spirit is "for everyone whom the Lord our God calls to him" (2:39) but not, according to some, for the house of Cornelius (11:1–2). Later Gentiles are accepted (11:18) only for a concern to arise again over converts in Antioch (11:21–22, 15:1). Finally, Gentile believers are accepted into fellowship (15:11, 19, 23–29). (3) Conflict over table fellowship with Gentiles (11:3), followed by acceptance without condition (11:18), only later to add a provision (15:29). (4) Apostles lead and manage the affairs of the church (2:42–45; 4:33–35; 5:12–13; 6:2; 8:14) but later share the administration, preaching, and healing ministry with others (6:6–8, 8:4–7; 9:27–29; 11:29; 12:17; 15:6, 19, 23; 21:18–25).

5. For examples in ancient novels concerning the suspension of events, consider Heliod. *Eth.* 1.1 (opening in the middle of a scene whose background does not appear until 5.28–33); 2.11; 2.25–4.21; Philost. *Hrk.* 25.16–17; and Cicero *Verr.* 2.5.5.10–11.

6. Concerning literary seams see Dibelius, *Acts*, 134–35; 140–50, esp. 149. Conzelmann, *Acts*, 80.

what may account for these so-called seams? Again, setting aside concerns of historicity, viewing Acts as a literary tale offers an explanation. An answer befitting the narrative evidence lies with distinguishing between Luke's text-order (linear narrative) and his story-order (plot).[7] Such a proposal is not inconsistent with other ancient historiographies or novels.[8] As Keener remarks,

> Temporary suspension of narrative and other forms of suspense were common in ancient novels, but they also appear in other genres. Thus Polybius leaves Carthage about to destroy Rome at the end of book 3 of his History of the Roman Republic, then shifts to an account of Greece during the same period, returning to Rome only later. This approach fits the needs of chronology (geography and chronology offer competing demands) but also creates suspense.[9]

We see this in Luke's grammatical use of the phrase, "Now those who were scattered." in Acts 8:4 and 11:19.[10] This phrase reconnects his story to events previously introduced and already in progress. Essentially, Luke is stating, "Now, back to our story," or "Returning to the present."[11] In light of this, we argue the reason literary seams are noticeable in Acts 9:32–14:28 is (1) because the events are not in sequence and often overlapping in time and (2) because Luke intends for the audience to notice them.[12]

---

7. I am indebted to work of Rimmon-Kenan for her analysis concerning the literary category of "narrative time" and text order vs. story order. See Rimmon-Kenan, *Narrative Fiction*, 44–46. For additional support see Osborne, *Hermeneutical Spiral*, 206–7; Keener, *Acts*, 2:1863; Talbert, *Reading Acts*, 113–14.

8. See Keener, *Acts*, 2:1863 n. 305–6. For additional support also see Schwartz, *Agrippa I*, 122, 213–16, esp. 216.

9. Keener, *Acts*, 2:1863.

10. Gr. μὲν οὖν διασπαρέντες (NA28). For textual support see Culy and Parsons, *Acts Handbook*, 150, 225; Levinsohn, *Textual Connections in Acts*, 137–50, esp. 143.

11. As Bennema states, "The recurring phrase μὲν οὖν διασπαρέντες in 8:4 and 11:19 . . . indicates the start of simultaneous accounts." Bennema, "Ethnic Conflict in Early Christianity," 756. For Keener, "11:19 picks up where 8:4 leaves off; 11:30 leaves off where 12:25 will pick up." See also Keener, *Acts*, 2:1830. For text-critical support see Levinsohn, *Textual Connections in Acts*, 11.

12. For support of an interrupted timeline, see Keener, *Acts*, 2:1863; Talbert, *Reading Acts*, 113–14; B. Longenecker, "Lukan Aversion to Humps and Hollows," 185–204, esp. 191–201. Cf. Conzelmann, *Acts*, 80. Dibelius also appeals to literary methods for detecting narrative seams. Dibelius, *Acts*, 137–44.

Following this line of argument, the text-order, as presented by Luke in Acts 9:31–11:18 and 12:1–23, occurs during the following story-order: Acts 9:1–31 followed by 11:19–30 followed by 12:24 to the end of Acts. Moreover, we maintain the episodes concerning Peter (Acts 9:31–11:18) and the persecution by Herod (12:1–23) are told in *reverse order* since the events in Acts 12 provide the occasion for Peter's departure from Jerusalem, his subsequent travels to "another place," and introduces the prominence of James.[13] The following timeline demonstrates this process.

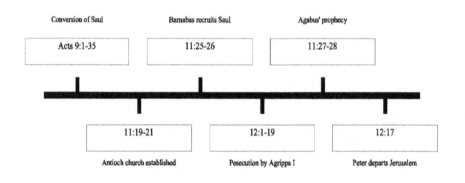

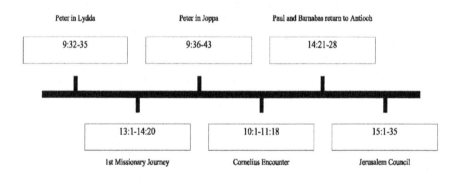

13. For similar argument of this technique in Acts see Benoit, *Exégèse et théologie III*, 285–99. Benoit argues Acts 13–14 rightfully belong between 11:26 and 11:27.In narrative terms, this would make Acts 9:32–11:18 a *prolepsis* (flash-forward) and 12:1–23 an *analepsis* (flashback). Rimmon-Kenan describes a *prolepsis* as "a narration of a story-event at a point before earlier events have been mentioned" with the purpose of arousing "the readers expectations." Furthermore, she describes an *analepsis* (flashback) as the "narration of a story-event at a point after later events have been told" with the purpose of providing "information necessary to the reader." See Rimmon-Kenan, *Narrative Fiction*, 46, 120.

This sequence scenario narratively explains why the Antioch delegation (15:2–3) seems unaware of the events concerning Peter in Caesarea and supports our argument concerning sequence and time in Acts 9:32–14:28.[14] With Herod's death (12:23), Luke once again returns to the "present" in Acts 12:24–25. He has set the stage for the first missionary journey of Barnabas and Saul (13–14) and the council at Jerusalem (15). The gathering of the "whole church" (15:4–29) serves as the end of the narrative (that began with the conversion of Saul in Acts 9:1) concerning Luke's tale of the conversion and acceptance of Gentile Christians.

The Effect of the Gentile Pentecost on Characterizing the Community

As noted above, Luke's narrative tale of the Gentile Pentecost is also essential to understanding the characterization of the first-century community of believers engaging in theological creativity. Luke's story concerning Gentile converts begins with a Roman Centurion named Cornelius who lives

14. Consequently, within the scope of Luke's plot development, the story of the death of the Apostle James and Peter's imprisonment (Acts 12:1–5) as well as Peter's escape from prison (12:6–19a) occurs sometime after Barnabas is sent to Antioch (11:22) and before the famine-relief visit (11:27–30). This narratively explains why the community in Antioch delivers the famine relief to "the elders" and not the apostles (11:30). James becomes the newly appointed leader while Peter and (supposedly) the other apostles are in hiding. Concerning the rise of new leadership in Jerusalem see Haenchen, *Acts*, 391; Hann, "Judaism and Jewish Christianity," 344–45. Also see Campenhausen and Chadwick, *Jerusalem and Rome*, 59–61. Since the focus of the persecution in 12:1 appears only against the apostles, we maintain the story structure suggests all of the apostles either leave the region or go into hiding (12:17). Furthermore, Peter's escape from Jerusalem and travel to "another place" (Acts 12:17b) transpires sometime during the yearlong ministry of Barnabas and Saul in Antioch (Acts 11:25–27). For support, see Keener, *Acts*, 2:1953; Marshal, *Acts*, 211; R. Longenecker, *Acts*, 411. In opposition, see Hengel, *Acts and the History*, 93. Since these areas were under Agrippa's control, some doubt Peter would have traveled to Lydda and Joppa during this particular timeframe. For studies on Agrippa I, see Schwartz, *Agrippa I*, 145–49. Also see Goldblatt, "Agrippa I and Palestinian Judaism," 7 -32, esp. 9 and n. 15; Meyshan, "Coinage of Agrippa the First" 186–200 ; Wirgin, *Herod Agrippa I*, 1:102–51. During this time, Peter travels to Lydda (Acts 9:32–35) and Joppa (9:36–43). His encounter with Cornelius in Caesarea (10:1–11:18), perhaps following the death of Herod (12:23), narratively occurs during the first missionary journey of Barnabas and Saul (13–14). Concerning the death of Agrippa I, Josephus indicates it was three years after the ascension of Claudius (41–54 CE), *Ant.* 19.8.343–52; *J.W.* 2.11.214–19. He goes on to recount the joy the city expressed following his death (*Ant.* 19.9.354–59).

in Caesarea.[15] According to Luke, an angelic visitation affirms his earnest devotion to God, and he receives instructions in minute detail to send for the Apostle Peter (Acts 10:1–8).

The next day, Peter also experiences a vision in which he witnesses a sheet (tablecloth or picnic spread) coming down from heaven replete with animals, reptiles, and birds of all kinds. "A voice" tells him to approach the spread, kill the creatures, and eat them (10:13). When Peter objects, the voice responds, "What God has made clean, you must not call unclean" (10:14–15).[16] This experience is repeated two additional times (10:16).

Luke devotes significant space and detail to the tale of the Gentile Pentecost. In this critical section in Acts, Luke depicts Gentiles being filled with the Spirit and receiving water baptism without embracing aspects of the Law that are important to those in the Jerusalem church.[17] The story introduced in Acts 10–11 identifies a key development in the overall plot and prepares the reader for the events of chapter 15.[18] Indications of its importance are evident given Luke's extended structure and repetition of the vision (Acts 10:9–16; 11:4–10) and by its pivotal use and reference by Peter at the Jerusalem Council, both of which critical in altering the community's theological outlook (15:7–11, 22, 28).

Luke's use of irony is evident in the contrast between the submissive and obedient nature of Cornelius concerning his vision with the reluctant response of Peter during his vision.[19] Peter's acceptance of the situation is progressive and only complete when he states, "I truly understand that

---

15. The consensus view places the Gentile Pentecost in or around 37 CE. For a review, see Schnabel, *Paul and the Early Church*, 987. Cf. Fitzmyer, *Acts*, 447–48; R. Longenecker, *Acts*, 394. Dibelius maintains Luke adapts various traditions together to form the narrative. See Dibelius, "Conversion of Cornelius," 109–22. Cf. Conzelmann, *Acts*, 80.

16. Conzelmann argues that the original intention of the vision was concerning foods. However, at the time of narrative, "the two themes (Jews and Gentiles, foods) were already mixed together." Conzelmann, *Acts*, 80. Parsons provides a unique exposition on the difference between "defiled AND unclean" and "defiled OR unclean." Parsons, "Nothing Defiled AND Unclean," 263–74, esp. 263–65.

17. Initially, Luke includes the issue of circumcision only as it applies to Peter as a Jew having table fellowship with non-Jews. It is important to note the criticism by the elders in Jerusalem concerns Peter entering the home of and eating with the uncircumcised and not the uncircumcised receiving the Gospel per se (11:3). This detail will once again be a central concern at the Jerusalem Council (Acts 15).

18. Conzelmann, *Acts*, 80. See also Fitzmyer, *Acts*, 447. R. Longenecker, *Acts*, 383–84; J. Scott, "The Cornelius Incident in the Light of its Jewish Setting," 475–484.

19. Compare Acts 10:1–8 and 30–33 with 10:11–17a and 27–28a.

God shows no partiality" (Acts 10:34). In light of the verb structure, an apt translation is, "I am [just now] coming to realize that God does not show partiality."[20] In contrast, those present with Cornelius respond to the Spirit in a single moment: "While Peter was still speaking, the Holy Spirit fell on all who heard the word" (11:44).[21]

Having considered the narrative impact of Luke's storytelling method and the importance of the Gentile Pentecost, we are now able to proceed with identifying the first-century community of believers. In the following subsections, we will once again consider the way Luke characterizes the first-century community of believers as "groups within a group." In so doing, we will see that Luke combines diverse and often competing groups within the community of believers so they might ultimately function as a unified character, the "whole church," engaging in theological creativity.[22]

The Whole Church

Luke uses a variety of terms to identify the community of believers in Acts.[23] Thus far in his story, Luke variously refers to the followers of Jesus in Acts as

---

20. Gr. καταλαμβάνομαι, present tense, middle voice. D05 indicates a "realization that is dawning on Peter as the scene unfolds." Rius-Camps and Read-Heimerdinger, *Message of Acts*, 2:235, 269–70. Culy translates, "to come to understand something which was not understood or perceived previously." Culy and Parsons, *Acts Handbook*, 209. See also Scott, "Cornelius Incident," 483. Cf. Dollar, "Conversion of the Messenger.," 13–19.

21. Granted, Cornelius responds eagerly and promptly to "an angel of God" much earlier in the story, Acts 10:1–8.

22. Bruce argues "the whole assembly" in 15:12 includes "the [whole] Christian community" and that other members of the church were present. Nevertheless, he maintains that only the leadership participated in the debate. Bruce, *Acts*, 292, 295. Conzelmann states, "Vs. 4–5 provide a summary of the discussion which follows. They make clear that the author is not describing two assemblies here . . . but one plenary assembly (v. 12)." Conzelmann, *Acts*, 116. Also, see Schnabel, *Paul and the Early Church*, 1013. For a similar outline of events and history of debates, see Schnabel, *Paul and the Early Church*, 1007–20, esp. 1010–11 n. 91; Keener, *Acts*, 3:2207–10, 2239–41. Witherington argues Acts 15 does not record a single event but "a series of events" and multiple sources, thus explaining why Barnabas is once again listed first (compare vv. 4 and 12) and why the two speak on multiple occasions. Witherington, *Acts*, 444 n. 361, 449–50. For a synopsis of various views on chronology and a history of the debates, see Barrett, *Critical and Exegetical Commentary on Acts*, 2:709–12.

23. For a review of names for the community of believers in Acts see Cadbury, "Names for Christians" 5:375–92; Cf. Twelftree, *People of the Spirit*, 52–64.

brother(s)/sister(s),[24] believers,[25] disciples,[26] the Way,[27] and saints.[28] In the course of this narrative development, Luke steadily broadens his description of the community from brothers (believers), to disciples, and finally, to the church.

Luke's first use of the term church (ἐκκλησία, ekklesia) to describe the community of believers is as a summary statement concerning the whole region ("the whole church and all who heard of these things," Acts 5:11).[29] However, Luke does not use the term again until after the introduction of Saul and the subsequent mass exodus of disciples from Jerusalem due to severe persecution (8:1–3). Following its use in Acts 9:31, where it encompasses all believers in Judea, Galilee, and Samaria, Luke increasingly refers to diverse communities of believers as "the church."[30] This narratively indicates that the use of the word church, to describe the catholic community of believers, is rooted in its expansion beyond Jerusalem with particular emphasis on the churches in Jerusalem and Antioch.

---

24. Brothers—Acts 2:37; 6:3; 9:17, 30; 10:24; 11:1, 12, 29; 12:17; 15:1, 3, 7, 13, 22, 23, 32, 33, 36, 40; 16:2, 40 (adds sisters); 17:6, 10, 14; 18:18, 27; 21:17, 20; 22:13; 21:7; 28:14, 15. However, Luke also uses the term brothers to address groups other than the followers of Jesus in 2:29; 3:17, 22; 7:2, 13, 23, 25, 26, 37; 13:15, 26, 38; 14:2; 22:1, 5; 23:1, 5, 6; 28:17, 20. Luke's uses it for siblings in 1:14 (Jesus') brothers, 12:2 (John the brother of James), and 23:16 (Paul's sister).

25. For Luke's use of "believers" in Acts see 4:32; 5:14; 9:32; 10:45; 11:21, 29; 12:17; 13:48; 14:1; 15:7, 23; 17:34; 19:18; 21:25. NRSV translates ἀδελφός (brother/brothers) as "believers" in Acts 1:15; 9:30; 15:3, 23, 32, 33, 36, 40; 16:2; 17:6, 10, 14; 18:18, 27; 20:2; 21:7; 28:14, 15. NRSV adds "believers" for clarification in 11:2; 15:5; and 19:2. For support see von Soden, "ἀδελφός," TDNT, 1:144–46; BDAG, "ἀδελφός," xxviii, 18–19.

26. For Luke's use of "disciples": in Acts see 6:1, 2, 7; 9:1, 19, 25, 26 (fem.), 36, 38; 11:26, 29; 13:52; 14:20, 21, 22, 28; 15:10; 16:1; 18:23, 27; 19:1, 9, 30; 20:1, 30; 21:4, 16.

27. For Luke's use of "the way" in Acts, see 9:2; 18:25, 26; 19:9, 23; 22:4; 24:14, 22.

28. For Luke's use of "saints" in Acts see 9:13, 32, 41; 26:10.

29. For Luke's use of "church" in Acts see 5:11; 8:1,3; 9:31; 11:22, 26; 12:1, 5; 13:1; 14:23, 27; 15:3, 4, 22, 41; 16:5; 18:22; 20:17, 28. NASV translates ἐκκλησία as "congregation" in 7:38 and "assembly" in 19:32, 39, and 41 to distinguish it from the community of believers (church) in Acts. Schmidt states, "Whereas the ἐκκλησία was first a single congregation, it now covers several congregations, so that we do better to translate 'church' rather than 'congregation.'" For background and usage see Schmidt, "ἐκκλησία," TDNT, 3:487–536, esp. 3:504–5; BDAG, "ἐκκλησία," 303–4, esp. 3bβ. For analysis and review of Luke's use of ἐκκλησία (church), see Bovon, Luke the Theologian, 329–462.

30. See Acts 5:11; 9:31; 12:1; 13: 1; 15:3; 15:4, 22; 18:22; 20:17. Cf. Dunn, Acts, 1.

The Church in Jerusalem

Luke describes the church beginning with one hundred and twenty persons gathering together in a large meeting room (Acts 1:15). This community of believers in Jerusalem stand at the center of his story through Acts 8. In these early days Luke emphasizes the disciples' efforts to spread the message of Jesus in Jerusalem and immediate region.[31] However, as the disciples increase numerically and geographically into the surrounding region, Luke characterizes the Jerusalem community as the group who take responsibility for general oversight for all the churches.[32] With the disciples scattering "throughout the countryside of Judea and Samaria" (5:11–16; 8:1, 4) and going "from place to place proclaiming the word" (8:4), the remnants of the community in Jerusalem continue to face a concern for the integrity of the apostolic message.[33]

Luke indicates that the church in Jerusalem goes through significant upheaval in the days following Stephen's death (Acts 8:1–2). For example, the persecution that arises results in a sizeable exodus of believers from Jerusalem ("all except the apostles," Acts 8:1), which may help explain why Luke characterizes the remaining community of believers in Jerusalem suffering economically and needing assistance following the famine (11:29). Yet despite all these changes, Luke continues to characterize the Jerusalem church as the "mother church" explicitly through Acts 15 and implicitly throughout the remainder of the narrative.[34]

---

31. See Acts 2:42, 46; 4:29–30; 5:12–16.

32. For oversight of the church and churches see 2:45; 4:32–35; 6:2; 8:14; 9:26–30; 11:1, 22; 15:1–6.

33. Consider the progression in Acts 2:42; 4:31, 33; 6:4; 8:14; 11:1–3, 18, and 22; 15:2, 6, 12, 19, 22, 28, 30–31; 21:17–25.

34. For additional support see Bauckham, "James and the Jerusalem Church," 415–80, esp. 450–51. Codex Bezae (D05) presents the church in Jerusalem more directly as the mother church with authorial oversight. For support, see Ellis, "Codex Bezae at Acts 15," 134–40. Paul's multiple encounters with James and the elders in Jerusalem further leads the audience to conclude the ongoing and high regard for the Jerusalem church (see Acts 15:22, 30; 21:17–26).

The Church in Antioch

According to Luke's story the church in Antioch is like no other group of disciples in its day.[35] What Luke describes is *sui generis* and of the first-order in terms of integration with an ethnically diverse membership worshipping side by side as the church (Acts 11:20–21). Ironically, Luke provides no hint of internal difficulties in forging such a community. He only provides insight into the struggle facing the *Jerusalem* church (11:22; 15:1–5). The matter-of-fact way Luke writes the story suggests that the emergence of a diverse church was an inevitable or obvious outcome in a community such as Antioch and one in which Luke and his audience must have been familiar. Led by a group of five prophets and teachers (13:1), Luke presents this community as one experiencing radical transformation (11:21–22, 27–30; 13:1–3) and also offers a hint of how outsiders viewed the expanding movement (11:26).[36]

The church in Antioch sends a delegation to represent its interests to Jerusalem to meet with the apostles and elders (Acts 11:2–4). However,

35. See description concerning its members and activities in Acts 11:20–26, 27–30; 13:1–4; 14:27; 15:1–2, 4, 11–12, 30–33.

36. The church at Antioch acquires the name Χριστιανος (Christian), a description with theological significance rather than one rooted in the name of Jesus ('Ιησοῦς, Yeshua). For the first time, Χριστὸν (Christ) functions as a proper name rather than as a title, suggesting the believers spoke of "the Christ" with such frequency and clear purpose that officials and/or locals labeled the movement in this manner. See Taylor, "Why Were the Disciples," 76. Cf. Hengel and Schwemer, *Paul between Damascus and Antioch*, 228; Grundmann, "Χριστιανος," *TDNT*, 9:576–80; Danker defines it as *"Christ-partisan,"* BDAG, "Χριστιανος," 1090. The testimony of the church in Antioch concerning the Christ prompts a nickname for a new mix of Gentile and Jewish believers and establishes it as tradition altogether different from traditional Judaism. Stenschke, *Luke's Portrait of the Gentiles*, 330–31. Whether the term was derogatory or political in nature see the survey by Taylor, "Why Were the Disciples," 75–94. For a critique of this debate, see Fitzmyer, *Acts*, 474–76; Keener, *Acts*, 2:1847–50. Cf. Dunn, *Acts*, 156; Haenchen, *Acts*, 369–70; Pervo, *Acts*, 294–95. The only other NT occurrence is in 1 Pet 4:16. Here, the use of Christian suggests a term of contempt or ridicule and possessing a pejorative sense. See Yong, *Renewing Christian Theology*, 1. According to Taylor, the earliest known usage of Χριστιανος as a self-description is from the *Didache* (12:4). See Taylor, "Why Were the Disciples," 77. Moreover, he argues the *Didache* was written, mostly likely from Antioch, sometime between 50 and 70 CE. For date and composition, he is dependent on Audet, *Didachè*, 187–210. Other descriptors by outsiders in Luke include Paul acknowledging that some might view the movement as a sect; his response at trial in Jerusalem indicates his preference for "the Way" (24:14a); "Galileans" by the crowd at Pentecost (Acts 2:7); and "sect of the Nazarenes" by Tertullus (24:5). Also see Tacitus, *Ann.* 15:44; Pliny, *Ep.* 10:96–97; Lucian, *Alex.* 25:38; Jos. *Ant.* 18:64.

when they arrive they are greeted by the whole church (15:4, 12). Even though Paul becomes Luke's primary character as the plot unfolds, Paul and Barnabas hold a relatively minor role in the Jerusalem deliberations. While their testimony is verified on two occasions no direct dialogue is provided.[37] Instead, Luke narrates their participation and characterizes their contribution as a testimony of praise and as an affirmation of their experience rather than as a defense. Evidence that the Antioch delegation is included in the consent of the "whole church" (15:22) is both direct, in that Paul and Barnabas are part of the team designated to deliver news of the outcome, and indirect, by the way the message is received in Antioch upon their return (15:30–35).

SUMMARY

For Luke, the believing communities in Jerusalem and Antioch are part of the "whole church" and partner together to resolve the issue of conversion of and fellowship with Gentile believers (Acts 15:4, 12, 22). It is unclear if all the believers in attendance participate in the debate given the transition noted in 15:6. However, Luke makes it clear that the church unites to resolve the matter. He carefully describes how the Jerusalem community openly welcomes the delegation from Antioch (15:4), he identifies the gathering as the "whole assembly" (15:12), and he presents the "whole church" resolving the issue (15:22).

The Sect of the Pharisees

Luke introduces the conflict that leads to the so-called "Jerusalem Council" with a visiting group of teachers from Judea concerned with a procedural method for salvation involving the Jewish rite of circumcision.[38] Although he does not provide a name for this group in Acts 15:1, he does use the word *sect* to describe a faction within the church (15:5) who defend the actions of "certain individuals from Judea" (15:1).

From a narrative point of view it is possible "the sect of the Pharisees" (Acts 15:5) is coterminous with other Lukan characters introduced

---

37. See Acts 15:4, 12; although 15:4 may be an overview of events with 15:12 being a more specific depiction of their presentation.

38. See Acts 15:1–5, 10–11, 24.

earlier in the story such as the "circumcised believers" (11:2) and "certain individuals from Judea" (15:1, 24) in light of the common theological concern for the necessity of circumcision.[39] While we cannot be certain, it is a reasonable conclusion given the narrative circumstances. Notwithstanding, the initial resolution concerning Peter's encounter with Cornelius ends with at least some associated with this group acknowledging that, "God has given even to the Gentiles the repentance that leads to life" (11:18). Consequently, Luke characterizes this group as loosely connected by a theological belief in the necessity of circumcision while not unified in other aspects.[40]

In light of the comment by James (Acts 15:24), Luke's story implies that those affiliated with the sect of the Pharisees felt some sense of justification in going to Antioch and felt a measure of authorization to do so (15:1, 24). But what may account for the change in disposition from acceptance by "the circumcised believers" at the Jerusalem church in Acts 11:1–18 to "certain individuals . . . from Judea" in 15:1? Luke does not say. Perhaps, upon learning of the success of Barnabas and Paul (13:4–14:28) and in the wake of the Cornelius episode (10:1–11:18), a sub-faction within this group once again takes exception and sends a delegation to Antioch (15:1). Either the matter was not truly resolved following Peter's return from Caesarea or the circumstances continue to evolve.[41] In any event, we

---

39. Later, James refers to a group as individuals who are "zealous for the law" who may also be part of the sect of the Pharisees (Acts 21:20). In support of similarities between those in 11:2 and 15:5, Wilson concedes the possibility. See Wilson, *Luke and the Law*, 73. Wikenhauser more broadly defines the circumcision party as "the narrow-minded members of the community." Wikenhauser, *Apostelgeschichte*, 101. Keener draws on Hanson for support to state, "'Those who were from the circumcision' is Luke's [anachronistic] title for the Jerusalem believers." See Keener, *Acts*, 2:1818, also n. 854; Hanson, *Acts in the Revised Standard Version*, 126. However, Conzelmann insists, "For Luke οἱ ἐκ περιτομῆς, 'the circumcision party,' is not a group, but the whole Jerusalem congregation." See Conzelmann, *Acts*, 86. Cf. Haenchen, *Acts*, 354 n. 2; Barrett, *Acts*, 1:537. For Rius-Camps, Acts 11:2b (D05), "But the brethren of the circumcision raised objections," simply identifies those of the circumcision as believers and not as a defined subgroup within the church. Rius-Camps and Read-Heimerdinger, *Message of Acts*, 2:287, 294. For a review of "Christian Pharisees" in Acts, see Sanders, *Jews in Luke-Acts*, 94–98, 110–12, 114–15.

40. For example, Bockmuehl demonstrates differences in halakic observation and practice during first-century Palestinian and Diaspora Judaism indicate many Jews did not see eating with Gentiles particular problematic. See Bockmuehl, *Jewish Law in Gentile Churches*, 58–61.

41. While events at the home of Cornelius in Caesarea are the result of a vision and divine encounter, events in Antioch are methodic and progressive. For support concerning the church's possible acceptance of Cornelius as an exception, see Dunn, *Beginning*

argue Luke resolves this confusion in the story by revealing that what is of primary concern is not whether the gospel of Jesus extends to Gentiles but rather how they join the faith tradition and under what circumstances they might fellowship with Jewish believers. For even if they accept that Jesus, through direct intervention with accompanying charismatic phenomenon, saves a Gentile household, the church may still need a general method for reaching and disciplining new Gentile converts.[42] In all fairness to Luke's character, the sect of the Pharisees attempt to clarify this issue (15:5).

Apostles and Elders

By Acts 15, Luke has hinted of a transition in leadership from the apostles to a group of elders.[43] At the head of this new leadership is James.[44] What becomes of the apostles, namely the Twelve, after the persecution of Agrippa I is left unstated by Luke. He does indicate that more than one apostle is present during Peter's first defense concerning events in Caesarea (Acts 11:1) and at the Jerusalem Council.[45] Although Luke characterizes the leadership of the Jerusalem Council as a shared event, the prominence of James is unmistakable (15:13, 19). Peter's testimony at the council (15:7-11) marks the end of all reference by name of the founding apostles.

---

from Jerusalem, 401-2, 446. In opposition, Schnabel indicates the agreement in Acts 11:18 is "paradigmatic for all conversion of Gentiles." See Schnabel, *Paul and the Early Church*, 462-68. Cf. Wilson, *Luke and the Law*, 72. The only experience Jews have for receiving Gentiles into their religious tradition and fellowship is through the formal process of proselytization, although many were received simply as God-fearers. Concerning proselytes and God-fearers in Luke's writings, see Schnabel, *Jesus and the Twelve*, 124-33; Sanders, *Jews in Luke-Acts*, 137-42; Stenschke, *Luke's Portrait of the Gentiles*, 310-18, 328, 382-83; Keener, *Acts*, 1:512-15; 2:1284-87; Fitzmyer, *Acts*, 243; Loader, "Explanation of the Term *Proselutos*," 270-77; Kuhn, "προσήλυτος," *TDNT*, 6:727-44.

42. See Acts 9:27-28; 11:2; and 15:1, 5 in contrast with 15:11, 28-29.

43. See Acts 11:2, 22, and 30; 12:17b; 15:6, 13-21, 22-23.

44. Luke never identifies James as the brother of Jesus. Consider Acts 11:30 (presumably); 12:17b; 15:4, 6, 13, 22; 21:18.

45. See Acts 15:2, 4, 6, 22, and 23. In this episode, more than one apostle is present. pl., ἀπόστολοι (apostles). In addition to ἀπόστολοι in Acts 11:1 and 15:6, Luke uses ἀἀποστόλων in 15:4 and ἀποστόλοις in 15:22.

Summary

Having analyzed Luke's characterization of the groups comprising the community of believers in Acts 15, it is now possible to identify them as the "whole church" who are present on that day and provide consent for the unanimous decision proffered by the apostles and elders (Acts 15:4–5, 12a, 22, 25). As we have argued in previous chapters, Luke utilizes conflict and the need for resolution to bring the community, as a unified character within the narrative, to the forefront resulting in action.[46]

While we see Luke highlight the prominence of Peter and James in the proceedings (15:7–11, 13–21), we have argued that Luke structures the story as he does to demonstrate the whole community of believers' engagement in theological creativity. Individual contributions are overshadowed by the engagement of various subgroups and by the affirmation of the whole community concerning the conversion of and fellowship with Gentile believers. Thus, as we will see in the following section, the community of believers in Jerusalem engage in theological creativity by accepting the salvation of Cornelius' household specifically without coming to a definitive conclusion concerning the *process* for salvation for Gentiles in general (Acts 11:15–18). The gathering of the believing communities from Jerusalem and Antioch provide the disciples with a second occasion (comp. 11:1–18 with 15:6–29) to clarify their theological position on the acceptance of Gentiles.

As we have seen, the conversion of and fellowship with Gentiles within the churches in Jerusalem and Antioch have profound and far-reaching consequences for the community of believers.[47] Moreover, we have argued that Luke relates his story in a series of overlapping episodes. Since, as we maintain, events in Acts 9:1–12:25 are not sequential we can see why the community of believers in Antioch are not aware of Peter's experience among Gentiles and why the community of believers in Jerusalem are just coming to terms with the Cornelius event when "certain individuals from Judea" send their own delegation to Antioch (15:1). Having accounted for the literary seams in the story as well as Luke's characterization of the "groups within a group," we may now see how Luke fashions them into the "whole church" engaging in theological creativity.

46. For the role of conflict in characterization see Hochman, *Character in Literature*, 51, 138–40; Moore, *Literary Criticism and the Gospels*, 15.

47. See earlier in this chapter concerning the pivotal nature of Luke's narrative tale of the conversion of the Gentiles. For similar conclusions see Conzelmann, *Acts*, 115–22, esp. 121–22; Fitzmyer, *Acts*, 538–61; R. Longenecker, *Acts*, 442–45.

The Community in Theological Creativity

According to Luke, the community's perception of its experience with Gentile converts is heavily influenced by the prophetic vision Peter experiences while staying in the home of Simon the Tanner (Acts 9:43).[48] Their theological view of prophetic encounters coupled with the testimony of the evidential work of the Spirit in saving Gentiles leads them to modify critical theological assumptions.

Using Scripture to Support Experience

After considerable debate (Acts 15:7), Peter provides testimony of his experience at the home of Cornelius (10–11).[49] According to Peter, it is God who cleanses their hearts, making "no distinction between them and us" (15:9). However, Peter then remarks that to impose the requirement of circumcision on the Gentile believers challenges God by "placing on the neck of the disciples a yoke that neither our ancestors nor we have been able to bear" (Acts 15:10). John Christopher Thomas suggests the yoke to which Peter refers is the necessity of certain aspects of Jewish law.[50]

While maintaining fundamental agreement with Thomas on this issue, we argue Peter's point is that culturally derived mandates, when imposed on other cultures, challenge God's evidential work among other nations.[51] It seems highly unlikely Luke's story would have Peter speak negatively of either the law or insult the sect of Pharisees by claiming that neither they

48. See Acts 10:1–23, 11:1–18; 15:7–11, 13. Other episodes that likely influenced the community's decision include Philip's evangelism among the Samaritans (Acts 8:5–25) and the Ethiopian eunuch (8:26–39) as well as the large influx of Gentile (Greek) believers in Antioch (11:20–24).

49. D05 adds emphasis to Peter's testimony by stating, "Peter rose up in the Spirit and said to them." Ellis states, "The Speech of Peter is introduced in D in a way which accords it pneumatic authority." Ellis, "Codex Bezae at Acts 15," 137. Epp suggests the import in D05 is intended to show a difference between Peter's speech (inspired by the Spirit) and James' speech (speaking on behalf of the consensus view). See Epp, *Theological Tendency*, 103–4.

50. See Thomas, "Women, Pentecostals," 44. See also Fitzmyer, *Acts*, 548; Cf. Conzelmann, *Acts*, 117.

51. For support, see Keener, *Acts*, 3:2235; Nolland, "Fresh Look at Acts 15.10," 105–15. Alternatively, Fitzmyer argues Peter is alluding to examples in the OT of the Jews testing God, i.e., Exod 15:22–27; 17:2, 7; Num 14:22; Isa 7:12; Ps 77:18, 41, 56; and Wis 1:2. For Fitzmyer, to test God is to "approach God in a spirit of unbelief and mistrust." See Fitzmyer, *Acts*, 547.

nor their Jewish ancestors had been able to keep the law (Acts 15:10).[52] In light of his declaration (15:11), we may conclude that Peter is in effect stating, "They (Gentiles) cannot take on our (Jewish) culture any more than we (Jews) might take on their (Gentile) culture. Fortunately, we (Jews and Gentiles) are both saved through the grace of the Lord Jesus."[53]

Following the testimonies of Peter, Paul, and Barnabas Luke reports that it is James who interprets all the testimony given as proof of the Spirit's evidential work among the Gentiles (15:13–22). Moreover, James concludes his assessment is consistent with the prophets (15:15). Luke's narrative indicates James does not begin with Scripture but rather with the community's experience.[54] On this occasion, their experience alters an interpretation of formerly held views.[55] We may conclude this for the following reasons. First, in order to interpret their experience through Scripture, James combines Peter's prophetic encounter among the Gentiles with Scripture using a creative interpretation of Amos 9:11–12 with allusions to Isa 45:20–25 and Jer 12:15–16.[56] On this occasion, James applies and interprets Scrip-

---

52. On the contrary, Luke favorably presents the importance of law-keeping among the Jews. See Luke 1:6, 15, 59; 2:21, 22–24, 39, 41; 4:16; 5:14; 10:26–28; 16:16–18; 22:7; Acts 3:1; 10:14, 28; 16:31; 17:2; 21:20–24, 26; 23:4–5; 24:17; 26:4–5. Cf. Wilson, *Luke and the Law*, 61. For a review of various arguments see Haenchen, *Acts*, 446 n. 3. Witherington cites examples of Jewish literature with a favorable view of the "yoke of the law." See Witherington, *Acts*, 454 n. 387–88. Cf. Nolland, "Fresh Look at Acts 15.10," 105–15.

53. Peter's line of reasoning is valid whether applied to Jews or Gentiles. For support see Bennema, "Ethnic Conflict in Early Christianity," 753–63, esp. 755–56; Nolland, "Fresh Look," 107–8. In opposition, see Haenchen, *Acts*, 446 n. 3.

54. Johnson states, "The work of God precedes the perception of the text's agreement." Johnson, *Acts*, 265. For Shelton, the meaning of the text has not altered, only the perception of the church upon receiving a greater understanding of events. He argues, "[In Luke] the Scripture does not determine the meaning of the Heilsgeschichte–event. . . . The Old Testament as previously interpreted does not compel God to conformity." J. Shelton, "Epistemology and Authority," 238. Cf. Fitzmyer, *Acts*, 555–56; Conzelmann, *Acts*, 117.

55. For a similar assessment see Johnson, *Acts*, 271; Witherington, *Acts*, 451. In opposition to the view argued here, Bauckham insists James relies solely on Scripture since "the issue is a matter of *halakha*, which can only be decided from Scripture (Cf. b. B. Mes. 59b)." See Bauckham, "James and the Jerusalem Church," 452.

56. See Amos 9:11, "ἐν τῇ ἡμέρᾳ ἐκείνῃ ἀναστήσω τὴν σκηνὴν Δαυὶδ τὴν πεπτωκυῖαν καὶ ἀνοικοδομήσω τὰ πεπτωκότα αὐτῆς καὶ τὰ κατεσκαμμένα αὐτῆς ἀναστήσω καὶ ἀνοικοδομήσω αὐτὴν καθὼς αἱ ἡμέραι τοῦ αἰῶνος, 12 ὅπως ἐκζητήσωσιν οἱ κατάλοιποι τῶν ἀνθρώπων καὶ πάντα τὰ ἔθνη, ἐφ᾽ οὓς ἐπικέκληται τὸ ὄνομά μου ἐπ᾽ αὐτούς, λέγει Κύριος ὁ Θεὸς ὁ ποιῶν πάντα ταῦτα" (LXX). For an analysis of textual variations concerning Amos 9:11–12, see Meek, *Gentile Mission*, 56–61, 77–81, 93. Bauckham argues that

---

ture in a manner consistent with the community's perception of the Spirit's evidential work. Consequently, it is more interpretation than quotation.[57]

Second, for the believing community in Luke's story, experiences concerning the Spirit's evidential work in the form of prophetic occurrence and testimony directly influences their use and interpretation of Scripture.[58] Here, Luke shows the community actively engaging both Spirit and Scripture in theological creativity (Acts 15:7-11, 12, 13-18).

The experience of the churches in Jerusalem and Antioch is clear: Gentiles join the faith and experience Spirit baptism without the Jewish rite of circumcision and observance of dietary laws (11:18; 15:11, 19, 28). As we have argued, the reason the community in Jerusalem engages in theological creativity in Acts 11:30 only to repeat the process again in Acts 15 is due to the manner in which Luke unfolds the chain of events and because of the narrative time it takes for all the characters involved in the story to come together and, so to say, "compare notes."

Criteria for Fellowship Dinners

Luke characterizes the whole church as an active participant in theological creativity concerning Gentile conversion without condition while stipulating essential concessions for communal meals.[59] Their address to

---

James' use of Amos 9:11-12 "shows that it is far from simply a quotation of the LXX text. . . . What appears to be merely a quotation of a scriptural text turns out to be in fact also an interpretation of the text [pesharim]." See Bauckham, "James and the Jerusalem Church," 453-58. Parsons refers to it as an "intricate exegesis." Parsons, *Acts*, 213-14. Johnson doubts an allusion to Isa 45:21 is intended. See Johnson, *Acts*, 265. For Lake and Cadbury, James' quote in Acts 15:16-18 differs from Amos 9:11-12 "with small variations." See Lake and Cadbury, *Acts*, 176. For further discussion on James' nuanced use of Amos 9:11-12 see Fitzmyer, *Acts*, 554-56; Conzelmann, *Acts*, 117; Thomas, "Women, Pentecostals," 46-49; Johnson, *Acts*, 271; Shelton, "Epistemology and Authority," 243-44; Whitlock, "Exposition of Acts 15:1-29," 377. For more on combining prophetic experience with Scripture, see chapter 5.

57. Bauckham, "James and the Jerusalem Church," 453; Cf. Parsons, *Acts*, 213.

58. For example, Acts 2:1-4, 14-36; 8:26-35; 10:9:16, 15:7-11, and 15:15-18. For additional support see Ellington, "History, Story, and Testimony," 258.

59. See Keener, *Acts*, 3:2259. Bauckham and Zetterholm (from differing perspectives) cast doubt on table fellowship being the central concern for the prohibitions. See Bauckham, "James and the Jerusalem Church," 463-64; Zetterholm, "Didache, Matthew, James," 84-85. Elsewhere in the NT, the issue of table fellowship is a central point of contention for Paul. For him, the Gentile Christians gain access to the family of God by faith in Christ and are in need of no further requirement (Gal 2:11-13, 15-21; 3:3).

the "believers of Gentile origin in Antioch and Syria and Cilicia" with the declaration "we impose on you no further burden" implicitly acknowledges the genuineness of their faith (Acts 15:23, 26, 28).[60] However, the mandates for table fellowship are explicit and include the following:

1. No consumption of food from markets dedicated to the gods (idols),[61]

2. No meat prepared rare or cooked in blood,[62]

3. No talk or acts of fornication at the table.[63]

60. For critical and textual issues concerning the decree see Metzger, *Textual Commentary*, 379–83. Pervo sees the decree as a "fabricated official document, like the letters in Esther, *Maccabees*, the *Alexander Romance*, and a number of ancient historical novels and tracts." See Pervo, *Profit with Delight*, 77, also 166 n. 14.

61. See NA28 Acts 15:20, "ἀλισγημάτων τῶν εἰδώλων" (pollutions of idols); 15:29, "ἀπέχεσθαι εἰδωλοθύτων" (abstain from meat sacrificed to idols); 21:25, "φυλάσσεσθαι αὐτοὺς τό τε εἰδωλόθυτον" (that they should abstain from what has been sacrificed to idols). B03—"idol sacrifices." D05—"pollutions of idols." Stenschke argues the prohibitions address a general assessment of how Gentiles worship god(s); through the ritual use of idols and food dedicated for its purpose, eating meat cooked with blood, and through indulgence in illicit sexual activity. See Stenschke, *Luke's Portrait of Gentiles*, 74–77, also 75 n. 106.

62. B03 "Abstain from . . . meat cooked in its juices and blood" (15:20). Furthermore, Codex Vaticanus indicates a connection between πνικτοῦ and αἵματος, as if πνικτοῦ serves to qualify αἵματος, in order to specify its meaning in a ritual or cooking sense. We argue each phrase ("καὶ τοῦ πνικτοῦ καὶ τοῦ αἵματος, 15:20; "καὶ αἵματος καὶ πνικτῶν," 15:29; "καὶ αἷμα καὶ πνικτὸν," 21:25) indicates a manner or method of cooking, hence, "and [meat] marinated or prepared in blood." Wedderburn agrees: "Philo, too, in *Spec. leg.* 4.119 . . . may be referring 'to a method of preparing gourmet dishes.'" Wedderburn, "'Apostolic Decree,'" 366. Cf. Wilson, *Luke and Law*, 89–90, 94–99. However, Klinghardt argues dual sense in Philo: (1) a Jewish sense (strangle) and (2) culinary sense (marinate or cook with blood). See Klinghardt, *Gesetz und Volk Gottes*, 203. Savelle reveals, "The term does occur in Athenaeus and other Greek writers as a culinary term (e.g., smothered)." See Savelle, "Reexamination of the Prohibitions," 449–68, esp. 456. For more traditional analysis see Bietenhard, "πνικτός," *TDNT*, 6:455–58. Danker states, "In non-biblical Greek with another meaning . . . 'steamed, stewed, baked.' Not in LXX nor in Hellenistic Jewish writings." Yet, despite no earlier precedent in ancient literature, he claims, "In Acts it plainly means strangled, choked to death [in Acts 15:20, 29; 21:25]." See BDAG, "πνικτος," 838. Alternatively, Codex Bezae (D05) indicates an ethical dimension to the prohibitions (idolatry, fornication, murder, and the Silver Rule (aka, negative Golden Rule), and thus the Western text eliminates πνικτόν/πνικτά altogether. For analysis see critical apparatus in Rius-Camps and Read-Heimerdinger, *Message of Acts*, 3:182.

63. Acts 15:20, "καὶ τῆς πορνείας" (and from fornication); 15:29, "καὶ πορνείας" (and fornication); 21:25, "καὶ πορνείαν" (and fornication). B03 and D05 indicate "illicit sexual relations." In light of the context (table fellowship), we maintain that the prohibition is to *prevent* illicit behavior during dinner-fellowship between Jews and Gentiles since that

Since the context indicates the matter of salvation is taken for granted (i.e., resolved without dispute), the community turns its focus to the other issue of concern—namely the gathering together of Jews and Gentiles for a festive or celebratory meal (i.e., possibly the Sabbath day; Acts 15:14).[64] Whereas some argue the prohibitions are intended to prevent future participation at pagan festivals or celebrations,[65] in practical terms, we argue Luke's narrative specifically seeks to prevent such activity during communal gatherings among *believers* since his story elsewhere limits the conflict to Jews and Gentiles eating together and not how Gentiles eat in general.[66]

The manner in which the whole church engages the issue indicates an unconditional acceptance of equality between Jews and Gentiles in terms of salvation while guarding the cultural sensibilities of more conservative Jews.[67] Luke indirectly reveals through the edict a reformulation of former-

---

is what the rest of the resolution concerns. For evidence see Acts 10:13–16, 28–29; 11:3, 17. Moreover, compare with the real issue of concern in 15:19–20, 29. For analysis, see Hauck and Schultz, "πορνεία," *TDNT*, 6:579–95, esp. 580–84, 592–93; BDAG, "πορνεία," 854.

64. Bauckham argues the decrees' mandate for table fellowship are already part of Torah Law and binding on "Gentile members of the eschatological people of God." He argues the four prohibitions indicated in the decree are the same universal prohibitions noted Leviticus 17–18. See Bauckham, "James and the Jerusalem Church," 58–62. However, his argument is not without its problems and critics (which he attempts to account for on pp. 460–62). In particular, see Wilson, *Luke and the Law*, 76–92; Wedderburn, "Apostolic Decree," 362–89, esp. 362–70. Other supporters of Lev 17–18 as a source for the prohibitions in Acts 15 include Conzelmann, *Acts*, 118–19; Dunn, *Beginning from Jerusalem*, 466; Fitzmyer, *Luke the Theologian*, 194; Schnabel, *Paul and the Early Church*, 1017–18. For opposing views, see Wilson, *Luke and the Law*, 76–77; Barrett, *Acts*, 2:734–35; Witherington, *Acts*, 464; Gaventa, *Acts*, 222. For a synopsis of arguments concerning the inspiration behind "the four (or three) prohibitions," see Keener, *Acts*, 3:2260–69; Wilson, *Luke and the Law*, 84–102. Codex Bezae indicates an ethical dimension to the prohibitions (idolatry, fornication, murder, and the Silver Rule). D05: "Abstain from the pollutions of idols, illicit sexual relations and blood, and whatever they do not wish to happen to themselves, stop doing to others." See critical apparatus in Rius-Camps and Read-Heimerdinger, *Message of Acts*, 3:182.

65. Such as described in 2 Macc 6:4–5; see Witherington, *Acts*, 463 n. 420.

66. See Acts 10:13–16, 28–29 11:3, 17; and compare with the real issue of concern in 15:19–20, 29. The point of contention between "those of the circumcision" and Peter is that he ate with Gentiles (11:2). The problem needing clarification is how Jews and Gentiles may fellowship (eat) together, not what Gentiles do in general. Suffice it to say, the communal aspect of eating together involves everyone in the community and is, in its most practical application, something begging for ground rules and supports our argument.

67. In opposition, Witherington doubts the whole church was involved in approving

ly held theological views. They engage in theological creativity by deciding that issues once considered moral imperatives are now regarded as cultural differences necessitating reasonable consideration and accommodation.[68]

Rather than as a demand, an imposition, or as an act of scorn or hubris the church in Jerusalem invites the churches of Antioch, Syria, and Cilicia to graciously meet them, so to say, "halfway" at the table of fellowship. Whereas Luke reveals that the act of salvation is solely between one's heart and God (Acts 10:47; 11:17–18; 15:11), the act of fellowship occurs among diverse people (10:28; 11:2; 20, 28–29). His story indicates that the churches of Jerusalem and Antioch are able to differentiate between vertical relationships (human and divine) and horizontal relationships (human to human). That Luke narrates the way the church in Antioch "rejoices" when the letter is read back in Antioch serves as evidence for this claim (Acts 15:31).[69]

Summary and Conclusions

Luke crafts a linear story with coinciding events, requiring the reader to follow the narrative clues inherent in the story. At a gathering hosted by the Jerusalem church, Peter testifies of his experience in Caesarea among Gentile converts. Moreover, he compares the imposition of cultural expectations and mores of one group upon another to a heavy yoke not easily borne by anyone. His argument is that Gentiles as a whole need not follow Jewish customs in order to join the community of faith (Acts 15:11). Following the testimony of Peter, Barnabas, Paul, and the verdict of James the whole community concludes that Gentile believers need not follow prescribed rituals in Jewish law and custom to be saved. Consequently, they impose no ritual requirements for salvation while setting minimum criteria for ongoing table fellowship between Jewish and Gentile believers. Their decision directly concludes culturally derived mandates imposed on

---

the decree but does acknowledge "some decisions were made by the leaders with the consent of the assembly of believers." See Witherington, *Acts*, 451. We argue the ground rules for table fellowship between Jews and Gentiles is the decision the leaders made with the consent of the whole church.

68. On this "mystery," Dunn states, "How it was that Christian Jews felt able thus to disregard the explicit injunctions of Gen 17:9–14 is one of the great unsolved mysteries of Christianity's beginnings." See Dunn, *Theology of Paul's Letter*, 70.

69. For additional support see Keener, *Acts*, 3:2279–80.

other cultures test God by challenging the Spirit's evidential work among the nations.

The combined-communities from Jerusalem and Antioch base their decision on a theological predilection for prophetic revelation and experience through testimony and use Scripture to affirm its decision. Here, Luke shows the community actively combining their experience with both the Spirit and Scripture in theological creativity in at least two ways, (1) by applying and interpreting Scripture in a manner consistent with the community's perception of the Spirit's evidential work, and (2) by deciding that issues once considered moral imperatives are now regarded as cultural differences necessitating reasonable consideration. At the end of their deliberations, representatives are chosen to deliver the community's decision to the Syrian churches. In sum, the decision by the whole church in 15:1–31 fundamentally alters the trajectory of the early church in Luke's story and demonstrates the way the church perceives itself in light of the evidential work of the Spirit. Thus, Luke's presentation of the believing community demonstrates the community's role in an interpretive process involving Spirit-Community-Scripture.

5

DISCERNING THE SPIRIT
—ACTS 11:27–30; 13:1–4; AND 21:4, 8–14

SO FAR, WE HAVE drawn attention to the manner in which Luke demonstrates the role of the first-century community of believers engaging in theological creativity as it grapples with (1) how it perceives itself both theologically and publicly, (2) its understanding of Jesus Messiah as Servant and Son of God, (3) a growing need for extended leadership, and (4) the manner in which a prophetic vision and testimony of the Spirit's evidential work alters their interpretation of Scripture.[1] In this chapter, we will see how Luke demonstrates the effect prophetic utterances and its interpretation has on the theological creativity of the first-century community of believers in Acts 11:29–30, 13:1–4, and 21:4, 10–14.

Early in Acts, the community of believers accepts prophetic events (happenings) rooted in Scripture.[2] As the story unfolds and the geographic

---

1. Theological creativity is the act of reformulating formerly held theological interpretations in light of testimony concerning the Spirit's evidential work and an emerging understanding of applicable Scripture followed by commensurate action. The Spirit's evidential work is known only through the community's testimony. Therefore, theological creativity is the outcome of the interpretive process since it is theology in action, functional in nature, and situationally pragmatic in scope. Consequently, it involves the process of theological justification and action or reaction in light of current circumstances. In this sense, to be creative with theology is to take what is already a theological assumption and broaden or adapt it to current circumstances in light of the Spirit's evidential work and a consensus understanding of Scripture.

2. For example, the community of believers act in response to scripture in Acts 1:20; 2:16–21, 25–28, 31, 34–35; 4:25–26; 15:15–18; 28:23–28.

98

center of the disciples broadens from Jerusalem to the surrounding region, a shift occurs in the source and nature of prophetic utterance.[3] Studying Luke's characterization of prophets and prophetic encounters, along with the community's interaction with both, provides fresh insight concerning the role of the community in theological creativity.

In this collection of prophetic encounters, Luke foregrounds the community as a central character that is active in recognizing and testifying to the Spirit's evidential work. We will see the high value Luke places on the prophetic in shaping theological decisions by the community of believers. In the context of this research, *the prophetic* includes prophets, prophecy, and prophetic-type utterances and experiences (e.g., dreams, visions, and trances). However, we concede that Luke does not clearly define his view of the prophetic as broadly as we will in Acts beyond his use of Scripture (as a fulfillment of the prophets)[4] or beyond the attention he draws to those who speak prophetically or those who "spoke by the Spirit."[5]

Finally, we will see that the community responds favorably when its interpretations are heeded and how it responds when its interpretations are ignored. Through analysis of the characters and their actions engaging the prophetic, we will show the integral role the community of believers play in adjudicating prophetic utterance. This chapter will conclude with a summary of the main points and evidence to demonstrate Luke's view of the community as a character engaging in theological creativity.

Identifying the Community

To demonstrate this claim, we must first consider the manner in which Luke identifies the community in the selected passages. Following this, we will address the significance he places on the prophetic in the context of his story. In the first section, we will see how Luke characterizes those who

3. In similar fashion, the community of believers act in response to the prophetic in Acts 8:26, 29; 9:10-19, 27-28; 10:1-44; 11:1-18, 17-30; 13:1-4; 15:6-14; 16:6-10; 21:4, 8-14; 27:21-26, 42-44. Notice the overlap in 15:6-18.

4. Consider Luke's use of Scripture in Acts 1:16-20; 2:17-35; 3:13-25; 4:11, 24-26; 7:2-53; 8:32-33; 13:16-52; 15:13-21; 23:5; 28:26-27. Also, see Luke's use of quotations from and allusions to OT passages concerning Jesus as the fulfillment of the prophets in Luke 1:46-55, 68-79; 2:14, 21-38, 41-52; 3:4-6, 23-38; 4:1-30; 7:22, 27; 8:10; 10:27; 13:35; 18:20; 19:38; 20:17, 28, 42-43; 24:21, 25-28, 32, 44:47.

5. Luke draws attention to those who speak prophetically by the Spirit see Acts 11:28; 13:1-3; 20:22-23; 21:4, 10-11.

operate with prophetic gifts, as well as the manner in which the community of believers acts and reacts to the prophetic. In doing so, we will see how and why their ministry among the churches affects the community in theological creativity.

We

In the passages under consideration, Luke refers to the community of believers as disciples (Acts 11:29–30; 21:4), the church (13:1), and we.[6] Having already addressed the community as disciples and as the church, we will focus our attention on Luke's use of the pronoun we.

Luke's use of first person is sporadic and not, in our view, always during the most interesting occasions.[7] Using "we" may indicate he is an eyewitness to the events.[8] However, it may be a narrative technique to simply bring the audience deeper into the story as the plot proceeds.[9] When Luke uses the pronoun we to describe the characters collectively in the story, the audience is invited to join the narrator in the action.[10] Since little is gained

---

6. "We" passages include 11:28 [D05]; 16:10–17; 20:5–21:18; 27:1–28:16. Luke's narrative use of we suggests he is present during the events. Further instances of we and us in Acts include 21:16, 17, 18; 27:1, 2, 3, 4, 5, 6, 7, 8, 15, 18, 27, 29, 37; 28:1, 2, 10, 11, 12, 13, 14, 15, 16. For research concerning Luke's use of "we" passages, see annotated bibliography in Green and McKeever, Luke-Acts, 140–43.

7. Most of which are during times of travel. Since little is gained by his presence, such usage favors his presence during these events. Or perhaps, that he is using a diary as a source. For support of Luke's presence, see Keener, Acts, 3:2350; Witherington, Acts, 481. Whether the narrator is the author or the source for the author in the so-called we-passages is beyond the scope of this research.

8. For analysis of prevailing views see Smith, "Sources in Acts," 63–73; Haenchen, Acts, 489–91; Barrett, Acts, 2:773; Keener, Acts, 3:2350–74. D05 includes the first "we" passage in Acts 11:28 by stating, " . . . and when we were gathered together, one named Agabus stood up and spoke." For support see Rius-Camps, who argues the observation is made from a "first-hand point of view." Rius-Camps and Read-Heimerdinger, Message of Acts, 2:323. Cf. Barrett, Acts, 1:564; Conzelmann, Acts, 90.

9. Haenchen also ponders the notion of Luke's use of we to draw the audience further into the narrative. See Haenchen, Acts, 491. Evidence suggesting it was a convention of Luke's day to record "sea voyages" using first-person narrative (as argued by Plümacher) is weak and sufficiently discredited by Praeder, "Problem of First Person Narration," 193–218, esp. 207–14. Cf. Plümacher, "Wirklichkeitserfahrung und Geschichtsschreibung," 2–22, esp. 14–22;

10. Hochman acknowledges the phenomenon of this literary technique. Hochman, Character in Literature, 50.

by Luke's presence (he does not contribute to the action), we maintain the primary effect of his use of we is to draw the audience into the story more deeply and to aid their awareness of the Spirit's evidential work among the churches outside of Jerusalem. Of central importance to this research is recognizing that "we-episodes" represent a group of people, who travel with Paul and are committed to his mission but not, as we will see, always in agreement with his actions.

Characterizing the Prophetic

Prophetic experience, or simply *the prophetic*, is prominent in Luke's writings.[11] The prophetic is evident through Old Testament quotation and allusion, through the words of Jesus, and through the preaching of the apostles.[12] In Luke's gospel, the active presence of and engagement with the Holy Spirit occurs within the matrix of human experience.[13] For example, Luke narrates for the reader (1) the Spirit coming upon Mary in the miraculous conception of Jesus (Luke 1:35); (2) Elizabeth and Zachariah being filled with the Spirit in prophetic exclamation (1:41–45, 67–79); (3) the Spirit resting on and guiding Simeon through the fulfillment of a revelation to see the Messiah before his death (2:25–35); (4) the fulfillment of John's message concerning baptism with the Holy Spirit and Jesus' message that "the heavenly Father [will] give the Holy Spirit to those who ask" through the experience of the disciples after the ascension;[14] (5) the Spirit resting on Jesus "in bodily form like a dove" (3:21–22); (6) Jesus being "full" of the Holy Spirit overcoming temptation in the wilderness and "filled" with the power of the Spirit returning to Galilee for public ministry (4:1–14); (7) the

11. In the context of this research, the expression *the prophetic* includes prophets, prophecy, and prophetic-type utterances and experiences (e.g., dreams, visions, and trances). With the exception of the book of Revelation, the writings of Luke contain more prophetic happenings than the rest of the New Testament combined. See Twelftree, *People of the Spirit*, 155; Johnson, *Acts*, 12–14.

12. For examples in antiquity see Josephus, *Life*, 208–10; Josephus, *J.W.* 3.350–51; Josephus, *Jub.* 32. Although, Dunn's assertion that Luke believes "all converts were given the gift of prophecy" seems to be overreaching. See Dunn, *Jesus and the Spirit*, 170.

13. We concede that Luke does not identify any of our examples as prophetic with the exception of particular sayings in Acts given by prophets in the first-century church (e.g., Acts 11:28, 13:2; 20:23, 21:4, 11). The following lists are intended to highlight events or actions in Luke's writing that seem inspired by the Holy Spirit.

14. Concerning the gift of the Spirit see Luke 3:16; 11:13; Acts 1:8; 2:4; 4:31; 8:14–20; 9:17–18; 10:44–48; 13:52; 16:6–10; 19:1–7.

Spirit of the Lord being upon Jesus through self-awareness (4:18–21); and (8) the Spirit teaching the disciples what to say.[15]

In Acts, we see that the prophetic also includes personal revelation. For example, (1) Peter's announcement to the lame man (Acts 3:4–6); (2) the condemnation of Ananias and Sapphira (5:3–4, 8–9); (3) Stephen's vision of Jesus (Acts 7:55–56); (2) Philip's guidance by an angel and transport to Azotus (8:26, 39–40a); (4) Paul's encounter with Jesus (9:3–6); (5) Ananias' directives (9:10–16); (6) the healing of Aeneas and Dorcas (9:34, 40); (7) Cornelius' directives (10:4–8, 30–33); (8) the revelation concerning the clean and unclean (10:19, 28–29); (9) Paul's directives;[16] and (10) circumstances concerning the initial call to Macedonia (16:6–10). Each episode possesses prophetic aspects without directly attributing the knowledge to prophecy.

Additionally, as we will see below, prophetic occurrences in Acts include the voice of the prophet (prophetic utterance).[17] Clearly Luke sees prophecy, whether spoken or in the form of dreams, visions, or directives as a defining sign of the Spirit's evidential work and as a source of divine communication. Consequently, as we will argue, the line between prophetic word and Scripture is blurred in Luke's accounting.[18]

Prophets from Jerusalem

In Luke's writings, the office of prophet is not directly defined. In the broadest sense, Luke indirectly identifies prophets in a classical sense, like those in Jewish antiquity.[19] In Acts, prophets operate as both an anonymous

15. Concerning the Spirit's guidance see Luke 12:12; Acts 4:8–12; 5:3–10; 6:10; 7:1–53; 13:9–11.

16. Concerning Paul's directives see Acts 16:6–10; 22:17–21; 23:11; 27:23–24.

17. Acts 11:27–28; 13:1–4; 19:21; 20:22–24; 21:4, 8–14. Since Acts 18:9–10; 23:11; and 27:23–26 are personal encounters for Paul and lack a community dimension, they are not under consideration in this chapter.

18. See below for more discussion under "The Community's Acceptance of Prophetic Utterance." In opposition, Witherington argues, "In view of 1 Cor 14, NT prophecy would seem to have had an authority of general content and was not taken as a literal transcript of God's words, but rather was something that needed to be weighed or sifted (see 1 Cor 14:29)." Witherington, *Acts*, 631. However, this does not seem to be Luke's view.

19. Prophets are identified in Acts 11:27; 13:1; 15:32; 21:9. For support see Jervell, *Unknown Paul*, 108. Other first-century sources concerning itinerate prophets include *Did.* 11:3–12; *Herm. Mand.* 11:1–17. See also Dunn, *Jesus and the Spirit*, 175; Hengel and

group (11:27) and as an identifiable group (13:1; 21:9) who occupy a welcome, respected, and necessary ministry among the churches.[20] Moreover, we see the ministry of prophets active in Jerusalem before they are active in Antioch (Acts 13:1). In Acts 11:27, prophets come from Jerusalem even though they are not identified as an official delegation. Notwithstanding, the context implies they come with the blessing of the Jerusalem elders.[21] Since Luke notes the prophets come from Jerusalem, Barrett's conclusion that Luke seems "to be introducing prophecy into Antioch and the presbyterate into Jerusalem" is overreaching.[22]

Finally, Luke characterizes the sayings of prophets as spontaneous (unplanned) and as predictive in nature (foretelling rather than forthtelling).[23] Whereas prophetic passages from Scripture in Luke's Gospel and Acts 1–8 possess a messianic sense are concerned with an issue of judgment, prophecy among the prophets in the remainder of story are informative and intended to prepare the church for upcoming experiences. Consequently, we find it ironic that prophets in Luke's writings do *not* interpret their sayings.[24]

Schwemer, *Paul between Damascus and Antioch*, 235. The conception of prophets as a group of believers endowed with a prophetic gift for the purpose of edification (as in 1 Cor 12, 14) is not under consideration in this research.

20. In support that prophets are welcome, respected, and considered necessary D05 adds the mood of the Antioch congregation upon the arrival of the prophets in Acts 11:27–28a. : "Ἐν ταύταις δὲ ταῖς ἡμέραις κατῆλθον ἀπὸ Ἱεροσολύμων προφῆται εἰς Ἀντιόχειαν, ἥν δὲ πολλὴ ἀγαλλίασις." As Rius-Camps demonstrates, "The joy that is expressed by ἀγαλλίασις is especially associated with experiencing something of the divine. Rius-Camps and Read-Heimerdinger, *Message of Acts*, 2:323. Luke limits the use of ἀγαλλίασις to special occasions in Luke 1:14, 44, and Acts 2:46. Other uses in scripture include Hab 1:9 and Jude 24. For analysis see Bultmann, "ἀγαλλίασις," *TDNT*, 1:19–21; BDAG, "ἀγαλλίασις," 4, describes it as a piercing exclamation, exultation. In the front material, Danker notes, "There are no secular occurrences of ἀγαλλίασις" (BDAG, xxi). See also Epp, *Theological Tendency*, 99. In contrast, NA28 (follows the Alexandrian text and omits the mood): "Ἐν ταύταις δὲ ταῖς ἡμέραις κατῆλθον ἀ ἀ ἀπὸ Ἱεροσολύμων προφῆται εἰς Ἀντιόχειαν." Same in B03, "Ἐν αὔταις δὲ ταῖς ἡμέραις κατῆλθον ἀπὸ Ἱεροσολύμων προφῆται εἰς Ἀντιόχειαν."

21. Possibly at the behest of the Jerusalem church. In opposition, Conzelmann maintains the prophets from Jerusalem are not delegates but "free charismatics" better known as wandering prophets. Conzelmann, *Acts*, 90. To this end, Dunn agrees. See Dunn, *Jesus and the Spirit*, 171. Haenchen's argument (among other points of contention) that itinerant prophets did not travel in groups in the mid-first century CE is without evidence. Haenchen, *Acts*, 376–78. Cf. Johnson, *Acts*, 208.

22. Barrett, *Acts*, 1:559.

23. Johnson, *Acts*, 205. Cf. Barrett, *Acts*, 1:561; Witherington, *Acts*, 372.

24. As we will see that function is left to the community of believers. See below

In Luke's story the prophetic, from Acts 9 and onward, always provides the disciples with an opportunity for action and serves as confirmation of the Spirit's evidential work.[25] Since the manner in which a prophetic utterance is perceived and processed by the local body of believers is important to this study, it will be necessary to see how Luke characterizes Agabus particularly and the community's interaction with him.[26]

Within the story, Agabus seems to be well-known among the churches. Aside from his travels to Antioch (Acts 11:27–28) and Caesarea (21:10), he does not seem to be characterized as a "wandering prophet" with an itinerant ministry—that is, as one traveling to a community or household to deliver prophetic words. Instead, his prophecies in Antioch and Caesarea narratively appear more serendipitous in nature.[27] First, Agabus predicts a famine that will affect the inhabitants of the whole region (Acts 11:27–28).[28] The church in Antioch receives the prophecy by Agabus and takes immediate action by sending financial support to the fledgling congregation in

---

under "The Community Acts upon Prophetic Guidance."

25. Examples include Acts 9:10–19; 10:1–29; 11:27–30; 12:6–9; 13:1–4; 16:6–10; 21:4–14; 23:11; 27:9–10, 21–26, 42–44; and 28:3–10.

26. Luke identifies others as prophets in Acts (e.g., Barnabas, Simeon, Lucius, Manaen, and Saul in Acts 13:1; Judas and Silas in Acts 15:32; daughters of Philip with the gift of prophecy in 21:9. However, only in the case of Agabus is a specific prophetic word linked to a specific individual. (The prophecy in Acts 13:1–3 is set within a group context, similarly in 21:4.) Furthermore, Luke narrates that Paul detects evil in and predicts calamity over various individuals (e.g., Elymas in 13:8–11 and the possessed slave girl in 16:11–18). However, Luke draws no specific attention to Paul functioning as a prophet, at least not like he does for Agabus.

27. Luke's story does not indicate that Agabus traveled to Antioch (Acts 1:27–28) to deliver a prophecy concerning the famine to the Antioch church or to Caesarea to deliver a prophecy to Paul (Acts 21:10). Rather, the prophecies of Agabus seem to occur serendipitously.

28. Gr. οἰκουμένην, lit. "inhabited world," or as "empire" in Luke 2:1 and 4:5. For other uses of the term οἰκουμένην in this manner, see Lucian, *Octogenarians*, 7, "…the emperor's world"; Josephus, *J.W.* 3.29, where the reference is to citizens of the empire. The prediction of a universal famine is widely disputed on historical grounds. See Haenchen, *Acts*, 376–77. Talbert refers to it as "poetic hyperbole." Talbert, *Reading Acts*, 117. For a more favorable view, see Josephus, *Ant.* 3:320–21; 20:51–53, 101; Suetonius, *Claud.* 18; Tacitus, *Ann.* 12:43. Cf. Barrett, *Acts*, 1:588–66; Johnson, *Acts*, 206–8; Riesner, *Paul's Early Period*, 132–34; Gapp, "Notes: The Universal Famine," 258–65, esp. 262. Concerning the second prophecy, some dispute on the grounds that it is not the *Jews* who bind Paul, rather it is the Romans (compare 21:11 and 33). But this detail seems trivial in nature.

Jerusalem (11:30, comp. 8:1-2). In doing so, Luke presents the community of believers in Antioch as self-sufficient and able to function on its own.[29]

Second, Agabus predicts the apprehension of Paul by the Jerusalem authorities (Acts 21:10-14). Whereas the church views the prophecy of Agabus as a warning against Paul's travel to Jerusalem, Paul interprets it as information or as a sign of what he might expect, like an intelligence report.[30] As noted earlier, prophets do not indicate a course of action; that is, we do not see them interpret their own prophesies. Rather, and as we will demonstrate, interpretation and action are left to the community of believers.

Prophets in Antioch

As we noted of prophets in general, Luke provides little information concerning the prophets in Antioch.[31] However, by naming each in Acts 13:1-3 and including their pivotal roles in the calling of Barnabas and Saul to missionary service, he elevates their stature in the story.[32] Though Luke

29. See Rius-Camps and Read-Heimerdinger, *Message of Acts*, 2:321.

30. For similar view, see Haenchen, *Acts*, 602, also 602 n. 1; Conzelmann, *Acts*, 178; Barrett, *Acts*, 2:996-99; Fitzmyer, *Acts*, 689-90. Cf. Keener, *Acts*, 3:3105-9.

31. As noted earlier. For the majority view that each member is both a prophet and teacher, see Haenchen, *Acts*, 395; Witherington, *Acts*, 391; Twelftree, *People of the Spirit*, 158. Here, Luke links prophets with teachers. However, he provides no context to designate or separate the two groups. Some suggest the first three (Barnabas, Simeon, and Lucius) are prophets and the latter two (Manaen and Saul) are teachers. See Dunn, *Acts*, 172-73; R. Longenecker, *Acts*, 212. However, such a claim is speculative and difficult to support.

32. See Keener, *Acts*, 2:1983-84. Barnabas' name appears first in the list suggesting his position of honor among the group. Aside from Saul, whose name appears last, Luke situates the remaining members with distinguishing marks. Luke's minimal information showcases their high-status, diversity, and foreign nature. Simeon is called Niger, suggesting he is African or dark-skinned. For support see Jervell, *Apostelgeschichte*, 340-41; Witherington, *Acts*, 392; Dunn, *Acts*, 172. Pervo indicates the evidence is not substantial enough to warrant a conclusion. Pervo, *Acts*, 322 n. 28. Lucius is from Cyrene. Cyrene (N. Africa) had a large Jewish population. See Josephus, *Ant.* 14.11544; Josephus, *Ag. Ap.* 2.44. Keener, *Acts*, 2:1987. It was Cyrenians who cofounded the mixed-ethnic Antioch congregation (Acts 11:20-21). It is unlikely Lucius is Luke the author. For support, see Bruce, *Acts*, 260; Hengel, *Acts and the History*, 72. Manaen was formerly a member (σύντροφος) of Herod's (Antipas) court. Gk. σύντροφος, "to be brought up with" suggests Manaen was either the son of a nobleman who was educated inside Herod's court as a schoolmate and childhood friend of Antipas (making him age 60+) or possibly a high-status servant to Antipas. See Keener, *Acts*, 2:1989, also 1989 n. 67; Bruce, *Acts*, 260-61;

provides no further activity of the prophets in Antioch, their role in acting upon the prophetic word to "set apart" Barnabas and Saul for a missionary expedition is a defining moment in the story. For the first time, Luke shows the expansion of the gospel as an organized and deliberate act. Whereas all previous expansions of the Gospel are either serendipitous or as a reaction to circumstance, persecution, or expulsion, now it is a planned and focused endeavor.[33]

Prophets among the Churches

Luke indicates that Paul and his traveling companions, described as we, book passage on a cargo vessel in Patara bound for Phoenicia (Acts 21:1–2). Along the way, they make extended stops in Tyre and Caesarea (21:3, 8). In both locations, Luke reports prophetic sayings warning Paul that he must not go to Jerusalem. In Tyre, one or more of the disciples offer a prophetic utterance. Luke collapses their saying and interpretation by stating, "Through the Spirit they told Paul not to go to Jerusalem" (Acts 21:4). Paul's response is not immediately disclosed. However, earlier in Acts 20:22–24, Paul testifies to receiving many such warnings concerning his fate in Jerusalem. For Paul, the messages do not address the appropriateness of his travel plans. However, in Tyre, the interpretation is directly aimed at the appropriateness of Paul's travel to Jerusalem (21:4).

In Caesarea, while staying in the home of Philip the Evangelist, Luke discloses the prophetic ability of Philip's four daughter but does not record any specific prophetic utterance from them concerning Paul's travel plans (21:8–9).[34] Nevertheless, that Luke mentions the prophetic daughters strongly suggests that prophetic gifts are prominent in the churches and commonplace in their experience.

Hemer, *Acts*, 166. For similar usage of σύντροφος in LXX see 1 Kgs 12:8, 10; 1 Macc 1:6; 2 Macc 9:29.

33. Compare events in Acts 2:1–42; 3:3–4:4; 4:31; 5:12–16; 6:1–7; 8:1–5; 9:32–11:18; 11:19–26; and 12:17 with 13:3–4.

34. For an analysis of prophetesses in antiquity, see excursus in Keener, *Acts*, 3:3093–3102. See also Witherington, *Acts*, 632–33; Barrett, *Acts*, 2:994.

SUMMARY

Using familiar language to identify the community of believers, namely *disciples* and *church*, Luke now refers to the community as *we* on specific occasions, thus drawing the audience deeper into the story through first person narrative. Within the plot, the audience encounters prophetic experience dynamically affecting the church while directing the characters through the story. Luke repeatedly demonstrates the Spirit's evidential work through the active presence of the prophetic in the life of the first-century community of believers. Furthermore, he shows the high value the community places on the prophetic by drawing special attention to both prophetic encounters and utterances and by the way he characterizes the prophets in his narrative tale.

The Community in Theological Creativity

Given Luke's characterization of the prophetic and its influence on the community, we see the first-century community of believers engaged in theological creativity in the following ways, (1) the community of believers is inclined to accept prophetic utterances as divine directive, and (2) the community, rather than the prophets, interpret and take commensurate action. In the following subsection, we will address these two aspects.

The Community's Acceptance of Prophetic Utterance

Early in Acts, the community of believers accepts prophetic occurrences in light of an applicable Scripture.[35] For example, Peter justifies his decision to replace Judas based upon his understanding of Ps 69:25 and 109:8 (Acts 1:16, 20).[36] In order to explain the unusual manifestation described in Acts 2:1–4, Peter draws on prophecy from Joel 2:28. Later, in Acts 4:27–28, the community is emboldened to resist the mandate by the Jewish authorities

---

35. For example, the community of believers act in response to Scripture in Acts 1:20; 2:16–21, 25–28, 31, 34–35; 4:25–26; 15:15–18; 28:23–28. For an analysis of Luke's use of Scripture see Bovon, *Luke the Theologian*, 78–121; Pao, *Acts and the Isaianic*, 5–17; J. Sanders, "Prophetic Use," 191–98; Meek, *Gentile Mission*, 1–23; Clarke, "Use of the Septuagint," 2:66–105; Keener, *Acts*, 1:477–85.

36. For discussion see chapter 1 under "Scripture as an Explanation for Experience."

to discontinue its preaching of Jesus. The community's *pesher* of Ps 2:1–2 is a messianic interpretation using contemporary events and persons.[37]

For Luke, at least throughout his Gospel and up through Acts 8, the word "Scripture," as divine communication, refers to quotations from and allusions to the words of the prophets.[38] However, as the geographical center of the church moves beyond Jerusalem, a shift occurs concerning the inspiration for prophetic happenings.[39] Whereas the foundation for the prophetic had been Scripture, we now see it as an emerging group within the community of believers who speak prophetically.

Given this shift, Luke's audience is left to assume the general acceptance and prominence of prophetic utterance originating from something *other* than Scripture. For Luke, the Spirit speaking through individuals and then interpreted by a community of believers is prophetic in nature as divine witness and functions authoritatively in the absence of an applicable Scripture.[40] Despite this shift in prophetic source, the effect on the community in theological creativity appears to be the same, it demonstrates the Spirit's evidential work.[41]

The community engages in theological creativity by acting and reacting to the prophetic in a manner like its earlier action and reaction to Scripture. Since the prophetic functions as a source of divine communication, we argue that the line between Scripture and the prophetic is blurred.[42] Consequently, in the absence of written Scripture, we conclude that the community in Luke's story relies on the prophetic to indicate divine will.[43]

37. For discussion see chapter 2 under "Evidence of Pesher."

38. As noted earlier in this chapter, particularly notes 4–5. Moreover, we have also argued that Luke seems to view the community's commitment to precedent established in its cultural past as action consistent with Scripture or divine will. See chapter 2 under "Selecting a Successor," chapter 3 under "The Laying on of Hands" and "Commitment to the Common God of All," and chapter 4 under "Criteria for Fellowship Dinners."

39. Compare Acts 1:20; 2:16–21, 25–28, 31, 34–35; 4:25–26; 15:15–18; 28:23–28; with Acts 8:26, 29; 9:10–19, 27–28; 10:1–44; 11:1–18, 17–30; 13:1–4; 15:6–14; 16:6–10; 21:4, 8–14; 27:21–26, 42–44. Notice the overlap in 15:6–18.

40. See Acts 5:3–6; 6:3–5; 11:27–30; 13:1–4; 15:28; 16:6–10; 20:22–23; 21:4, 10–14.

41. The community of believers act in response to the prophetic in 8:26, 29; 9:10–19, 27–28; 10:1–44; 11:1–18, 17–30; 13:1–4; 15:6–14; 16:6–10; 21:4, 8–14; 27:21–26, 42–44. Notice the overlap between the prophetic and Scripture as sources of authority in 15:6–18.

42. See above under "Characterizing the Prophetic."

43. While it may not be possible to prove Luke equates prophetic experience with Scripture, what may be concluded from the story is his willingness to rely on prophetic

The Community Acts upon Prophetic Guidance

With the rise of prophets among the community of believers, this new source of prophetic inspiration provides occasions for action. The community is engaged in theological creativity when its actions are based on its theological recognition of prophets.[44] Within Luke's writings, the ministry of prophets does not occur in private. Prophets speak within a group setting and a community decides what to do with their words.[45] Even the mention of Philip's four daughters who prophesy, despite the absence of a prophetic saying, is set within the context of the community of believers in Caesarea and their gift is known publicly (Acts 21:9).[46] Again, for Luke, prophecy is not a private affair. Prophetic statements are given among a community of believers and judged accordingly. By committing to this process and remaining faithful to it throughout the story, the first-century community of believers is engaged in theological creativity.

For example, the first prophetic message by Agabus warns the believers in Antioch of an impending event (Acts 11:28). In response, the Antioch church takes immediate steps to assist their fellow believers in Jerusalem (11:29-30). The second prophetic encounter involves prophets who settle in Antioch (13:2). On this one occasion, Luke mentions fasting during times of worship followed by prophetic utterance (13:2-3).[47] The

---

experience when no clear Scripture is in mind.

44. See earlier under "Prophets from Jerusalem."

45. For example, Acts 11:27-30; 13:3; 16:6-10; 21:4, 8-14.

46. See earlier under "Prophets among the Churches."

47. In contrast to the Pharisees and Jesus himself, fasting is absent among Jesus' followers (Luke 4:2; 5:33). Although uncommon among Romans and Greeks but more common among the Jews, the social custom of fasting is generally associated with mourning for the dead. As Keener notes, fasting "characterized Jewish tradition." Keener, *Acts*, 2:1991; Witherington, *Acts*, 393; Barrett, *Acts*, 1:606; Rius-Camps and Read-Heimerdinger, *Message of Acts*, 3:22. Fasting is also mentioned in Luke 18:12 as a sign of piety. For some Jewish circles, times of fasting also accompanied mourning associated with sorrow for sins and shame as seen in Saul's experience following his conversion in Damascus (Acts 9:9). Some evidence exists concerning Jewish fasts when seeking revelation (e.g., Dan 10:3; 2 Bar 20:5; 43:30). For an additional list of sources in ancient literature, see Keener, *Acts*, 2:1992 n. 108. While it is possible the prophets in Antioch theologically base their custom of fasting on their Jewish heritage, it is difficult to prove without further evidence. Evidence suggests that second and third generation Christians in the region rejected Jewish customs of fasting. For example, *Did.* 8:1; *Diogn.* 4:1; *Barn.* 3:1-3, 7:3-5; and *Herm.* 54:3-56:8 all elude to Isa 58:5-7 for support in curbing Jewish fasts.

narrative suggests Luke intends for his audience to conclude that fasting during times of worship aids the process of interpretation. After fasting and praying, the community confirms the prophetic word by commissioning Barnabas and Saul by laying their hands on them and then they "sent them off."[48] Whether the Antioch church provides funding for the trip is not revealed but may be implied considering the church's participation in the commissioning and sending process (13:4).

The third prophetic event involves a group of utterances warning Paul against travel to Jerusalem. Luke introduces these communities to his audience as:

1. "Every" community of believers Paul encounters after the riot in Ephesus (Acts 20:1) and prior to his farewell speech with the Ephesian elders in Miletus (20:17–38, specifically v. 23),

2. Believers in Tyre (21:3–4),

3. Believers gathered at the home of Philip the Evangelist (21:8–14).[49]

The prophetic episodes in Luke's story are critical to understanding the community's engagement in theological creativity since the revelation concerning the famine (Acts 11:28), the sending of Barnabas and Saul (13:2), and the two warnings concerning the imprisonment of Paul (21:4, 10) are preemptive in nature, giving the churches time to evaluate and take action.

The first instance leads the community of believers in Antioch to assist the Jerusalem church (Acts 11:27–30). The second results in the first intentional and organized missionary journey (13:1–4). The third instigates a conflict between Paul and the churches concerning his travel to Jerusalem and results in an end to prophetic utterances among the churches concerning Paul and his ministry (21:4, 11). The end result is Paul's four-year imprisonment and the absence (or silence) of the believing community concerning Paul's defense.[50]

48. D05 indicates the whole community of believers participates in prayer and the commissioning, whereas "in B03 the response does not involve anyone outside the five prophets and teachers." Rius-Camps and Read-Heimerdinger, *Message of Acts*, 3:16, 22. Concerning the laying on of hands, see chapter 3. Barrett states, "Luke uses ἀπέλυειν in a variety of senses; here, 'sent them on their way'. Most often, in Greek generally, it means *to dismiss* (in various senses); for the present meaning see Tobit 10.12(ℵ); Josephus *Ant.* 5.97." Barrett, *Acts*, 1:607.

49. Philip the Evangelist is previously noted in Acts 6:5; 8:5–40; 21:8–10.

50. The four-year process includes two years imprisoned in Caesarea (Acts 24:27) and two years in Rome awaiting trial (28:16, 30).

Even though Luke does not present this encounter in a negative manner, as we will see, it signals a consequential change in relationship between the churches and Paul following his arrest. The ambiguity in the narrative leaves the audience in a quandary concerning the conflicting directions by the Spirit. For example, Luke narrates that Paul "resolved in the Spirit to go through Macedonia and Achaia, and then to go on to Jerusalem" (Acts 19:21). Later, during his farewell speech to the Ephesian elders, Paul indicates the motivation for his journey is that he is a "captive to the Spirit" (20:22).[51] The only other reference to a possible motive for his trip to Jerusalem is after his incarceration in Caesarea (24:17). Paul tells Felix, "I came to bring alms to my nation and to offer sacrifices" (24:17). Aside from this reference, which Luke offers in the form of a quotation, nothing further is indicated concerning Paul's offering.[52]

Moreover, Luke includes prophetic warnings from multiple communities of believers in diverse locations. Each group attempts to persuade Paul that going to Jerusalem is not God's will. Paul interprets the prophetic warnings as an attempt by the Spirit to prepare him for what lies ahead (Acts 20:22; 21:13).[53] Even the church in Jerusalem attempts to mitigate the consequences of Paul's arrival (21:20b–23a) by convincing him to join another group engaged in a rite of purification (21:24b). Before the rite

51. Paul's reference to "Spirit" could be in reference to his own spirit (i.e., he feels motivated internally). For support see Codex Bezae, Acts 20:22, "And now, here I am, bound by my spirit travelling to Hierosoluma." For support, see Rius-Camps and Read-Heimerdinger, *Message of Acts*, 4:130. Tannehill is doubtful but reluctantly concedes the reference could mean Paul's own spirit. See Tannehill, *Narrative Unity of Luke-Acts*, 239.

52. In his letters, Paul indicates an offering as the reason for his trip to Jerusalem. Concerning the offering, see Rom 15:25–27; 1 Cor 16:1–4; 2 Cor 8–9. Since no mention is made of Paul delivering the offering to the elders in the Jerusalem church (Acts 21:17–19) and since Paul's only reference to it (in Acts after his arrest) implies he was apprehended prior to completing his vow at the temple (24:17–18), it is unclear who actually received the funds. Luke remains silent on the issue, and Paul makes no mention of the offering in letters written after his imprisonment. If Paul was arrested before he could finalize the offering to the temple, then the money remained in his possession and might explain why Felix expected to receive a bride from Paul (Acts 24:26) and how Paul supports himself "at his own expense" while awaiting trial in Rome (28:30). See Tannehill, *Narrative Unity of Luke-Acts*, 266.

53. Much later in the story (at least two years later), Luke includes Paul's vision of Jesus and the comforting words, "Keep up your courage! For just as you have testified for me in Jerusalem, so you must bear witness also in Rome." (Acts 23:11). We see this as evidence that the Lord does not abandon Paul regardless of whether he should have gone to Jerusalem or not. However, it does not speak to the issue of whether he should have listened to the believers and not gone to Jerusalem.

of purification is complete, Paul is seized by "Jews from Asia" (21:27–30). What seems clear in light of the plot is that when the community is able to be fully engaged, the work or effort is supported. When the community is left outside the process or ignored, the work is unsupported and considered, perhaps, counterproductive altogether.

Notwithstanding, Luke does mention two groups of believers at the end of Paul's journey to Rome. The first is in Puteoli and the second involves a group of believers from Rome who hear of Paul's coming and meet his transport at the Forum of Appius and Three Taverns (Acts 28:13–15).[54] Yet, Luke's account of believers in Puteoli meeting Paul seems serendipitous and the encounter with Roman disciples so far outside the city narratively suggests that no churches in Judea or abroad have notified believers in Italy of Paul's coming. Moreover, we get the impression that the church in Rome, so to say, "keeps its distance from Paul."

We may conclude this since Paul's initial audience in Rome are not identified as disciples but Jews eager to hear more about "this sect we know that everywhere it is spoken against" (Acts 28:22).[55] Ironically, they too are unaware of his pending arrival or reason for coming (28:21). Not only have the believing communities in Jerusalem or Antioch taken no action but neither has anyone else. Aside from a small band of traveling companions (we), Paul is on his own.[56]

The narrative concludes with Paul under house arrest for two years at his own expense with no mention of fellowship with the believing community in Rome, although, Luke does indicate that Paul entertains guests from time to time (28:30–31). The lack of prior correspondence from anyone and the circumstances of Paul's accommodations in Luke's story serve as evidence to our claim that Paul's disregard for the community's interpretation of prophetic utterance concerning his trip to Jerusalem leaves Paul ostracized from the community at large.[57] The community of believers is

54. Ancient Puteoli is approximately 140 miles south of Rome on the Bay of Naples. The Forum of Appius and Three Taverns is 43 miles south of Rome. The impression one gets from a cursory reading of the Epistle to the Romans is of a thriving community of believers in and around Rome (Rom 15:13; 15:30–33; 16:1–21).

55. Upon arriving in Rome, Paul meets first with a delegation of leading Jews and then later with a larger group of Jews (Acts 28:17–23). The latter encounter ends poorly (28:24–29).

56. Paul attests to his feeling of abandonment on at least one occasion in 2 Tim 4:9–11, 16.

57. We are aware that Paul's letters indicate receiving some correspondence and

engaged in theological creativity by declaring, "The Lord's will be done" (21:14), followed by, at least in Luke's story, no further contact or fellowship with Paul.

It seems unusual to us that Luke offers no evaluation of the situation.[58] Tannehill concludes that the passages concerning prophecy in Acts show it to be "incomplete (Acts 20:22–23), inexact (21:11), and that it may even lead to false conclusions (21:4)."[59] But by remaining silent, we argue that Luke allows the characters in his story to deal with this conundrum on their own theological assumptions. Consequently, and given the unfolding plot, we conclude that Luke, though attempting to be as impartial as possible also intends for his audience to conclude that the interpretation of the various communities should have been followed. The commensurate action taken by these first-century communities of believers concerning the famine prophecy as well as in the call and commission of those for missionary service serve as evidence for this claim. Luke's story suggests that had Paul followed the community's interpretation, all involved would have acted on their theological assumptions concerning prophecy and assisted Paul in accomplishing his goal (whatever it was) through other means.

Summary and Conclusions

Careful analysis of prophetic occurrences in Acts supports the thesis of this study by showing the first-century community of believers actively engaged in theological creativity. Luke presents three instances in which prophetic utterances shape the way the community of believers theologically act and react. Despite differences between the various communities of believers involved, the results are consistent. For Luke, those with prophetic gifts

---

assistance from some believers (e.g., Phil 4:10–20) . However, this is outside the scope of this study.

58. As Dunn notes, "The fact that Paul ignored what seem to have been regarded as clear directions of the Spirit through prophecy (21.4; Cf. 21.10–4 [sic]) is recorded without comment; no attempt is made to give guidance on what should be done when two inspired utterances, *both* from the Spirit (20.22; 21.4), not merely differ but contradict each other!" See Dunn, *Jesus and the Spirit*, 175–76. For conclusions that Luke shapes the narrative to demonstrate the misinterpretation by the prophetic members of the community, see Conzelmann, *Acts*, 178; Tannehill, *Narrative Unity of Luke-Acts*, 263, 266.

59. Tannehill, *Narrative Unity of Luke-Acts*, 266. However, Rius-Camps demonstrates that Codex Bezae most clearly demonstrates Paul's error in judgment. Rius-Camps and Read-Heimerdinger, *Message of Acts*, 4:169–70.

provide the utterance but the course of action is left to the community's evaluation and interpretation. The community of believers take commensurate action proactively when a consensus interpretation occurs.

As we have seen, the community of believers in Antioch receive a prophetic warning concerning the ill effects the Jerusalem church will suffer because of famine (Acts 11:27–30). Moreover, the first missionary endeavor of Barnabas and Saul into the interior of Asia Minor is initiated by the Spirit during a time of prayer and fasting and confirmed by a group of prophets leading the Antioch church (Acts 13:1–3). However, when the community's interpretation is not received, they commit the matter to God and relent. We see this indirect outcome after numerous communities of believers in diverse places attempt to assist Paul (20:23; 21:4b, 10–14).

What do these three instances of the prophetic and the community's reaction reveal concerning their engagement in theological creativity? Each reveals the high regard the first-century community of believers had for prophetic utterance and that it is predictive in nature, it reveals happenings (events). We see that the prophetic functions authoritatively in the absence of an applicable Scripture. On theological grounds, prophecy is received within the community of believers as a sign of the Spirit's evidential work and interpreted by consensus to determine divine direction. They, and not the prophets, decide how to interpret the prophecy and what action is required.

Once a consensus is reached the community of believers offer their response. If the response is not initially received, repeated efforts ensue, often by different groups of believers. If the consensus interpretation is ultimately rejected, the community relents, and prophetic utterances cease. As a result, the community commits the matter into God's hands. Considering the way the community engages with Spirit and their regard for prophetic utterance as divine communication, we conclude Luke's presentation of the believing community demonstrates the community's role in an interpretive process involving Spirit-Community-Scripture.

6

The Community
in Theological Creativity

IN THIS STUDY, WE have presented the first-century community of believers in Acts functioning as an indispensable character in Luke's story that is actively engaged in theological creativity. We have demonstrated that from Luke's perspective the community confirmed and acknowledged divine activity by taking decisive steps in response to its understanding of Scripture and its testimony of the Spirit's evidential work.[1] In Luke's narrative, the community has done this by addressing various crises and by affirming or rejecting the words or deeds of other characters.

Bringing It All Together:
Spirit–Community–Scripture

As we defined early in this project, theological creativity is the act of reformulating formerly held theological views in light of testimony regarding the Spirit's evidential work and an emerging understanding of applicable Scripture followed by commensurate action. The Spirit's evidential work is known only through the community's testimony. Therefore, theological

---

1. Since identifying the Spirit's work, or the Spirit's activity, is a subjective event we have referred to the Spirit's activity as testimony of the Spirit's evidential work. The Spirit's evidential work (evidence of the Spirit) in Acts is expressed through the testimony of the community of believers (e.g., Acts 1:26; 2:2–4, 14–16; 3:3–9, 12–16; 4:7–10, 24–25, 6:5–6; 7:55–56;) or revealed by the narrator (e.g., Acts 1:2; 2:5–11, 41; 4:7–8, 31; 5:11–16, 19–21; 6:7, 15; 8:18–24, 26, 39–40).

creativity is the outcome of the interpretive process since it is theology in action, functional in nature, and situationally pragmatic in scope. Consequently, it involves the process of theological justification and action or reaction considering current circumstances. In this sense, to be creative with theology is to take what is already a theological assumption and broaden or adapt it to current circumstances in light of the Spirit's evidential work and a consensus understanding of Scripture.

Having surveyed five instances in which the first-century believing community functions as a unified character in Luke's story,[2] the time has come to bring all the pieces together in order to establish our findings. Following this, we will bring this research and its findings into dialogue with the renewal views of Amos Yong, Kenneth Archer, and Simon Chan on the significance of the community in the hermeneutical process. In so doing, we will see that Luke's perspective provides a hermeneutical approach in which the community's role in the interpretative process does *not* overshadow Spirit or Scripture. To the contrary, we will see the community positioned cooperatively between Spirit and Scripture, like a bridge, so that both may interact with the community in theological creativity and aid in its course of action. In the following sections, we will review and summarize our findings concerning Luke's portrayal of the first-century community of believers engaging in theological creativity.

Chapter 1: Reestablishing the Twelve–Acts 1:15–26

Luke characterizes the community of Acts 1 as a dynamic group acting and reacting to its circumstance. He demonstrates the impetus for action by portraying the Eleven's expectation concerning the restoration of Israel (Luke 22:28–30; Acts 1:6) and by portraying Judas' purchase of property and gruesome death as a public scandal (Acts 1:18–19). Peter's use of Scripture validates their experiential need to replace Judas, and the selection of Matthias by casting lots brings it to a resolution. Even though the Spirit is not explicitly mentioned in this episode, as we demonstrated, Luke does connect the call of the Twelve to the work of the Spirit (1:2) and the Spirit's role is implied given the community's decision to cast lots for divine direction (1:24–26).

---

2. (1) Acts 1:12–26 in chapter 1, (2) 4:23–31 in chapter 2, (3) 6:1–7 in chapter 3, (4) 15:1–35 in chapter 4, and (5) 11:27–30 and 21:4, 8–14 in chapter 5.

We have argued that in Luke's narrative the first-century community of believers engages in theological creativity by linking their theological interpretation of a restored nation of Israel with Jesus' selection of twelve apostles (Luke 6:12–16; 22:28–30) and by drawing on an ancient custom from Scripture to identify the replacement for Judas (Acts 1:24–26). Luke's plot in Acts 1:15–26 begins and ends with resolving the Judas issue. The community responds to its circumstance by finding validation in Scripture. Furthermore, it utilizes a method for discerning the divine choice by using an ancient custom from Scripture, casting lots.

Chapter 2: Revealing Jesus as Servant and Son–Acts 4:23–31

In Acts 4:23–31, Luke presents the community as the only character in this episode. The community hears the report (4:23), raises its voice (4:24), corporately experiences the shaking of the building and the infilling the Holy Spirit (4:31), and feels emboldened to proclaim the word of God (4:31). In addition, Luke goes on to portray them with "one heart and soul" (4:32), sharing their possessions for the common good of all (4:32, 34–35), and witnessing the great power of God through the apostles' preaching (4:33).

We argued that the community engages in theological creativity in two ways. First, by identifying Jesus Messiah as Servant and Son in terms coterminous with King David. The community's understanding of Jesus as the Servant/Son is inextricably linked to its understanding of David as God's servant and son. Jesus is God's servant as David is God's servant. Jesus is God's son as David is God's son. Following the structure of Psalm 2, the community expresses the prophetic nature of its circumstance as well as its theological understanding of and identification with Jesus as Messiah.

Second, we saw the community in Acts 4 engaged in theological creativity by connecting their interpretation of God's sovereign protection of God's Servant Jesus with their own situation. The community now views their persecution and suffering in light of the sufferings and persecution of Jesus. Since Jesus suffered unjustly, so they too must suffer.

In the process of connecting the sufferings of Jesus with the sufferings of the community, Luke portrays the community's character in contrast to the community in Psalm 2. Rather than retribution against its enemies, the community seeks boldness to continue preaching and a manifestation of God's glory. The community experiences the witness of the Spirit, mentioned both in the preamble and in God's response to the prayer, and applies Scripture to its circumstance.

Chapter 3: Selecting the Seven–Acts 6:1–7

In our view, the crisis in Acts 6:1–7 is a community-wide social issue concerning the welfare of Hellenist widows in Jerusalem. In turn, the disciples work together as the "whole community" to devise a solution to assist all Hellenist widows living in Jerusalem. Luke portrays the implementation of a solution that successfully meets a societal woe of this magnitude in Jewish culture as a contributing factor for why many priests joined the community of disciples. In Luke's view, the care and concern for the weakest members of society touches a social nerve among the population of Jerusalem, resulting in exponential growth.

We argued that from Luke's perspective the disciples responded on theological grounds by first addressing a critical social need and then by ritually laying hands on those chosen for ministry, both of which are rooted in the characters' awareness of ancient stories found in Scripture. In this story, the disciples' theological need to care for widows is met by formulating a new level of leadership. Luke portrays their actions as both broadening their theological assumptions concerning the welfare of widows while narrowing the ministry focus of the Twelve.

Their ritual use of the laying on of hands as an act of transference demonstrates that Luke sees the community engaging in theological creativity. Their testimony of the Spirit's evidential work in the lives of the Seven ("full of faith and the Holy Spirit") and the continued numeric growth of the community provide indirect evidence of divine approval.

Chapter 4: Accepting the Gentiles–Acts 15:1–31

The encounter with the house of Cornelius (Acts 10–11) and the influx of Gentile converts in Antioch (11:20–21) culminate in a meeting of the apostles, elders, and "the whole assembly" (15:4–6, 12, 22). As Luke has it, the community's perception of its experience with Gentile converts is shaped, in no small part, by the prophetic vision Peter experiences while staying in the home of Simon the Tanner (10:1–23). Peter's vision and subsequent interaction with the house of Cornelius, along with James' prophetic interpretation of Amos 9:11–12, serve as evidence for the whole church that the missionary expansion to the Gentiles is a work of the Spirit. In Acts 15:1–31, the community of believers engage in theological creativity by combining testimony of the Spirit's evidential work with a reinterpretation of Scripture to shape its theological outlook concerning Gentile believers. In Luke's narrative, the way he depicts the whole church engaging the issue indicates an unconditional acceptance of equality between Jews and Gentiles while safeguarding the cultural sensibilities of Jewish Christians. Also, we demonstrated that Luke depicts the community engaged in theological creativity by determining that issues they once considered moral imperatives are now regard as cultural differences necessitating due consideration. In sum, the decision by the whole church gives rise to the ensuing plot and demonstrates how the church perceives itself in light of its testimony of the Spirit's evidential work and in light of an emerging understanding of Scripture.

Chapter 5: Discerning the Spirit–Acts 11:27–30; 13:1–4; 21:4, 10–14

Having used words like disciple and church to identify the community of believers, Luke now refers to the community on occasion as *we*, thus drawing the audience deeper into the story through first person narrative. Through prophetic encounters with Agabus (Acts 11:27–30; 21:10–14), prophets in Antioch (13:1–4), and even unnamed prophets among the churches in Greece, Asia Minor, Tyre, and Caesarea (20:23; 21:4–9), Luke describes for his audience how the prophetic affects theological creativity among the first-century community of believers depicted in his story. In so doing, Luke can portray the community engaging both the Spirit and what it believes to be divine communication.

In Acts 1–8, Luke describes the community accepting the prophetic when its manifestation is rooted in or associated with Scripture. However, as the geographic center of the disciples broadened from Jerusalem to the surrounding region, we detected a shift in Luke's depiction of the source and nature of prophecy. We demonstrated this by showing that for Luke the Spirit speaking through the community (Acts 9ff) functiones authoritatively in the absence of an applicable Scripture. As a result, we concluded that the line between prophetic words and Scripture, as a guiding source of authority in Luke's narrative, becomes blurred as the story progresses.

Within the plot, Luke portrays a community that possesses a high regard for prophets and prophetic experience. Moreover, we see that he characterizes the prophetic as something always prompting action from his characters, despite the unpredictable nature of its occurrence. For Luke, the first-century community of believers engage in theological creativity by accepting that the Spirit inspires prophetic utterances among its members. He then shows his audience that the community must evaluate or interpret those sayings to determine its validity as divine communication as well as to determine its course of action. When a consensus interpretation is determined and followed, the community remains engaged and support-ive. However, when its interpretation is unheeded, it relents and takes no further action.

Summary

In the passages selected for this study, Luke portrays the community engag-ing Spirit and Scripture in varying ways. Twice, the community engages Spirit and Scripture to determine its course of action (Acts 4:23–31; 15:1–31). On one occasion, the community engages Scripture without explicit mention of the Spirit (Acts 1:15–26). However, Luke does connect the call of the Twelve to the work of the Spirit (Luke 6:13; Acts 1:2) and the Spirit's role is implied given the community's decision to cast lots for divine direc-tion (1:24–26). For the remaining instances, the community reacts to the Spirit with Scripture implied or absent altogether.[3] In these latter episodes the prophetic functions as divine communication in place of Scripture.

What may we conclude from these findings? In our study, we find that Luke portrays the community deciding its course of action as if it is positioned *between* Spirit and Scripture, like a bridge, with testimony of the Spirit's evidential work on one side and a source of divine communication on the other. On some occasions, Luke depicts the community drawing on written Scripture.[4] However, when no direct correlation in Scripture seems relevant, he portrays the community (1) relying on prophetic utterance, which is then interpreted by the community,[5] or (2) drawing on ancient traditions described in Scripture (Acts 1:26; 6:6) to fill the gap created by an absence of applicable Scripture. Thus, we have argued that Luke pres-

3. See Acts 6:1–7; and 11:27–30; 13:1–4; 21:4, 10–14.

4. As in Acts 1:16, 20; 4:25–26; and 15:15–17.

5. As in Acts 11:27–30; 13:1–4; and 21:4, 10–14.

ents a harmonious and cooperative view of Spirit–Community–Scripture by positioning the community between Spirit and Scripture, not above or beneath, so that the community might discern its course of action. We will have more to say regarding this process following the next section.[6]

Engaging Contemporary Issues: Spirit–Community–Scripture

In the Introduction, we highlighted three Pentecostal scholars who have written substantially on the role of the community in the interpretive process. We will now engage their findings in light of our own.

Amos Yong

Yong offers a succinct theoretical outline of the philosophical complexities involved in a "triadic, trialectical, and trialogical" theological hermeneutic, what he refers to as Spirit–Word–Community.[7] In matters specific to the community, he promotes a view of the community of believers as a dynamic body existing within a culture and one existing within a wider society among other religions.[8] In its broadest sense, consequently, he argues that Christian community is much larger and as such rightly includes identification with the church through the ages as well as the "human community" at large.[9]

Existing within the larger society, the community, even in a Christian context, must always consider every other societal aspect that impinges on its identity.[10] Unfortunately, Yong does not provide a concrete example, let alone one from Scripture. Nevertheless, we see this aspect demonstrated in

---

6. See below under "Spirit–Community–Scripture in Lukan Perspective."

7. Yong, *Spirit–Word–Community*, 315. For comments specific to the Spirit's role, see pages 221–44; for Word, 245–74; for Community, 275–310. For a succinct assessment of Yong's trialectic configuration see Oliverio, *Theological Hermeneutics*, 240–47.

8. Yong, *Spirit–Word–Community*, 300–305.

9. Yong, *Spirit–Word–Community*, 17, 297.

10. Concerning aspects affecting nature and societal issues see Yong, *Spirit–Word–Community*, 297–303. Concerning engagement with global pluralism and gender relations, 305–10. According to Yong, such theological understanding is crucial for the development of a historic and contemporary Pentecostal ecclesiology (282–86, 297). See also Yong, *Spirit Poured Out*, 122–34.

Luke's portrayal of the community in Acts 1 when he indirectly introduces geopolitical concerns and a public scandal regarding Judas' demise as motivating factors in their theological creativity. We further see Luke's community of believers engaging the wider world in Acts 6:1–6, when it takes on the social issue of welfare for Hellenist widows in greater Jerusalem, as well as issues affecting ethnic diversity and integration in Acts 15:1–31, by distinguishing between matters of salvation (moral implications) and social engagement (ethical aspects). Our findings demonstrate that Luke's portrayal of the first-century community of believers engaging in theological creativity provides concrete biblical examples of Yong's call to consider the wider society in which we live.

Kenneth Archer

As we have already discussed, Archer maintains that the Pentecostal hermeneutical strategy suggested in his book involves a narrative approach "that embraces a 'tridactic' negotiation for meaning between the biblical text, the Holy Spirit, and the Pentecostal community."[11] He argues that his Pentecostal strategy will resist placing the community story over Scripture, and presumably over the Spirit, while maintaining that, "the primary filter for interpretation will be the Pentecostal narrative tradition."[12]

However, the manner in which Archer subsumes interpretive matters of Spirit and Scripture to the Pentecostal story makes it difficult to determine how the community could function cooperatively with the Spirit's evidential work in the church and world or negotiate an "underdeterminate" Scripture during socially changing times.[13] The process whereby the church or fellowship might reevaluate declining convictions (Archer's CNCs) in favor of new convictions or even how a new encounter with Spirit baptism, for example, might affect traditional convictions seems to be at worst an impossibility or at best a painful experience resulting in division.[14] Con-

11. Archer, *Pentecostal Hermeneutic*, 157.

12. Archer, *Pentecostal Hermeneutic*, 156. However, he claims this process is not "simply a linear process because Pentecostals *will* allow for the bilbical stories to challenge and reshape their tradition. Therefore, there is a dialogical and dialectical enncounter betwen the Bible and the Community" (italics added). Archer, *Pentecostal Hermeneutic*, 99. Unfortunately, he does not tell us how this could occur.

13. See Archer, *Pentecostal Hermeneutic*, 94–126, esp. 98–99, and our discussion in the Introduction, "Kenneth Archer."

14. For Archer, CNCs are "central narrative convictions." See Archer, *Pentecostal*

sequently, we find it difficult to see a cooperative "tridactic process" function of Spirit–Community–Scripture as Archer describes for the following reasons.[15]

First, as we have seen, he suggests that all written communication is "underdeterminate" and "needs" the reader to complete the communicative event.[16] However, at the same time, he maintains that this claim does not suggest that a text could possess unlimited meaning.[17] Although we can appreciate why he would want to maintain a hope for limiting possible meaning(s), how can he predict future situations in which the community might decide upon a meaning beyond a "Pentecostal narrative" tradition? Moreover, if the narrative tradition is the lens whereby Scripture is read, and if Scripture is underdeterminate, and if the Spirit's evidential work is discerned through Scripture then how can either the Spirit or Scripture continue to guide or expand the Pentecostal story? In other words, how can Spirit or Scripture "speak" beyond the Pentecostal narrative in its current form? For if the hermeneutical process is tied too closely to denominational origins, the interpreter runs the risk of subsuming both Spirit and Scripture to a past understanding of identity and neglect the current living community altogether. Our study of Acts 1:15–26, 4:23–31, and 15:1–31 demonstrated that the believing community's use of Scripture in Luke's story went well beyond the community's traditional or narrative "story" in ways that could not be anticipated.[18]

Second, Archer suggests that the application of suspicion and retrieval will serve to prevent rampant subjectivism.[19] Unfortunately, he does not articulate the vehicles for this suspicion and retrieval clearly. However, we see in Luke's portrayal of the community a biblical example for his claim

---

Hermeneutic, 114–18.

15. For an additional assessment with similar findings, see Oliverio, *Theological Hermeneutics*, 227–32, esp. 231.

16. Archer, *Pentecostal Hermeneutic*, 158–64, also 175.

17. Archer, *Pentecostal Hermeneutic*, 158–63.

18. In Acts 1, the community could not predict that Judas would defect, let alone purchase a field with the proceeds of his betrayal and then commit suicide. In Acts 4, there is no evidence to suggest the community's perception of Jesus as Messiah had been contemplated by previous interpretation of Psalm 2. In Acts 15, we demonstrated that the Jewish disciples in Jerusalem had envisioned the inclusion of Gentiles through a process of proselytization. But the outcome of their meeting in Acts 15 came to a new and different conclusion.

19. Archer, *Pentecostal Hermeneutic*, 158.

by finding that testimony of the Spirit's evidential work functioned as an effective "hermeneutic of retrieval" and diverse perspectives from leading members of the community ("full of the Holy Spirit and wisdom"), that is, a consensus of an interpretive body of believers, functioned as a "hermeneutic of suspicion." In Luke's story the community's view is, so to say, "adjusted," in light of the testimony of the ongoing activity of the Holy Spirit, what we have referred to as the Spirit's evidential work and adjudicated by a consensus interpretation among the body of believers.

Simon Chan

As introduced earlier, Chan ascribes to the Christian community a specific identity.[20] First, he indicates that the Christian community is one that identifies itself with ancient Israel and apostolic experience.[21] We have seen Luke depict the community as one connected to its roots in ancient Israel by drawing on Scripture to explain its experience. Moreover, he anchored the theological decisions of the church (e.g., to accept Gentiles into the fellowship of believers) in apostolic tradition by depicting an apostle and the Jerusalem church front and center in reaching Gentiles.

Second, he claims the community of believers must acknowledge itself as a people with a history of successes and failures.[22] As we noted in the introduction, Chan argues that a common conception of *Sola Scriptura* takes an "ahistorical view of the church supported by an ahistorical view of Scripture, cut off from tradition."[23] For him, this view dislodges the biblical text from any former living community forcing Scripture to function as a series of propositional truth claims that function independent of tradition. However, for Chan, without tradition a community of believers cannot understand its true identity."[24]

---

20. Since Chan's items 2 and 4 are similar in that address a historical recognition, we will link them together. Furthermore, we will link aspects 3 and 5, which address the peculiar nature of the community of believers as "divine humanity."

21. Chan, *Liturgical Theology*, 24. The church community does not replace ancient Israel or the apostolic community, rather it is adopted into the same family.

22. Chan, *Liturgical Theology*, 26, 32.

23. Chan, *Liturgical Theology*, 30.

24. Chan, *Liturgical Theology*, 30–31. For additional analysis of Chan's view of tradition see Oliverio, *Theological Hermeneutic*, 306–8.

We see the value of tradition in Luke's depiction of the community when he characterizes them with an expectation of a restored Israel and by taking Jesus' call for Twelve "to sit on thrones judging the Twelve tribes of Israel" (Lk 22:30; Acts 1:6, 26) in a literal sense.[25] We demonstrated the community's awareness of its history as a people who care for the disenfranchised (widows) and an awareness of its own successes and failures when the apostles accept the need for expanded leadership in Acts 6:1–6. Moreover, we argued that Luke portrays the community linking their identity and circumstance to Jesus through messianic prophecies in Psalm 2 (Acts 4:25–27), with ancient customs such as casting lots for Matthias and laying their hands on the Seven (1:26; 6:6), and by accepting the role of prophets in their daily experience. In Luke's story, the early community of believers see themselves to an eschatological community rooted in past tradition.

Finally, Chan describes the community as a peculiar people whose community ethos is defined by specific rituals and doctrines and defined as a "community of character."[26] Consequently, the community functions as Christ's bodily presence on earth, a divine humanity—as an "available something."[27] In so doing, Chan envisions the community as a Pneumatological construct called to embody the very presence of Christ to the world.[28] We see Chan's description of a "community of character" as an "available something" in Luke's portrayal of the first-century community (1) when they recognize the public effect its failures have had on the community at-large (Acts 1:18–19), (2) when they are resolved to endure persecution and call upon God for miracles and blessing rather than judgment for their persecutors (4:29–30), (3) when they care for the disenfranchised (Acts 6:1–6), and (4) when they work together to find a solution that mitigates division and is sensitive to ethnic diversity (15:11, 19, 28–29).[29] In light of our findings, we conclude that Luke's portrayal of the community engaging in theological creativity provides concrete examples of the kind of community Chan envisions.

---

25. Which we discussed in chapter 1 under "The Agenda of the Community of Believers" and "Scripture as an Explanation for Experience."

26. Chan, *Liturgical Theology*, 26, 27.

27. Chan, *Liturgical Theology*, 27–39, esp. 28.

28. Chan, *Liturgical Theology*, 37.

29. See Chan, *Liturgical Theology*, 28–31, 37. Chan maintains throughout his book that the church community is generally uncomfortable if not ignorant of this conception to which we agree and is particularly critical of evangelical hermeneutics on this point.

Summary and Analysis

In our view, Yong, Archer, and Chan have contributed significantly to the conversation concerning the community's role in the interpretive process. Yong's challenge for the church to envision itself in relationship to a wider society calls for more deliberate reflection on ecclesiological matters. Since Luke portrays the community engaging social issues in the community-at-large on numerous occasions, we may conclude that it was his intention for his audience to envision a community that understands what it means to be part of a historic people as well as its function in the community in which it lives. Consequently, we join with Yong in calling upon the Pentecostal community to reevaluate its self-conception and develop a more refined ecclesiology.

Archer draws attention to the fact that the present community's story plays a considerable role in the way it interprets Scripture. However, considering our findings concerning Luke's portrayal of the first-century community of believers engaged in theological creativity, we conclude that it is *testimony* of the Spirit's evidential work and not a "narrative tradition" that functions as the lens though which Scripture is interpreted.

Finally, Chan calls for the Christian community to see itself as a peculiar people distinguished by its commitment to the markers of faith and by its function in the world as the body of Christ, as "an available something." Unfortunately, his lofty challenge also lacks concrete description. As we have demonstrated, Luke portrays a community of believers committed to its traditions and one committed to being an available "something" to those in the community-at-large.

In the process of engaging these writers, we can see that Luke's portrayal of the first-century community of believers engaging in theological creativity is able to complement their work by illustrating the triadic notion of Spirit–Community–Scripture. As we will see in our final section, Luke's portrayal provides concrete examples of the community functioning as a bridge whereby Spirit and Scripture interact with and engage the community of believers.

Spirit–Community–Scripture in Lukan Perspective

As we noted in the Introduction, a triadic interpretive process involving a trialectical relationship between Spirit–Community–Scripture has been conceived in various ways and through a variety of models and seems to have achieved a measure of acceptance within the present discussion. By approaching Acts as a novel with characters and by analyzing the characters and their actions in the story, we may now show how Luke's portrayal of the believing community engaging in theological creativity demonstrates a harmonious, cooperative, and balanced view of the community's role in an interpretive process involving Spirit-Community-Scripture.

We have argued that the audience is able to imagine the community engaged in the process of theological creativity while demonstrating that the community in Luke's narrative is an identifiable group of believers. For Luke, the community is not a single group of believers but various groups of believers who are active and indispensable characters in the narrative and who share a commitment to the apostles' message concerning Jesus Messiah and to each other. We demonstrated this process in our analysis of Acts 1:12–26, 4:23–31, 6:1–7, 15:1–35, and 11:27–30, 13:1–4, and 21:4, 8–14.

Set within this Lukan perspective, we find that the community is positioned neither above nor below Spirit or Scripture in the hermeneutical or interpretive process, as if one or both directed its actions. Rather, we maintain that Luke's portrayal of the community, so to say, "negotiates" between its testimony of the Spirit's evidential work and its understanding of Scripture in order to determine its course of action.[30] Our research shows that for Luke the community of believers is positioned (stands) between Spirit and Scripture, like a bridge, so that (1) the community may interact with either one as it engages in theological creativity and so that (2) both Spirit and Scripture may influence its course of action.

Given these observations, we propose a reworking of the hermeneutical spiral as a visual metaphor to describe the interpretive process.[31] A

30. Or, we may even say that the community adjudicates both Spirit and Scripture. The calling of the Twelve in Luke 6:12–16, their commissioning in 9:1–6, along with the revelation of an eschatological function in 22:28–30 provides the apostles with a sense of who they are and what they are called to do. However, as the story of Acts proceeds, we have shown that the community (apostles, communities of believers, etc.) develops their understanding of "who they are" and "what they are called to do" in a practical manner through their testimony of the Spirit's evidential work and their understanding of Scripture.

31. A spiral is one image often used to describe the hermeneutical process with each aspect (Spirit–Community–Scripture) appearing on the spiral at various points along the interpretive path. See Osborne, *Hermeneutical Spiral*, 22–23. Despite Osborne's warning to view the spiral as "a cone, not twirling upward forever with no end in sight but moving

model based on Luke's view of the first-century community of believers engaging in theological creativity better accounts for the way in which Spirit and Scripture interact with each other through the believing community. In our findings, Spirit does not interact with Scripture except through the community's experience (corporately or individually). Conversely, Scripture, as a written text or oral tradition, does not interact with the Spirit except through the community's act of hearing, reading, or proclaiming (corporately or individually).

By faith we claim that the Spirit illumines Scripture and that Scripture reveals the Spirit's work. Yet, we also claim, demonstrated through Luke's story, that both events are actualized through the community only. To be clear, we *believe* that the Spirit of God is active in the world and in the life of the believer and that Scripture is the divine Word of God. However, we maintain that until one or both intersect with the community's experience the community is unable to understand or process it in practical terms. Thus, both Spirit and Scripture must enter the experience of the community on some level if either is to assist or influence the community in theological creativity.

As illustrated in the infinity-shaped model (below), we see that the community stands as the connection point, the hub, between the Spirit's activity and Scripture's inspiration. In an ongoing fashion, the work of the Spirit illuminates or inspires the community while the community interprets and appropriates Scripture. Moreover, we see that Scripture informs or engages the community while the community seeks divine guidance from the Spirit.

---

ever narrower to the meaning of the text and its significance today" (22), in practical terms, the nature of a spiral as a visual image necessarily requires a start and an end or a start with no end, which we feel causes hermeneutical confusion. In light of this concern, I propose two models that may (1) serve to represent the manner in which the hermeneutical process works and (2) demonstrate how the community functions cooperatively with both Spirit and Scripture, using Luke's view of the community in theological creativity as evidence.

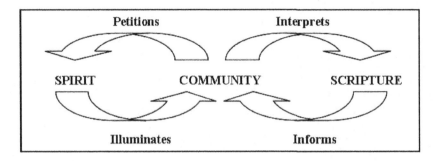

Alternatively, if this model were constructed as a circle with Scripture on one side and the Spirit on the other, we find the community at two points on the circle—at the top and on the bottom.

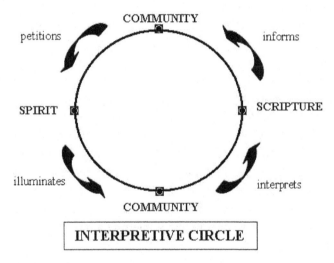

INTERPRETIVE CIRCLE

Thus, Scripture informs the community while the Spirit illuminates the community, facilitating interpretation. We might well regard this as a *balanced* circle because the community is responding to Scripture and Spirit while at the same time engaging both in a communicative process. Both models demonstrate Luke's view of the community in theological creativity.

For example, in Acts 1:15–26, we saw how Luke portrayed the community interpreting Scripture to justify the replacement of Judas as one of the Twelve. After selecting two candidates, the community prayed for the will of God to be revealed through the activity of casting lots. The lot "fell on" Matthias, which in the story functioned as a sign of divine approval, and he joined the Twelve.

In Acts 4:23–31, Luke depicted the community praying to the sovereign Lord who spoke through David via the Spirit. Scripture provided an explanation for both Jesus' persecution and their own persecution. In the narrative, the community's interpretation of Scripture led it to seek an outpouring of divine blessing and boldness to continue preaching rather than to seek retribution on its enemies. Luke characterized the witness of the Spirit as both physical (the place was shaken) and materially consequential (they spoke with boldness, accompanied by miracles).

In Acts 6:1–7, the community selected Seven from among their ranks who were known for being full of faith, the Spirit, and wisdom. From the way Luke sets up his narrative, we concluded that his unified character, the whole community, would have been aware of the Scriptural mandate concerning the care of widows. Moreover, we maintained that they would have also been aware of the commissioning of the Levites for ancient Israel when they decided to "lay hands" on the Seven as an act of transference.

In Acts 15:1–31, Luke portrays the community adjudicating both testimony of the Spirit's evidential work among the Gentiles alongside a reinterpretation of Scripture to conclude that Gentile converts need not follow the customs of Moses to be saved. In this episode, he depicts the Spirit revealing and Scripture confirming their perception of the divine will.

Finally, in the prophetic encounters,[32] the story reveals the Spirit speaking through the community in prophetic utterance, who in turn prayed for interpretation so that they might determine a proper course of action. In each episode prophets spoke, the community prayed, and the community acted upon its consensual interpretation.

What Does This All Mean for Us?

Not only do we see a community adjudicating between its testimony of the Spirit's evidential work and its understanding of Scripture, we also find that they do both with a clear understanding of "who they are" and "what they are called to do." The community in Luke's narrative understands that it possesses an apostolic calling as witnesses for Jesus endowed with a sense of mission to the community-at-large.[33] Consequently, we agree with Yong,

32. Acts 11:27–30; 13:1–4; and 21:4, 8–14.

33. For examples of "who it is" in Luke's portrayal see Luke 6:13; 9:1–2; 10:1; 22:28–30;

Archer, and Chan that if the community is to fulfill its function in the inter-pretive process of Spirit–Community–Scripture, it must understand who it is and why it exists. The call for the Pentecostal community to reflect more seriously upon its ecclesiology seems to be more pressing now than ever if it is to understand its role in the interpretive process.

Perhaps a good starting point for ecclesiological reflection might in-clude, for example, exploring a Lukan view of Scripture as testimony of the community's historic tradition. Even in situations far removed from its original context, the canon of Scripture embodies the testimony of its beginnings and of its founders, which is, after all, the heritage of the church. This testimony is both fixed in time and objective in so far as it is revered as divine Scripture. But, as we have shown in Luke's view of the community in theological creativity, how it is interpreted and applied is left to the living community of believers.

Since Scripture embodies the testimony of the founders (stories of the patriarchs, prophets, and apostolic witness), we suggest that the point of contention concerning the relationship of the community to Scripture stems from a misconception of the *nature* of Scripture—that is, its prac-tical function. Issues of infallibility and inerrancy ultimately weaken the power of Scripture by fixing its meaning in the past. Furthermore, issues of individuality, relativism, and contextualization likewise complicate the interpretive process by failing to recognize Scripture as part of the historic community's tradition. Even if applied to new contexts, the canon of Scrip-ture still embodies the testimony of its beginnings and of its founders. As we have already stated, Scripture embodies the heritage of the church.

Again, Scripture's heritage—that is, the testimony of the founders—is a fixed and objective event. But, as we have shown in Luke's view of the community in theological creativity, how it is interpreted is left to the com-munity of believers. Throughout time, as new communities emerge, former (now past) communities join the tradition of the saints and add their voice to the historic church. New applications and understandings of Scripture emerge with each generation as the Spirit continually inspires and informs the community of believers. By faith we believe the Spirit abides over this process as the bond of love.

24:47–49; Acts 1:2, 8, 21–22; 2:14–16; 4:19–20, 29; 5:20–21, 32; 6:2; 8:4, 25, 26, 29, 40; 9:20; 10:20, 33; 11:13, 19–22; 13:2, 4–5. For examples of "what it is called to do" in Luke's portrayal see Luke 9:1–2; Acts 2:41–42, 44–47; 3:6; 4:32–37; 5:12–16; 6:1–6; 8:6–7, 38; 9:10–17, 34, 40; 10:47–48; 11:25–26, 29–30.

Finally, another area of ecclesiological reflection that may benefit from a Lukan perspective of community would be in a reconsideration of why the church exists. Only as the believing community recognizes itself as an "available something" to those outside the church, can it read Scripture in an ever-changing world continually energized by the power and life of the Spirit. Only then may we demonstrate that we are a part of a community of believers who knows "who it is" and "what it is called to do."

We maintain such an exploration would be consistent with a *twentieth*-century "Pentecostal story" that must now engage the many complex issues of the twenty-*first* century. For even E. N. Bell stated, "We must keep our skylights open so as not to reject any new light God may throw upon the old Word. We must not fail to keep pace in life or teaching with light from heaven."[34] As the church continues to engage the world in which it lives, we may expect that new applications and understandings of Scripture will continue to emerge as the Spirit continually inspires and informs the community of believers. Not only that, but we should expect for the Spirit to continually bring the community into closer contact with the concerns of a wider society. If we embrace this challenge, we believe the community of believers, the Church, will be able to remain consistent with its historic past and relevant to the world whenever both its testimony of the Spirit's evidential work and its understanding of Scripture require it to change.

34. E. N. Bell and J. R. Flower, "In Doctrines," *The Christian Evangel*, 1 August 1914, 2. Also quoted in Blumhofer, *Assemblies of God*, 1:209. Bell was the first general superintendent of the Assemblies of God, USA.

APPENDIX

THINKING FORWARD
IN RENEWAL HERMENEUTICS

IN THE INTRODUCTION TO this research, we asked if Luke's portrayal of the function of community in theological creativity could offer an acceptable solution to the concern of community overshadowing Spirit or Scripture in the hermeneutical process of interpretation. In our view our findings do offer an acceptable solution. However, our conclusions may prompt new discussions and debates in other areas of interest in renewal studies.[1] In the context of this research, the term renewal refers to Pentecostal and Charismatic traditions that emphasize the work of the Holy Spirit within creation in general and in the life of the Christian community in particular.

For example, does Luke's Gospel foreshadow the notion of theological creativity in the life and ministry of Jesus, as one adjudicating Spirit and Scripture, in the same manner as the community of believers in Acts? In other words, does Jesus engage in theological creativity in Luke's Gospel? Or, in light of our discussion in chapter one concerning the importance of the Twelve to Jesus and their declining importance in Acts, what events in Luke's gospel may have precipitated such a radical change and lead to Jesus to "retask" his closest followers (Acts 1:4–8)? For example, does Luke's depiction of Jesus's rejection and crucifixion or his resurrection necessitate this change in emphasis? Or, does Luke offer any hint or explanation in his gospel for this abrupt change?

1. In the context of this research, the term *renewal* refers to Pentecostal and Charismatic traditions that emphasize the work of the Holy Spirit within creation in general and in the life of the Christian community in particular.

Other points of discussion and debate might include: (1) In chapter 2, we focused attention on similarities between Jesus Messiah and King David as Servant and Son of God. How does Luke's portrayal of the Jerusalem community's view of Jesus in the first century CE compare and contrast with an orthodox Trinitarian view that emerged during the third and fourth centuries? Specifically, do the events leading up to and following the Nicene Council and Creed represent the community's engagement in theological creativity in a manner similar to Luke's portrayal in Acts 4? (2) In chapter 4, we addressed Luke's portrayal of divergent communities of believers meeting to resolve the most difficult issue of its day. What are the implications of our findings on contemporary issues facing the church today? For example, how might diverse communities of believers join together to address issues facing many churches today such as:

1. Ongoing conflicts concerning matters of inclusiveness,

2. Recognizing and implementing accommodations that promote or foster fellowship between diverse cultural traditions once considered incompatible,

3. Advancing the ever-expanding role of women and minorities in upper-level ministerial leadership in order to meet pressing societal needs and,

4. Difficult and complex issues concerning socio-economic disparity, gender inequality, and human sexuality.

In each of these extended areas of discussion and debate, at least at this juncture, we are not prepared to offer any conclusions. More research is needed. It is our hope that this study might prove helpful in such endeavors, particularly on elevating the importance of the community (not just its leaders) in discerning the work of the Spirit in the world today while experiencing an ever-emerging understanding of Scripture.

BIBLIOGRAPHY

All biblical citations are from the NRSV unless otherwise noted. The Greek text follows Nestle-Aland, 28th edition, unless otherwise noted.

Abrams, Meyer H. *A Glossary of Literary Terms*. 9th ed. Boston: Wadsworth Cengage Learning, 2009.

Agnew, Francis H. "The Origin of the NT Apostle-Concept: A Review of Recent Research." *JBL* 105 (1986) 75–96.

Aichele, George, ed. *The Postmodern Bible: The Bible and Culture Collective*. New Haven, CT: Yale University Press, 1995.

Alter, Robert. *The Art of Biblical Narrative*. New York: Basic Books, 1981.

Archer, Kenneth J. *A Pentecostal Hermeneutic for the Twenty-First Century: Spirit, Scripture and Community*. New York: T. & T. Clark, 2004.

———. "Pentecostal Story: The Hermeneutical Filter for the Making of Meaning." *Pneuma* 26 (2004) 36–59.

———. "A Pentecostal Way of Doing Theology." *IJST* 9.3 (2007) 301–14.

Arnold, Bill T. "Luke's Characterizing Use of the Old Testament in the Book of Acts." In *History, Literature, and Society in the Book of Acts*, edited by Ben Witherington, 300–323. Cambridge: Cambridge University Press, 1996.

Arrington, French L. "The Use of the Bible by Pentecostals." *Pneuma* 16 (1994) 101–7.

Audet, Jean Paul. La Didachè: *Instructions des apôtres, Études Bibliques 43*. Paris: Gabalda, 1958.

Baker, Robert O. "Pentecostal Bible Reading: Toward a Model of Reading for the Formation of Christian Affections." *JPT* 7 (1995) 34–48.

Barrett, C. K. *A Critical and Exegetical Commentary on the Acts of the Apostles: Preliminary Introduction and Commentary on Acts I–XIV*. Edinburgh: T. & T. Clark, 1994.

Barthes, Roland. *The Semiotic Challenge*. Translated by Richard Howard. Oxford: Blackwell, 1988.

Barthes, Roland, Richard Miller, Richard Howard, and Honoré de Balzac. *S/Z*. Translated by Richard Miller. New York: Hill & Wang, 1974.

Bates, Matthew W. "Cryptic Codes and a Violent King: A New Proposal for Matthew 11:12 and Luke 16:16–18." *CBQ* 75 (2013) 74–93.

Bauckham, Richard. *The Book of Acts and Its Palestinian Setting*. Grand Rapids: Eerdmans, 1995.

———. "James and the Jerusalem Church." In *The Book of Acts and Its Palestinian Setting*, edited by Richard Bauckham, 415–80. Grand Rapids: Eerdmans, 1995.

———. "Kerygmatic Summaries in the Speeches of Acts." In *History, Literature, and Society in the Book of Acts*, edited by Ben Witherington, 185–217. Cambridge: Cambridge University Press, 1996.

Baur, Ferdinand C. "Die Christuspartei in der korinthischen Gemeinde, der Gegensatz des petrinishcen und paulinishen Christenthums in der ältesten Kirche, der Apostle Petrus in Rom." *TZT* 4 (1831) 61–206.

Beardslee, William A. "The Casting of Lots at Qumran and in the Book of Acts." *NovT* 4 (1960) 245–52.

Bennema, Cornelis. "The Ethnic Conflict in Early Christianity: An Appraisal of Bauckham's Proposal on the Antioch Crisis and the Jerusalem Council." *JSNT* 56 (2013) 753–63.

Benoit, Pierre. *Exégèse et théologie III*. Paris: Éditions du Cerf, 1968.

Bird, Michael F., and Jason Maston, editors. *Earliest Christian History: History, Literature, and Theology: Essays from the Tyndale Fellowship in Honor of Martin Hengel*. Tübingen: Mohr Siebeck, 2012.

Black, Matthew, and H. H. Rowley, editors. *An Aramaic Approach to the Gospels and Acts: With an appendix on the Son of Man, by Geza Vermes*. 3rd ed. Oxford: Clarendon, 1967.

Blumhofer, Edith L. *The Assemblies of God: A Chapter in the Story of American Pentecostalism*. Vol. 1. Springfield, MO: GPH, 1989.

Bockmuehl, Markus. *Jewish Law in Gentile Churches: Halakhah and the Beginning of Christian Public Ethics*. Edinburgh: T. & T. Clark, 2000.

Bovon, Francois. *Luke the Theologian: Fifty-Five Years of Research (1950–2005)*. 2nd ed. Waco, TX: Baylor University Press, 2006.

Brawley, Robert L. *Centering on God: Method and Message in Luke-Acts*. LCBI. Louisville: Westminster John Knox, 1990.

Brehm, H. Alan. "The Meaning of Ἑλληνιστής in Acts in Light of a Diachronic Analysis of ἑλληνίζειν." In *Discourse Analysis and Other Topics in Biblical Greek*, edited by Stanley E. Porter and D. A. Carson, 180–99. JSNTSup 113. Sheffield: Sheffield Academic, 1995.

———. "The Role of the 'Hellenists' in Christian Origins: A Critique of Representative Models in Light of an Exegetical Study of Acts 6–8." PhD diss., Southwestern Baptist Theological Seminary, 1992.

Brooke, George J. "Qumran Pesher: Towards the Redefinition of a Genre." *RevQ* 10.40 (1981) 483–503.

Brown, Jeff. *Corporate Decision-Making in the Church of the New Testament*. Eugene, OR: Pickwick, 2013.

Bruce, F. F. *The Acts of the Apostles: The Greek Text with Introduction and Commentary*, 3rd ed. Grand Rapids: Eerdmans, 1990.

Burgess, Stanley M., and Eduard M. Van Der Maas, eds. *The New International Dictionary of Pentecostal and Charismatic Movements*. Rev. and exp. ed. Grand Rapids: Zondervan, 2002.

Cadbury, Henry J. "The Hellenists." In *The Beginnings of Christianity*, part 1, *The Acts of the Apostles*, edited by Frederick J. Foakes Jackson and Kirsopp Lake, 5:59–73. Grand Rapids: Baker, 1979.

———. *The Making of Luke-Acts*. London: SPCK, 1927.

———. "Names for Christians and Christianity in Acts." In *The Beginnings of Christianity*, part 1, *The Acts of the Apostles*, edited by Frederick J. Foakes Jackson and Kirsopp Lake, 5:375–92. Grand Rapids: Baker, 1979.

———. "The Titles of Jesus in Acts." Pages in *The Beginnings of Christianity*, part 1, *The Acts of the Apostles*, edited by Fredrick J. Foakes Jackson and Kirsopp Lake, 5:364–70. Grand Rapids: Baker, 1979.

Campenhausen, Hans von, and Henry Chadwick. *Jerusalem and Rome: The Problem of Authority in the Early Church*. Philadelphia: Fortress, 1966.

Cargal, Timothy B. "Beyond the Fundamentalist-Modernist Controversy: Pentecostals and Hermeneutics in a Postmodern Age." *Pneuma* 15.2 (1993) 163–87.

Carpenter, Levy L. *Primitive Christian Application of the Doctrine of the Servant: With Special Reference to Isaiah 49–55*. Durham, NC: Duke University Press, 1929.

Chan, Simon. *Liturgical Theology: The Church as Worshiping Community*. Downers Grove, IL: InterVarsity, 2006.

Chatman, Seymour. *Story and Discourse: Narrative Structure in Function and Film*. Ithaca, NY: Cornel University Press, 1978.

Clarke, William Kemp Lowther. "The Use of the Septuagint in Acts." In *The Beginnings of Christianity*, part 1, *The Acts of the Apostles*, edited by Frederick J. Foakes Jackson and Kirsopp Lake, 2:66–105. Grand Rapids: Baker, 1979.

Conzelmann, Hans. *Acts of the Apostles: A Commentary on the Acts of the Apostles*. Translated by James Limburg, A. Thomas Kraabel, and Donald H. Juel. Edited by Eldon Jay Epp and Christopher R. Matthews. Philadelphia: Fortress, 1987.

———. *The Theology of St. Luke*. Translated by G. Buswell. New York: Harper & Row, 1961.

Corrington, Robert S. *The Community of Interpreters: On the Hermeneutics of Nature and the Bible in the American Philosophical Tradition*. StABH 3. Macon, GA: Mercer University Press, 1987.

Cousland, J. R. C. *The Crowds in the Gospel of Matthew*. Leiden: Brill, 2002.

Cross, Terry L. "A Proposal to Break the Ice: What Can Pentecostal Theology Offer Evangelical Theology?" *JPT* 10.2 (2002) 44–73.

Crossan, John Dominic. *Who Killed Jesus?: Exposing the Roots of Anti-Semitism in the Gospel Story of the Death of Jesus*. San Francisco: Harper, 1995.

Cullmann, Oscar. "The Significance of the Qumran Texts for Research into the Beginnings of Christianity." *JBL* 74 (1955) 213–26.

Culpepper, R. Alan. *Anatomy of the Fourth Gospel: A Study in Literary Design*. Philadelphia: Fortress, 1987.

Culy, Martin M., and Mikeal C. Parsons. *Acts: A Handbook on the Greek Text*. Waco, TX: Baylor University Press, 2003.

Danker, Frederick W., William Bauer, William F. Arndt, and F. Wilbur Gingrich. *Greek-English Lexicon of the New Testament and Other Early Christian Literature*. 3rd ed., rev. and ed. by Frederick W. Danker. Chicago: University of Chicago Press, 2000.

Darr, John. *Herod the Fox: Audience Criticism and the Lukan Characterization*. JSNTSup 163. Sheffield: Sheffield Academic, 1998.

———. *On Character Building: The Reader and the Rhetoric of Characterization in Luke-Acts*. LCBI. Louisville: Westminster John Knox, 1992.

Davies, W. D. *Paul and Rabbinic Judaism: Some Rabbinic Elements in Pauline Theology*. 4th ed. Philadelphia: Fortress, 1980.

Dayton, Donald, and Robert K. Johnston, editors. *The Variety of American Evangelicalism.* Downers Grove, IL: InterVarsity, 1993.

Denova, Rebecca I. *The Things Accomplished among Us: Prophetic Tradition in the Structural Pattern of Luke-Acts.* Sheffield: Sheffield Academic, 1997.

Dibelius, Martin. "The Conversion of Cornelius." In *Studies in the Acts of the Apostles,* edited by H. Greeven, 109–22. London: SCM, 1956.

Dibelius, Martin, and K. C. Hanson. *The Book of Acts: Form, Style, and Theology.* Minneapolis: Fortress, 2004.

Dollar, Harold. "The Conversion of the Messenger." *Missiology* 21 (Jan 1993) 13–19.

Dowd, Michael B. "Contours of a Narrative Pentecostal Theology and Practice." In *The Distinctiveness of Pentecostal-Charismatic Theology.* Society for Pentecostal Studies Papers, 1985, E1–E40.

Dunn, James D. G. *The Acts of the Apostles.* NC. Valley Forge, PA: Trinity, 1996.

————. *Beginning from Jerusalem.* Vol. 1 of *Christianity in the Making.* Grand Rapids: Eerdmans, 2009.

————. *Jesus and the Spirit: A Study of the Religious and Charismatic Experience of Jesus and the First Christians as Reflected in the New Testament.* Grand Rapids: Eerdmans, 1997.

————. *The Theology of Paul's Letter to the Galatians.* Cambridge: Cambridge University Press, 1993.

Ellington, Scott A. "History, Story, and Testimony: Locating Truth in a Pentecostal Hermeneutic." *Pneuma* 23 (2001) 245–63.

Elliot-Binns, Leonard E. *Galilean Christianity.* London: SCM, 1956.

Ellis, Ian M. "Codex Bezae at Acts 15." *IBS* 2 (1980) 134–40.

Epp, Eldon Jay. *The Theological Tendency of Code Bezae Cantabrigiensis in Acts.* SNTSMS 3. Cambridge: Cambridge University Press, 1966.

Ervin, Howard M. "Hermeneutics: A Pentecostal Option." In *Essays on Apostolic Themes: Studies in Honor of Howard M. Ervin,* edited by Paul Elbert, 23–35. Peabody, MA: Hendrickson, 1985.

Evans, , Craig A., and Stanley E. Porter, editors. *Dictionary of New Testament Background.* Downers Grove, IL: InterVarsity, 2000.

Fee, Gordon D. "Hermeneutics and Historical Precedent: A Major Problem in Pentecostal Hermeneutics." In *Perspectives on the New Pentecostalism,* edited by Russell P. Spittler, 118–32. Grand Rapids, Baker, 1976.

Fish, Stanley. *Is There a Text in This Class?: The Authority of Interpretive Communities.* Cambridge: Harvard University Press, 1980.

Fitzmyer, Joseph A. "The Aramaic and Hebrew Fragments of Tobit from Qumran Cave 4." *CBQ* 57 (1995) 655–75.

————. "David, 'Being Therefore a Prophet . . .'" *CBQ* 34 (1972) 332–39.

————. *The Gospel According to Luke I–IX: A New Translation with Introduction and Commentary.* AB 28. New York: Doubleday, 1981.

————. "Jewish Christianity in Acts in Light of the Qumran Scrolls." In *Studies in Luke-Acts: Essays Presented in Honor of Paul Schubert,* edited by Leander E. Keck and James L. Martyn, 233–57. Nashville: Abingdon, 1966.

————. *Luke the Theologian: Aspects of His Teaching.* New York: Paulist, 1989.

Frei, Hans W. *The Eclipse of Biblical Narrative: A Study in Eighteenth and Nineteenth Century Hermeneutics.* New Haven, CT: Yale University Press, 1974.

————. *The Identity of Jesus Christ: The Hermeneutical Basis of Dogmatic Theology.* Eugene, OR: Wipf & Stock, 1997.

————. "The 'Literal Reading' of Biblical Narrative in the Christian Tradition: Does It Stretch or Will It Break?" In *The Bible and the Narrative Tradition*, edited by Frank McConnnell, 36–77. New York: Oxford University Press, 1986.

Foakes Jackson, Frederick J. *The Acts of the Apostles.* MNTC. London: Hodder & Stoughton, 1931.

Fornara, Charles W. *The Nature of History in Ancient Greece and Rome.* Berkeley: University of California Press, 1983.

Frye, Northrup. *The Harper Handbook to Literature.* New York: Harper & Row, 1985.

Funk, Robert W, and Jesus Seminar. *The Acts of Jesus: The Search for the Authentic Deeds of Jesus.* 1st ed. San Francisco: HarperSanFrancisco, 1998.

Gallagher, Robert L. "From 'Doingness' to 'Beingness': A Missiological Interpretation." In *Mission in Acts: Ancient Narratives in Contemporary Context*, edited by Robert L. Gallagher and Paul Hertig, 45–58. Maryknoll: Orbis, 2004.

Gapp, K. S. "Notes: The Universal Famine under Claudius." *HTR* 28 (1935) 258–65.

Garrett, James Leo, Jr. "The Congregation-Led Church." In *Perspectives on Church Government*, edited by Chad Owen Brand and R. Stanton Norman, 157–208. Nashville: Broadman & Holman, 2004.

Garvey, James. "Characterization in Narrative." *Poetics* 7 (1978) 63–78.

Gaventa, Beverly R. *The Acts of the Apostles.* Nashville: Abingdon, 2003.

————. "To Speak Thy Word with all Boldness." *Faith and Mission* 3 (1986) 76–82.

Goldblatt, David. "Agrippa I and Palestinian Judaism in the First Century." *JH* 2 (1987) 7–32.

Goldingay, John. *Models for Interpretation of Scripture.* Grand Rapids: Eerdmans, 1995.

Gowler, David B. *Host, Guest, Enemy and Friend: Portraits of the Pharisees in Luke and Acts.* Emory Studies in Early Christianity 2. New York: Peter Lang, 1991.

Grabbe, Lester L. *An Introduction to Second Temple Judaism: History and Religion of the Jews in the Time of Nehemiah, the Maccabees, Hillel and Jesus.* New York: T. & T. Clark, 2010.

Hamm, Dennis. "Acts 4:23–31—A Neglected Biblical Paradigm of Christian Worship (Especially in Troubled Times)." *Worship* 77 (2003) 225–37.

Haenchen, Ernst. *The Acts of the Apostles: A Commentary.* Translated by Bernard Nobel, Gerald Shinn, and Robert McL. Wilson. Philadelphia: Westminster, 1971.

Hann, Robert R. "Judaism and Jewish Christianity in Antioch: Charisma and Conflict in the First Century." *JRH* 14 (1987) 341–60.

Hanson, R. P. C. *The Acts in the Revised Standard Version, with Introduction and Commentary.* Oxford: Clarendon, 1967.

Harnack, Adolf von. "Die Bezechnung Jesu als 'Knecht Gottes' und ihre Geschichte in der alten Kirchen." In *Sitzungsberichte der Bayerischen Akademie der Wissenschaften: Philosophisch-Philologische und Historische Klasse* (1926), 212–38. Berlin, 1926.

Harper, Michael. *A New Way of Living: How the Church of the Redeemer, Houston, Found a New Life-Style.* Plainfield, NJ: Logos, 1973.

Harvey, William J. *Character and the Novel.* Ithaca, NY: Cornell University Press, 1965.

Hengel, Martin. *Acts and the History of Earliest Christianity.* Translated by John Bowden. Eugene, OR: Wipf & Stock, 2003.

————. *Between Jesus and Paul: Studies in the Earliest History of Christianity.* Translated by John Bowden. London: SCM, 1979.

————. *Judaism and Hellenism: Studies in Their Encounter in Palestine during the Early Hellenistic Period.* Translated by John Bowden. 2nd ed. London: SCM, 1981.

Hemer, Colin J. *The Book of Acts in the Setting of Hellenistic History.* WUNT 49, edited by Conrad H. Gempf. Tübingen: Mohr Siebeck, 1989.

Hengel, Martin, and Anna Maria Schwemer. *Paul between Damascus and Antioch: The Unknown Years.* Translated by John Bowden. Louisville: Westminster John Knox, 1997.

Hesselgrave, David J., and Edward Rommen. *Contextualization: Meanings, Methods, and Models.* Pasadena: William Carey Library, 2000.

Hey, Sam. "Changing Roles of Pentecostal Hermeneutics." *ERT* 25 (2001) 210–18.

Hiebert, Paula S. "When Shall Help Come to Me?: The Biblical Widow." In *Gender and Difference in Ancient Israel,* edited by Peggy L. Day, 125–41. Minneapolis: Fortress, 1989.

Hill, Craig C. "Acts 6:1–8:4: Division or Diversity." In *History, Literature, and Society in the Book of Acts,* edited by Ben Witherington, 129–53. Cambridge: Cambridge University Press, 1996.

————. *Hellenist and Hebrews: Reappraising Division within the Earliest Church.* Minneapolis: Fortress, 1992.

Hinze, Bradford E., and D. Lyle Dabney, editors. *Advents of the Spirit: An Introduction to the Current Study of Pneumatology.* Milwaukee: Marquette University Press, 2001.

Hochman, Baruch. *Character in Literature.* Ithaca: Cornell University Press, 1985.

Iser, Wolfgang. *The Act of Reading: A Theory of Aesthetic Response.* Baltimore: John Hopkins University Press, 1978.

————. *The Implied Reader: Patterns of Communication in Prose Fiction from Bunyan to Beckett.* Baltimore: John Hopkins University Press, 1978.

Israel, Richard D., Daniel E. Albrecht, and Randal G. McNally. "Pentecostals and Hermeneutics: Texts, Rituals and Community." *Pneuma* 15 (1993) 137–61.

Jeremias, Joachim. *Jerusalem in the Time of Jesus.* Translated by F. H. and C. H. Cave. London: SCM, 1969.

————. *New Testament Theology: The Proclamation of Jesus.* Translated by John Bowden. London: SCM, 1971.

Jervell, Jacob. *Die Apostelgeschichte.* 17th ed. KEK 3. Göttingen: Vandenhoeck & Ruprecht, 1998.

————. *The Unknown Paul: Essays on Luke-Acts and Early Christian History.* Minneapolis: Augsburg, 1984.

Johns, Jackie D. "Pentecostals and the Postmodern Worldview." *JPT* 7 (1995): 13–96.

Johnson, Luke Timothy. *The Acts of the Apostles,* SP 5. Collegeville: Liturgical, 1992.

————. *Scripture and Discernment: Decision-Making in the Church.* Nashville: Abingdon, 1996.

Johnston, Robert K. "American Evangelicalism: An Extended Family." In *The Variety of American Evangelicalism,* edited by Donald Dayton and Robert K. Johnston, 252–72. Downers Grove, IL: InterVarsity, 1993.

Kahle, Paul. *The Cairo Geniza. The Schweich Lectures for 1941.* London: Oxford, 1947.

Kaiser, Walter C., Jr. "The Promise to David in Psalm 16 and Its Application in Acts 2:23–33 and 13:32–37." *JETS* 23 (1960) 219–229.

Kärkkäinen, Velli-Matti, ed. *The Spirit in the World: Emerging Pentecostal Theologies in Global Contexts.* Grand Rapids: Eerdmans, 2009.

Kilgallen, John J. "'The Apostles Whom He Chose Because of the Holy Spirit': A Suggestion Regarding Acts 1:2." *Bib* 81 (2000) 414–17.

Kilpatrick, George D. "ΛΑΟΙ at Luke 2.31 and Acts 4.25–27." *JTS* 16 (1965) 127.

Kittel, Gerhard, and Gerhard Freidrich, editors. *Theological Dictionary of the New Testament.* Translated by Geoffrey W. Bromiley. 10 vols. Grand Rapids: Eerdmans, 1964–76.

Kitz, Anne Marie. "The Hebrew Terminology of Lot Casting and Its Ancient Near Eastern Context." *CBQ* 62 (2000) 207–14.

Klinghardt, Matthias. *Gesetz und Volk Gottes: Das lukanische Verständnis des Gesetzes nach Herkunft, Funktion und seinem Ort in der Geschichte des Urchristentums.* WUNT II, 32. Tübingen: Mohr Siebeck, 1988.

Kraabel, Thomas A. "The Roman Diaspora: Six Questionable Assumptions." *JJS* 33 (1982) 445–64.

Kraft, Robert A. "The Multiform Jewish Heritage of Early Christianity." In *Christianity, Judaism, and Other Greco-Roman Cults: Studies for Morton Smith at Sixty*, part 3 of *Judaism Before 70*, edited by Jacob Neusner, 174–99. Studies in Judaism in Late Antiquity 12. Leiden: Brill, 1975.

Kraft, Robert A., and George W. E. Nickelsburg, editors. *Early Judaism and Its Modern Interpreters.* BMI 2. Philadelphia: Fortress, 1986.

Krieger, Murray. *A Window to Criticism: Shakespeare's Sonnets and Modern Poetics.* Princeton, NJ: Princeton University Press, 1964.

Kurz, William S. *Reading Luke-Acts: Dynamics of Biblical Narrative.* Louisville: Westminster, 1993.

Lake, Krisopp, and Henry J. Cadbury. *The Beginnings of Christianity*, part 1, *The Acts of the Apostles.* Edited by Frederick J. Foakes Jackson and Krisopp Lake. 5 vols. Grand Rapids: Baker, 1979.

Lienhard, Joseph T. "Acts 6:1–6: A Redactional View." *CBQ* 37 (1975) 228–36.

Lightfoot, J. B., and J. R. Harmer. *The Apostolic Fathers.* 2nd ed. Edited by Michael W. Holmes. Grand Rapids: Baker, 1989.

Lim, Timothy H. *Pesharim.* New York: Sheffield Academic, 2002.

Lindars, Barnabas. "Matthew, Levi, Lebbaeus, and the Value of the Western Text." *NTS* 4 (1958) 220–22.

Lindbeck, George A. *The Nature of Doctrine: Religion and Theology in a Postliberal Age.* Louisville: Westminster John Knox, 1984.

Loader, J. A. "An Explanation of the Term Proselutos." *NovT* 15 (1973) 270–77.

Lohfink, Gerhard. "Bemerkungen zur neuen Einheitsübersetzung der Bibel: Übersetzungsfehler in der Apostelgeschichte" (Comments on the New Bible Translation: Misunderstandings in the Acts of the Apostles) *TQ* 155 (1975) 244–46.

Longenecker, Bruce W. "Lukan Aversion to Humps and Hollows: The Case of Acts 11.25–12.25." *NTS* 50 (2004) 185–204.

Longenecker, Richard N. *The Acts of the Apostles.* EBC. Grand Rapids: Zondervan, 1981.

Lund, Nils Wilhelm. *Chiasmus in the New Testament: A Study in the Form and Function of Chiastic Structures.* Peabody, MA: Hendrickson, 1970.

Lyons, John. "The Fourth Wave and the Approaching Millennium." *Anvil* 15 (1998) 169–81.

Manson, William. *The Epistle to the Hebrews: An Historical and Theological Reconsideration.* London: Hodder & Stoughton, 1951.

Mare, W. Harold. "Acts 7: Jewish or Samaritan in Character?" *WTJ* 34 (1971) 1–21.

Marshal, I. Howard. *The Acts of the Apostles: An Introduction and Commentary*. Grand Rapids: Eerdmans, 1980.

———. "Palestinian and Hellenistic Christianity: Some Critical Comments." *NTS* 19 (1973) 271–87.

Martin, Francis. "Spirit and Flesh in the Doing of Theology." *JPT* 18 (2001) 5–31.

Meek, James A. *The Gentile Mission in Old Testament Citations in Acts: Text, Hermeneutic and Purpose*, LNTS 385. London: T. & T. Clark, 2008.

Meier, John P. "The Circle of the Twelve: Did It Exist during Jesus's Public Ministry?" *JBL* 116 (1997) 635–72.

Ménard, Jacques E. "PAIS THEOU as Messianic Title in the Book of Acts." *CBQ* 19 (1957) 83–92.

Metzger, Bruce M. "Antioch on the Orontes." *BA* 11 (1948) 70–88.

———. *A Textual Commentary of the Greek New Testament*. 2nd ed. Stuttgart: Deutsche Bibelgesellschaft, 1994; reprint 2012.

Meyshan, J. "The Coinage of Agrippa the First." *IEJ* 4.3/4 (1954) 186–200.

Moore, Rickie D. "Canon and Charisma in the Book of Deuteronomy." *JPT* 1 (1992) 75–92.

———. "A Pentecostal Approach to Scripture." *Seminary Viewpoint* 8 (1987) 4–11.

Moore, Stephen D. *Literary Criticism and the Gospels: The Theoretical Challenge*. New Haven, CT: Yale University Press, 1989.

Moule, C. F. D. "The Christology of Acts." In *Studies in Luke-Acts: Essays Presented in Honor of Paul Schubert*, edited by Leander E. Keck and J. Louis Martyn, 159–85. London: SPCK, 1966.

———. "H. W. Moule on Acts 4:25." *ExpTim* 65 (1953–54) 220–21.

———. "Once More, Who Were the Hellenists?" *ExpTim* 7 (1958) 100–102.

Munck, Johannes. *The Acts of the Apostles*. Revised and edited by William F. Albright and C. S. Mann. AB 31. Garden City, NY: Doubleday, 1967.

Nolland, John L. "A Fresh Look at Acts 15.10." *NTS* 27 (1980) 105–15.

Novick, Tzvi. "Succeeding Judas: Exegesis in Acts 1:15–26." *JBL* 129 (2010) 795–99.

Oliverio, L. William, Jr. *Theological Hermeneutics in the Classical Pentecostal Tradition: A Typological Account*. Leiden: Brill, 2012.

Osborne, Grant R. *The Hermeneutical Spiral: A Comprehensive Introduction to Biblical Interpretation*. 2nd ed. Downers Grove, IL: InterVarsity, 2006.

Pao, David W. *Acts and the Isaianic New Exodus*. WUNT 2. Grand Rapids: Baker Academic, 2002.

———. "Waiters or Preachers: Acts 6:1–7 and the Lukan Table Fellowship Motif." *JBL* 130 (2011) 127–44.

Parsons, Mikeal C. *Acts*. Paideia. Grand Rapids: Baker Academic, 2008.

———. "Nothing Defiled AND Unclean: The Conjunction's Function in Acts 10:14." *PRSt* 27 (2000) 263–74.

Parsons, Mikeal C., and Richard I. Pervo. *Rethinking the Unity of Luke and Acts*. Minneapolis: Fortress, 1993.

Penner, Todd C. "Madness in the Method?: The Acts of the Apostles in Current Study." *CurBR* 2 (2004) 223–93.

Pervo, Richard I. *Acts: A Commentary*. Edited by Harold W. Attridge. Minneapolis: Fortress, 2009.

———. *Profit with Delight: The Literary Genre of the Acts of the Apostles*. Philadelphia: Fortress, 1987.

Phillips, Timothy R., and Dennis L. Okholm. A *Family of Faith: An Introduction to Evangelical Christianity*. Grand Rapids: Baker Academic, 2001

Phillips, Gary A. "You Are Either Here, Here, Here, or Here: Deconstruction's Troublesome Interplay." *Semeia* 71 (1995) 193–213.

Pinnock, Clark. "The Role of the Spirit in Interpretation." *JETS* 36 (1993) 494–95.

Plümacher, Eckhard. "Wirklichkeitserfahrung und Geschichtsschreibung bei Lukas: Erwgungen zu den Wir-Stücken der Apostelgeschichte." *ZNW* 68 (1977) 2–22.

Plymale, Steven F. *The Prayer Texts of Luke-Acts*. New York: Peter Lang, 1991.

Polhill, John B. "The Hellenist Breakthrough: Acts 6–12." *RevExp* 71 (1974) 425–36.

Porter, Stanley E. "Why Hasn't Reader-Response Criticism Caught on in New Testament Studies?" *JLT* 4 (1990) 278–92.

Porton, Gary G. "Diversity in Postbiblical Judaism." In *Early Judaism and Its Modern Interpreters*, edited by Robert A. Kraft and George W. E. Nickelsburg, 57–80. BMI 2. Philadelphia: Fortress, 1986.

Praeder, Susan M. "The Problem of First Person Narration in Acts." *NovT* 29 (1987) 193–218.

Pratt, Richard L. "Pictures, Windows, and Mirrors in Old Testament Exegesis." *WTJ* 45 (1983) 156–67.

Prince, Gerald. *Narratology: The Form and Function of Narrative*. Berlin: Mouton, 1982.

Reasoner, Mark. "The Theme of Acts: Institutional History or Divine Necessity in History." *JBL* 118.4 (1999) 635–59.

Reinhardt, Wolfgang. "The Population Size of Jerusalem and the Numeric Growth of the Jerusalem Church." In *The Book of Acts and Its Palestinian Setting*, edited by Richard Bauckham, 237–65. Grand Rapids: Eerdmans, 1995.

Rengstorf, Karl. "Die Zumwahl des Matthias (Apg 1,15ff)." *ST* 15 (1961) 35–67.

———. "Election of Matthias, Acts 1,15 Ff." Pages 178–92 in *Current Issues in New Testament Interpretation: Essays in Honor of Otto A. Piper*. New York: Harper, 1962.

Resseguie, James L. *Narrative Criticism of the New Testament: An Introduction*. Grand Rapids: Baker Academic, 2005.

Richard, Earl J. "Acts 7: An Investigation of the Samaritan Evidence." *CBQ* 39 (1977) 190–208.

———. "Kerygmatic Summaries in the Speeches of Acts." Pages 185–217 in *History, Literature, and Society in the Book of Acts*, edited by Ben Witherington III. Cambridge: Cambridge University Press, 1996.

———. "Luke: Writer, Theologian, Historian: Research and Orientation of the 1970's." *BTB* 13 (1983): 3–15 "James and the Jerusalem Church." Pages 415–80 in *The Book of Acts and its Palestinian Setting*, edited by Richard Bauckham. Grand Rapids: Eerdmans, 1995.

Riesner, Rainer. *Paul's Early Period: Chronology, Mission Strategy, Theology*. Translated by Doug Stott. Grand Rapids: Eerdmans, 1998.

Rimmon-Kenan, Shlomith. *Narrative Fiction: Contemporary Poetics*. 2nd ed. New York: Routledge, 2002.

Rius-Camps, Josep, and Jenny Read-Heimerdinger. *The Message of Acts in Codex Bezae: A Comparison with the Alexandrian Tradition*. 4 vols. LNTS 257, 302, 365, 415 (formerly JSNTSup). London: T. & T. Clark, 2004–9.

Robeck, Cecil M. "Prophetic Authority in the Charismatic Setting: The Need to Test." *TR* 24 (1983) 4–10.

Sanders, E. P. *The Historical Figure of Jesus*. London: Penguin, 1995.

―――. *Jesus and Judaism.* Philadelphia: Fortress, 1985.

Sanders, Jack T. *The Jews in Luke-Acts.* Philadelphia: Fortress, 1987.

―――. "The Prophetic Use of the Scripture in Luke-Acts." In *Early Jewish and Christian Exegesis: Studies in Memory of William Hugh Brownlee,* edited by Craig A. Evans and W. F. Stinespring, 191–98. Atlanta: Scholars, 1987.

Savelle, Charles H. "A Reexamination of the Prohibitions in Acts 15." *BSac* 161 (October–December 2004) 449–68.

Schille, Gottfried. *Die Apostelgeschichte des Lukas.* THKNT 5. Berlin: Evangelische Verlagsanstalt, 1983.

Schnabel, Eckhard J. *Early Christian Mission.* 2 vols. Downers Grove, IL: InterVarsity, 2004.

Schneider, Gerhard. *Die Apostelgeschichte.* HThKNT 5. Freiburg: Herder, 1982.

Scholes, Robert, editor. *Approaches to the Novel; Materials for a Poetics.* San Francisco: Chandler, 1966.

Schwartz, Daniel R. *Agrippa I: The Last King of Judaea.* Tübingen: Mohr Siebeck, 1990.

Schweizer, Eduard. "The Concept of the Davidic 'Son of God' in Acts and Its Old Testament Background." In *Studies in Luke-Acts: Essays Presented in Honor of Paul Schubert,* edited by Leander E. Keck and J. Louis Martyn, 186–93. London: SPCK, 1966.

Scott, J. Julius, Jr. "The Cornelius Incident in the Light of Its Jewish Setting." *JETS* 34 (1991) 475–84.

Shelton, James B. "Epistemology and Authority in the Acts of the Apostles: An Analysis and Test Case Study of Acts 15:1–29." *Spirit & Church* 2 (2000) 231–47.

Shepherd, William H., Jr. *The Narrative Function of the Holy Spirit as a Character in Luke-Acts.* SBLDS 147. Atlanta: Scholars, 1994.

Simon, Marcel. *St. Stephen and the Hellenists in the Primitive Church.* New York: Longmans, 1958.

―――. "St. Stephen and the Jerusalem Temple." *JEH* 2 (1951) 127–42.

Smail, Thomas A. "Decision and Discernment." *TR* 24 (1983) 2–3.

―――. "The Sign and the Signified: The Work of the Spirit in Event and Theology." *TR* 15 (1980) 2–8.

Smith, Morton. "Palestinian Judaism in the First Century." In *Israel: Its Role in Civilization,* edited by Moshe Davis, 67–81. New York: Seminary Israel Institute, 1956.

Smith, T. C. "The Sources of Acts." In *With Steadfast Purpose: Essays on Acts in Honor of Henry Jackson Flanders Jr.,* edited by N. H. Keathley, 55–75. Waco, TX: Baylor University Press, 1990.

Soards, Marion L. "The Historical and Cultural Setting of Luke-Acts." In *New Views on Luke and Acts,* edited by Earl J. Richard, 86–93. Collegeville, MN: Liturgical, 1990.

Spawn, Kevin L., and Archie T. Wright. *Spirit and Scripture: Exploring a Pneumatic Hermeneutic.* London: T. & T. Clark, 2012.

Spencer, F. Scott. "Neglected Widows in Acts 6:1–7." *CBQ* 56 (1994) 727–28.

Springer, Mary Doyle. *A Rhetoric of Literary Character: Some Women of Henry James.* Chicago: University of Chicago Press, 1978.

Stenschke, Christoph W. *Luke's Portrait of Gentiles Prior to their Coming to Faith.* Tübingen: Mohr Siebeck, 1999.

Stibbe, Mark. "This Is That: Some Thoughts Concerning Charismatic Hermeneutics." *Anvil* 15 (1998) 181–93.

Stock, Augustine. "Chiastic Awareness and Education in Antiquity." *BTB* 14 (1984) 23–27.

Strauss, Mark. *The Davidic Messiah in Luke-Acts: The Promise and Its Fulfillment in Lukan Christology.* JSNTSup 110. Sheffield: Sheffield Academic, 1995.

Strack Herman L., and Paul Billerbeck. *Kommentar zum Neuen Testament aus Talmud und Midrasch.* Munich: Beck, 1961.

Talbert, Charles H. *Reading Acts: A Literary and Theological Commentary on the Acts of the Apostles.* New York: Crossroad. 1997.

Taylor, Justin. "Why were the Disciples First Called 'Christians' at Antioch?" *RB* (1994) 75–94.

Tannehill, Robert C. *The Narrative Unity of Luke-Acts: A Literary Interpretation.* Minneapolis: Fortress, 1990.

Thomas, John Christopher. "Reading the Bible from within Our Traditions: A Pentecostal Hermeneutic as Test Case." In *Between Two Horizons: Spanning New Testament Studies and Systematic Theology,* edited by Joel B. Green and Max Turner, 108–22. Grand Rapids: Eerdmans, 2000.

———. "Women, Pentecostals, and the Bible: An Experiment in Pentecostal Hermeneutics." *JPT* 5 (1994) 41–56.

Thompkins, Jane. P., editor. *Reader-Response Criticism: From Formalism to Post-Structuralism.* Baltimore: Johns Hopkins University Press, 1980.

Torrey, Charles C. *The Composition and Date of Acts.* Cambridge: Harvard University Press, 1916.

Twelftree, Graham H. *People of the Spirit: Exploring Luke's View of the Church.* Grand Rapids: Baker Academic, 2009.

Tyson, Joseph B. "Acts 6:1–7 and Dietary Regulations in Early Christianity." *PRSt* 10 (1983) 145–61.

———. "Jesus and Herod Antipas." *JBL* 79 (1960) 239–46.

Vanhoozer, Kevin J. *The Drama of Doctrine: A Canonical-Linguistic Approach to Christian Theology.* Louisville: Westminster John Knox, 2005.

———. *Is There a Meaning in This Text?: The Bible, the Reader, and the Morality of Literary Knowledge.* Grand Rapids: Zondervan, 1998.

Wahlde, Urban C. von. "Acts 4:24–31: The Prayer of the Apostles in Response to the Persecution of Peter and John—and Its Consequences." *Bib* 77 (1996) 237–44.

———. "The Problems of Acts 4:25a: A New Proposal." *ZNW* 86 (1995) 265–67.

Wallace, Martin. *Recent Theories of Narrative.* Ithaca, NY: Cornell University Press, 1986.

Walton, Steve. "How Mighty a Minority Were the Hellenists?" In *Earliest Christian History: History, Literature, and Theology; Essays from the Tyndale Fellowship in Honor of Martin Hengel,* edited by Michael F. Bird and Jason Maston, 305–27. Tübingen: Mohr Siebeck, 2012.

Wedderburn, A. J. M. "The 'Apostolic Decree': Tradition and Redaction." *NovT* 35 (1993) 362–89.

Welch, John W. *Chiasmus in Antiquity: Structure, Analyses, Exegesis.* Hildesheim: Gerstenberg, 1981.

Whitlock, David B. "An Exposition of Acts 15:1–29." *RevExp* 92 (1995) 375–78.

Wikenhauser, Alfred. *Die Apostelgeschichte.* Regensburg: F. Pustet, 1961.

Wilson, Stephen G. *Luke and the Law.* SNTSMS 50. Cambridge: Cambridge University Press, 1983.

Wirgin, Wolf. *Herod Agrippa I: King of the Jews.* 2 vols. Leeds: Leeds University Oriental Society, 1968.

Witherington, Ben, III. *The Acts of the Apostles: A Socio-Rhetorical Commentary.* Grand Rapids: Eerdmans, 1998.

———. *History, Literature, and Society in the Book of Acts.* Cambridge: Cambridge University Press, 2007.

Yong, Amos. *Renewing Christian Theology: Systematics for Global Christianity.* Waco, TX: Baylor University Press, 2014.

———. *The Spirit Poured Out on All Flesh: Pentecostalism and the Possibility of Global Theology.* Grand Rapids: Baker Academic, 2005.

———. *Spirit-Word-Community: Theological Hermeneutics in Trinitarian Perspective.* Eugene, OR: Wipf & Stock, 2002.

Yung, Hwa. *Mangoes or Bananas?: The Quest for an Authentic Asian Christian Theology.* Oxford: Regnum, 1997.

Zetterholm, Magnus. "The Didache, Matthew, James—and Paul: Reconstructing Historical Developments in Antioch." In *Matthew, James, and the Didache: Three Related Documents in Their Jewish and Christian Settings,* edited by Hubertus Waltherus Maria van de Sandt and Jürgen Zangenberg, 73–90. SymS. Leiden: Brill, 2008.

Zwiep, Arie W. *Judas and the Choice of Matthias.* Tübingen: Mohr Siebeck, 2004.

Made in the USA
Monee, IL
03 March 2020

22664132R00095